SOUL FUEL

BEAR GRYLLS

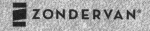

Soul Fuel

© 2019 by BGV Global Limited

Requests for information should be addressed to:
Zondervan, *3900 Sparks Dr. SE, Grand Rapids, Michigan 49546*

ISBN: 978-0-3104-5358-1

Art direction: Jennifer Showalter Greenwalt

Interior design: Emily Ghattas

Printed in China

19 20 21 22 23 DSC 10 9 8 7 6 5 4 3 2 1

A few special, great men and women have shaped my life and my faith, and this book could not have happened without them.

First, many of the stories and anecdotes have come from Nicky and Pippa Gumbel, who have been kind, loyal friends through so much of my journey.

Likewise, so much friendship and inspiration for the book has come from my best buddy, Charlie Mackesy, who has always lived with freedom, courage, and kindness.

To Jim Hawkins, whom I continue to do a daily reading with every morning by email, and who is such a loyal, fun, wise human being that I love very much.

And to Chris Stanley-Smith, who led me to faith as a nervous, awkward, and struggling teenager. What an incredible example of a man you have always been.

And finally to Shara and our three boys, who continue to show me day by day how to do faith in action— with love, kindness, generosity, fun, and loyalty.

CONTENT

INTRODUCTION

SOMETIMES PEOPLE ASK ME about stuff I've done. They'll mention my reaching the top of Everest or surviving a jungle or crossing an ocean—things that they think are successes. But to me these are the least interesting part of my story. And the truth is that behind every summit, every award or achievement that makes it into a neat headline, there is a string of failures. My life is much more of a collection of struggles, doubts, and fears, some of which I overcome, some I don't.

A more relevant question might be, where does my strength come from?

The honest answer is that I often don't feel very strong. Life can be a battle. We all feel that from time to time. But any strength I do have seems to come in the quiet moments at the start of my day. It comes when I am on my own, on my knees. It comes from taking time to be still with God.

God. For many of us, that's a difficult word. So might be the words *church* or *Father*. To some they might even be painful or negative. But let's try to see beyond the words to the force behind them. That force is love. Let's remember that if our Creator really is who He says He is, then He is good. He is calling us home, in a way that is powerfully unique to each of us. He's on our side, your side. He is holding out a hand, no matter how far we think we've fallen.

So God is love? I think so. I mean, that is all that Jesus ever wanted to share, isn't it? Love. The force He brought was goodness personified. This love is there to hold us, guide us, strengthen and rescue us. It's a power that I know I can turn to, however far away I feel.

I don't turn to God to be religious. In fact, I really battle with religion as such. It seems so divisive and full of rules. Both those things turn me off. Church often portrays itself as so neat and perfect. Life is neither of those things. I kneel simply because it is where I find strength. This book will reveal that. The whole notion of strength through weakness, connection through honesty, and power through humility is a journey, and I am not very far along the road. But I stay on it, as best I can, because my heart feels it is good.

Even with a lifetime of faith behind me, I find the journey hard. I often mess up. I find myself teetering on the edge more often than you would imagine. So for me, starting my day with God really helps. It is like food. Like good fuel for the soul.

That's what *Soul Fuel* is about. It's the chance to share with you the kind of fuel I rely on every day to try to keep my life on track. Like a firesteel or a length of good rope, my faith is another essential in my arsenal for survival. But it is so much more. It's my backbone, the heart of it all—the greatest source of any strength I have.

There are intentionally no formal dates on the entries in this book and no reading plan for you to struggle to follow. *Soul Fuel* is simply 360 separate entries, grouped around the twelve themes that I find myself returning to again and again—hope, purpose, determination, relationships, vision, wisdom, faithfulness, courage, forgiveness, freedom, and risk. And while this book no doubt has flaws, and there's so much more to say, it's a start. I really hope it can encourage you to stand strong and tackle life with courage and kindness, secure in the knowledge that you are truly loved and set free in Christ.

There will be days when you can't open this book. You might not visit it for weeks, months—years even. This cover's probably going to get a bit dusty, and that's okay. *Soul Fuel* is here only to help you, and there is no condemnation in these pages. We are all in the gutter more than we imagine, but we are also looking up at the Star. And He is good.

What matters most is that we find the courage to reach out and take the hand that's stretching toward us. That we keep on moving toward the light, inch by inch. And that we never give up.

Faith is a journey, and like all great journeys it is made up of small, faithful steps taken every day.

This book has fuel for your journey in its pages. Don't underestimate the power of the words of the Bible. So often they have been light to a dark path for me and strength to a failing body. Immanuel Kant said, "The Bible is an inexhaustible fountain of all truths. The existence of the Bible is the greatest blessing which humanity ever experienced."[1]

> Your word is a lamp for my feet,
> > a light on my path. (Psalm 119:105)

I truly hope this book blesses, enriches, and empowers you every day.

WHERE IT ALL STARTED

I WAS SIXTEEN WHEN IT HAPPENED. It was the end of an ordinary school day, and as the last of the lights in our house were turned off and the darkness finally settled, I quietly slipped out the ground-floor window.

There was enough moonlight to walk by, but I could easily have made the short walk in pitch black or a full-scale blizzard. I had done this a hundred times before. But that night was different.

I knew where I was going. To my favorite tree and my secret hideaway. I had always loved climbing high up into the sky, into her arms, hidden from view below by all the limbs and leaves beneath me.

The news that my godfather, Stephen, had died suddenly and without warning of a heart attack had hit me so hard. Stephen had been my father's best friend in the world, and he was like a second father to me. He came on all our family holidays. He'd helped me learn to do so much and always laughed and cheered me on. His death felt like someone had ripped my heart out.

The shock of his sudden passing had made me feel angry, confused, and lonely, all at the same time. It just felt so cruel and way too soon. In fact, I didn't even know what to feel anymore. I just needed some space and time—alone. That was why I was out that night, making my way toward that lone tree.

I climbed quickly. The feel of the bark, the angle of the branches, the way the tree started to move with my weight the higher I got—it all felt familiar. And when I was forty feet up and had reached the last limb that I knew could hold me, I stopped.

And then the tears came. And the anger. I held my head in my hands. I sobbed and hit the tree. Some would call it prayer.

I'd been silent on God for years. When I was younger, faith had felt so natural, as if somehow there was this thing inside and it was there just for me. Like a simple presence: quiet, nonjudgmental, strong, and always good.

But when I started going away to school as a teenager, I was forced to sit through endless religious services in chapel. Faith died a slow death. Death by boredom. Death by religion. Death by irrelevance. I assumed that belief belonged in the past, that growing up meant leaving any sense of the super-natural behind me. That was all kids' stuff.

Stephen's death had stirred up some deep coals of emotion in me, the flickering of an ember inside, like the pain was shaking everything up. And through it all, the quiet, calming presence of God was gently fanning that black ember of faith. That Presence was all I wanted again while I was up that tree. And then that ember gave the tiniest of flickers.

As the anger subsided for a few moments and the tears dried for a little while, I prayed the only prayer that ever really matters to the human heart: "Jesus, if You are real, if You are there, please be beside me this night."

See what the Bible says:

Have I not commanded you? Be strong and courageous! Do not be terrified or dismayed. (Joshua 1:9 AMP)

But how do we find that courage?

For the LORD your God is with you wherever you go. (v. 9 AMP)

Whatever fear we're facing, remember this: we do not face it alone. The Creator of the universe is good; He is beside us, within us, and for us.

4 THE LESSONS WE LEARN WHEN WE'RE ON OUR KNEES

LIFE CAN BE HARD, even brutal. It can so often be marked by pain, loss, grief, broken relationships, and ill health. No one can avoid all of these things, because they are part of the journey. And we wouldn't be human if we didn't at times feel desperate for help.

But the wonder of our faith is that those moments aren't times when we are hopeless or helpless. In fact, it is the opposite. They are our times of maximum power. We just don't always know it or feel it. But read this:

"You're blessed when you're at the end of your rope. With less of you there is more of God and his rule." (Matthew 5:3 MSG)

When we can no longer stumble on in our own "strength," we have no choice but to kneel down and cry out. And as people of faith, we are never taller than when we kneel down. Less of us. More of Him.

Remember the poem about the footprints in the sand, when the writer was wondering why she only saw one set of footprints when she needed Jesus most? He replied, "Because it was then that I carried you."[5]

In those times when we're aware of how desperately we need God, He is there. Right beside us. He is the closest He can be when we really need Him.

5 BE THANKFUL

Give thanks in all circumstances; for this is God's will for you. (1 Thessalonians 5:18)

THIS VERSE IS INTERESTING and challenging because it isn't what we first think of when the worst happens! Our default all too often can be to fall down and give up when things go badly wrong. But God has a better, smarter way. He says for us to be grateful in *all* circumstances. Instead of blaming and wailing, give thanks for all the good in your life. That's radical living.

At its most basic, that good is the truth that we are loved by God and given a future with Him for eternity. That in itself is crazy good news.

When it comes to living life on earth with power and purpose, it is scientifically proven that gratitude changes our state for the better. So let's make this a daily attitude and way to live: always in gratitude for our blessings, whether it be food, health, fortune, relationships, fun, family, or simply His promises for our futures.

Paul knew all about this too:

Whatever is true, whatever is noble, whatever is right, whatever is pure, whatever is lovely, whatever is admirable—if anything is excellent or praiseworthy—think about such things. (Philippians 4:8)

In other words, look for the positive and choose to be grateful.

He was right. When we look around us and focus on all that is good, it helps us see God in so many of the little things that we often overlook, whether it be the leap of a dog in delight at seeing us, or the smile and kindness of someone serving us a coffee. Christ is in it all. When we live like this, it is as though our eyes are being opened. And it starts with gratitude.

6 WORDS OF LIFE

GIVEN ENOUGH TIME and the right conditions, a river can slice through rock, leaving canyons that are thousands of feet deep. It's not because the river is powerful but because the river is persistent. It's the same way with the Bible. If we take time to read and reflect on it, it'll make an impact on our lives, almost without us knowing it.

David's Psalm 19 outlines some of the life-changing effects of Scripture. He explained how it

- pulls our lives together,
- point[s] out the right road,
- show[s] the way to joy, and
- warns us of danger (vv. 7, 8, 11 MSG).

It all points to a powerful truth: God loves you and promises to reveal Himself to you when you seek Him. But like the river working on the rock, there's got to be a point of contact. If we don't ask, He won't force Himself into our lives. So ask. Seek. Let the river water flow over you, carve you, and shape you into His likeness.

> For those who find me find life
> and receive favor from the LORD. (Proverbs 8:35)

Finding both life and favor from the Almighty—that's an amazing promise to claim on our lives today. So let's stay with our hearts wide open to His presence in our lives. And let's do it every day. It is the way to all good things.

7 WHAT DOES GOD REQUIRE?

ANY BIG JOURNEY OFTEN brings out mixed emotions at the start. A lot of the time we just want to hurry on and make it to our destination as quickly as possible. On the journey of faith, things are a little different. The destination is so far off that we won't even reach it in this lifetime. And the journey we take to get there is full of challenges. And it's long—so long that it will last until our final breath.

But here's the truth: we don't travel alone. God is both our destination and our guide, and He has promised to be with us every step of the way.

And what should those steps look like? The answer is beautifully clear:

> What does the LORD require of you? To act justly and to love mercy and to walk humbly with your God. (Micah 6:8)

You and I are definitely going to stumble from time to time, but when we do, let's not lose heart. Let's look up and see His hand outstretched above us, helping us back to our feet.

Act justly, love mercy, and walk humbly with our God.

WHO WAS JESUS?

WHO WAS JESUS? At some point in life, most people find themselves asking this simple question. We all have to make up our minds, just as people did back when He was walking on earth. For them—and us too—there seem to be only three credible, possible answers:

- He is out of his mind. (Mark 3:21)
- He is possessed by Beelzebul! (v. 22)
- [He is] the Son of God. (v. 11)

In other words, He was either insane, evil, or God.

I used to think, *Couldn't He simply have been a good teacher and good guy?* But then I looked at His life and words. Do good teachers repeatedly claim to be God? Do they claim to be one with the Father? Do they say they have come to die for all of mankind? Do they raise people from the dead and walk on water and calm storms? Those are strong claims and strong deeds.

C. S. Lewis reasoned that "a man who was merely a man and said the sort of things Jesus said would not be a great moral teacher. He would either be [insane] . . . or else he would be the Devil of Hell. You must make your choice. . . . But, let us not come up with any patronizing nonsense about his being a great human teacher. He has not left that open to us. He did not intend to."[6]

Who we decide Jesus is to us is a big question with big implications for our lives. But if we study the overwhelming and compelling evidence and then choose to believe that He is who He said He is—if we can take that leap of faith and ask, "Are You really there, and are You really good?"—it can be the start of an incredible journey and adventure. An adventure into life.

That's why the offer He made two thousand years ago still stands for us today:

"Come to me, all you who are weary and burdened, and I will give you rest." (Matthew 11:28)

Even today, for you and me, right now—that invitation has the power to change everything. If we let Him, He seeks us, saves us, strengthens us, supports us, and shows us how to live every day.

9 THE ROUTE

THERE ARE PLENTY OF good things that come with age. I like to say that any skills and experience I have are the sum of all my near misses. Experience becomes wisdom, the things we've failed at make us stronger, and all the learning we rack up can give us a solid footing in life.

Sadly, *wisdom* and *learning* are words whose worth have been badly eroded these days. We often see leaders being hypocrites. We're told we can be happy if we keep on buying more stuff. We can become so inward looking that we are blind to the power of God around us.

So how should we live?

Jesus gives us a perfect example to follow. His words are the best sort of wisdom and learning for us to follow:

"'Love the Lord your God with all your heart and with all your soul and with all your mind.' This is the first and greatest commandment. And the second is like it: 'Love your neighbor as yourself.'" (Matthew 22:37–39)

It's so simple yet so hard. But it is all we truly need.

WHOM JESUS CHOSE

I LOVE HOW JESUS interacted with women. He was such a revolutionary and visionary and so ahead of His time. (But then again, I guess that's to be expected if you are God!) But just look at the way Jesus interacted with Mary Magdalene when He found her weeping outside His empty tomb:

> He asked her, "Woman, why are you crying? Who is it you are looking for?"
>
> Thinking he was the gardener, she said, "Sir, if you have carried him away, tell me where you have put him, and I will get him."
>
> Jesus said to her, "Mary."
>
> She turned toward him and cried out in Aramaic, "Rabboni!" (which means "Teacher"). (John 20:15–16)

Of all the people He could have picked, Jesus appeared first to Mary Magdalene. Not a senior disciple, a leading Pharisee, or even His mother. He chose to make His first appearance to a woman whom no one in the world rated as important.

In the culture of the day, a woman's testimony would not have been considered as weighty as a man's. Or, to put it another way, if the disciples had been making the whole thing up, there's *no way* they would have said the first appearance of the risen Messiah was to Mary Magdalene.

But Jesus chose Mary—the loved one, the forgiven one—alone in a garden, with gentle love. Why? Because Jesus rewrote the rules about equality, justice, and love. He chose someone whom the world considered unqualified for the task, because that's what love does.

Today, let's be open to Christ surprising us, inspiring us, showing us how to live and love radically and kindly, and, above all, to treat women as Jesus did: with respect, gentleness, and favor.

11 NEVER ALONE

THE BIBLE USES MANY names for Jesus, but Immanuel is one of my favorites. It means "God with us," and it's a statement of truth that you can build your life on.

Through His Spirit, Jesus is always with us. Think about it for a moment: the same God who created the universe is with us right now. That's life changing, and it's not something to be taken lightly.

What it doesn't mean is that we get a free pass to miss all of life's hard times. A life of faith will not mean you avoid trouble. God doesn't ever promise a trouble-free life. Life is a series of battles. But He does offer something even better: He promises to be with us.

> "Because he loves me," says the LORD, "I will rescue him;
>> I will protect him, for he acknowledges my name.
> He will call on me, and I will answer him;
>> I will be with him in trouble." (Psalm 91:14–15)

This is what makes all the difference in life. Even in the darkest times, God is with us. Even when everything else appears lost, you are never alone. Ever.

12 KNOWN BY GOD

A LIFE OF FAITH can be tough. You'll have moments when you feel as if you're at the end of your rope. Doubt and obstacles can come thick and fast. Faith is a journey with many steep hills.

But if you want an enriched life—the sort that you were created to live—Christ leads us into a fullness of life that is unparalleled. How do we find the way? The trail is clearly marked:

> Command those who are rich in this present world not to be arrogant nor to put their hope in wealth, which is so uncertain, but to put their hope in God, who richly provides us with everything for our enjoyment. . . . So that they may take hold of the life that is truly life. (1 Timothy 6:17, 19)

It all starts in our heart, with trust. We were created for one thing—to be known by God. He longs to be beside us. He truly loves us in a way that is hard to put into words. Beyond convention, religion, and reason. Love. Love. Love.

Stop and take a moment to let it wash over you. Wash away the hurt and the pain and the fear. It is good. It is fuel. He asks nothing in return. Just receive. That's the place of power.

13 THE REAL DAVID

ONE OF MY HEROES is a man who went through every sort of human angst and emotion. He sank to the depths of despair yet soared to incredible heights. He was a true wilderness survivor, taking on the very worst that the elements could throw at him while he was still a boy. And as a scrawny kid standing in front of a violent, jeering crowd, he struck down a giant and won the freedom of his people. He went on to be king and a hero.

But there's another side to his story. He was a liar and a cheat. He was the kind of weak-willed man who conspired to send an innocent man to his death just so that he could satisfy his heart's desire.

King David had every reason to hate himself. He could have spent so much of his adult life as a prisoner to guilt, self-doubt, and remorse. Yet today he's still seen as one of the true heroes of the Bible.

Despite all his ups and downs, everything that he did well, and everything that he did wrong, the reason for David's greatness was simple. He knew he couldn't do it all alone. So King David looked beyond himself, putting his confidence in God, the only one who would never let him down.

> The LORD is my light and my salvation—
> whom shall I fear?
> The LORD is the stronghold of my life—
> of whom shall I be afraid? (Psalm 27:1)

I don't want to copy his mistakes, but I certainly want to love God the way David did. I want to start my days with his words on my heart: "Oh, let me rise in the morning and live always with you!" (Psalm 139:18 MSG).

14 COME AND DRINK

FROM ALL MY EXPERIENCES of cultures and people, I have learned one sure thing about human nature: we're all hungry and thirsty for purpose and satisfaction. But history shows us that when we try to find that purpose and satisfaction in ourselves, we rarely reach it. The way that Jesus lived showed that only His presence can truly satisfy the hunger and thirst in our hearts.

> Hey there! All who are thirsty,
> come to the water! (Isaiah 55:1 MSG)

The amazing truth is that this gift that Jesus offers us is free. We cannot earn this spiritual food and water. We cannot buy our way into the presence of God. We will never be worthy of it. It's a gift Jesus earned the hard way for us, His children.

> Come anyway—buy and eat!
> Come, buy your drinks, buy wine and milk.
> Buy without money—everything's free! (Isaiah 55:1 MSG)

The whole journey of faith is an awakening to the truth that God's love for us, His children, is extravagant. A life of faith in Christ should never be "religious" or somber. It is joyous, light, free, and empowering. Jesus' love and mercy are the greatest forces ever to have touched the earth, and they continue to transform lives today.

> Whoever accepts and trusts the Son gets in on everything, life complete and forever! (John 3:34 MSG)

15 WHERE TO FIND GOD

FOR SOME OF US, church can get in the way. We can assume that if the Sunday services are dull, loveless, and irrelevant, then God must also be dull, loveless, and irrelevant.

It can take a while before we begin to see things clearly. It takes time to understand that life with Jesus isn't a matter of dressing a certain way, singing a certain song, or telling people to behave better!

As C. S. Lewis put it, being a Christian "means to forgive the inexcusable, because God has forgiven the inexcusable in you."[7]

Church matters, that much is true. But being a Christian is not really about the quantity or quality of services we sit through. It's about the way that we *live*.

Whoever claims to live in him must live as Jesus did. (1 John 2:6)

Today, let's try to live in the knowledge that we are loved, and show love to others. Let's try to live in the knowledge that we are forgiven, and show forgiveness to others. And let's try to live in the knowledge that Christ helps us have a right relationship with God.

If we give our all in trying to get closer to God, these next twenty-four hours are going to be special.

16 HOW TO LIVE

CENTURIES AGO, when the people of God were in exile and despair, they cried out, "How then can we live?" (Ezekiel 33:10). It's a good question, and one that still needs asking today.

What does it mean to live a life that pleases God and keeps us close to Christ? How should our choices be different? Psalm 128 is one of the very best places we can go searching for answers: "All you who fear GOD, how blessed you are! . . . Enjoy the blessing! Revel in the goodness! . . . Stand in awe of God's Yes. Oh, how he blesses the one who fears GOD! Enjoy the good life" (vv. 1–6 MSG).

Fearing God is about simply knowing our place and understanding that we are flawed, far from God, and in need of restoration. Fear is knowing our brokenness. Fear is respect. We all make mistakes, and we all fall short, yet God offers every single one of us that same life-changing, hope-giving grace. Christ turns our fear into dancing.

It starts with knowing our need for forgiveness, and it leads us to a place of joy. That's how to live. When we reach up to Christ, He blesses us and restores us. We can stand in awe and revel in His goodness and truly begin to enjoy life.

17 TAKE TIME

WE CAN GO ROUGHLY three weeks without food, three days without water, and three minutes without oxygen. How long can we live effectively without refueling our faith?

Jesus never went long without praying. There was a time when the crowds were so desperate to get a piece of Him that there was no time to eat. People were running toward Him, predicting where He might be going next and waiting there. It was the busiest season in His life, but Jesus knew that He needed time alone in prayer, even more so when it was busy. Jesus always seemed to stick to this routine as a clear source of power for the day ahead.

"Come with me by yourselves to a quiet place and get some rest." (Mark 6:31)

Jesus' words to His disciples are also words to us today. That's why I try my best to start every day in a quiet place, getting my soul fuel in, even if for just a few minutes. And you know what? He's always ready and waiting for me, and He's never late.

So make that little time and protect it, even if it is with your eyes closed while you are on the train into work. Breathe it in; know His presence around you. Let His words soak in; let His strength empower you. Know you are forgiven, healed, restored. Ask for those things afresh, and be thankful and pray for the day ahead. Be still and know that He is with you.

Be still, and know that I am God. (Psalm 46:10)

Now we are ready to hit the day.

JOY, NOT RELIGION

WILLIAM WILBERFORCE WAS LOVED as much as he was respected. Driven by his faith, he joined with others and campaigned to end the slave trade. It was a long, wild ride, and at times he was said to be both the most admired and the most hated man in England.

Jesus was both admired and hated too. And those of us who are trying to live with Christ inside us can expect to face moments of negative reaction. But when we're properly rooted and looking to Him, those extremes won't matter so much. We have something greater inside ourselves than the opinions of others. We hold the keys to life and freedom in our hearts. Christ brings that to us, quietly and with love. He brings joy, never religion.

When I was a kid growing up, church services so often were lacking in joy. They seemed to be about rules and solemn voices—no wonder I assumed that God was cold and impersonal.

But Jesus wants to show us the truth about what it means to live with Him.

"I have come that [you] may have life, and have it to the full." (John 10:10)

When we try to live in Jesus' footsteps, things get put into perspective. The highs and lows that used to turn our heads can begin to lose their power. And the quiet, still, unsung moments can excite our hearts. The joy of Jesus creeps up on us. Finally—perhaps for the first time in our lives—we begin to discover what true freedom really looks like.

19 THE FOOT OF THE CROSS

SOME PEOPLE DOUBT WHETHER Jesus actually died on the cross. They say it was a hoax, a conspiracy to fool the world. Even the Qur'an has bought the myth, stating, "They did not kill him, neither did they crucify him; it only seemed to be so" (Sura 4:157). But John is careful to provide detailed evidence of Jesus' death.

We know that death by crucifixion could be sped up by breaking the person's legs. In Jesus' case this was not necessary, because He was already dead. "Instead, one of the soldiers pierced Jesus' side with a spear, bringing a sudden flow of blood and water" (John 19:34). At death the clot and serum of the blood separates, which would look like blood and water.

For some people, this isn't enough. Why? Because if Jesus really was who He said He was, and if He really did do what He said He was going to do—including rising from the dead—the implications for our lives are massive.

Can we acknowledge that our mistakes have a cost? Can we accept that Jesus paid for them on our behalf? Will we decide to ignore Him or to follow where He leads us?

Wherever we all are on our journey of faith right now, these are strong questions to ask. Be relentless; be persistent; don't be afraid to search for answers. We are following in the footsteps of some of the greatest minds ever to have walked this earth. And so often those footsteps have led those souls to the foot of the cross of Christ, where they have found love and mercy flowing down.

BEFORE HE WAS ARRESTED, tried, and crucified, Jesus used some of His final moments with His followers to reaffirm and strengthen them:

> "The Friend, the Holy Spirit whom the Father will send at my request, will make everything plain to you." (John 14:26 MSG)

The Greek word used for the Holy Spirit (*parakletos*) literally means "one called alongside." It has a multifaceted meaning: counselor, advocate, comforter, encourager, helper, someone to stand by and support us. For example, a mother is a *paraclete* for her child. She takes away the anguish of loneliness. She brings presence, security, peace, and love. She guides, especially when there is trouble around.

That's the promise of Christ, that the Holy Spirit will always be around and within us, including the times when we feel overwhelmed and tempted to do things that hurt us or others.

> God is faithful; he will not let you be tempted beyond what you can bear. But when you are tempted, he will also provide a way out so that you can endure it. (1 Corinthians 10:13)

When we're facing temptation, the Holy Spirit is always there to guide us to a way out. And God always provides an exit.

GOD ALWAYS PROVIDES AN EXIT.

21 WHY SO SERIOUS?

THE WHOLE WORLD IS seeking happiness. Happiness is a good thing to pursue, but like a butterfly, often when we chase it, it flies away. So how do we find happiness?

The Bible shows us how both laughter and joy lead to an enriched life. Where laughter and joy are, so also there will be happiness. And the Bible reminds us that "a cheerful heart is good medicine" (Proverbs 17:22).

Let's not take ourselves too seriously. We need to laugh at situations—and ourselves. Laughter is like an internal workout. It exercises our spirit and helps keep our hearts and minds healthy. (By the way, my mum and dad used to say, "Laugh with people, not at people." That was good advice.)

And what about joy? What is it? Joy runs deep and is less transient than just happiness. Joy goes beyond simply a pleasing emotion—joy brings peace, strength, and light. Joy goes right down to the heart of our very being.

The joy of the LORD is your strength. (Nehemiah 8:10)

Laughter, happiness, and joy. These might sound like simple things, but don't underestimate their power to bring life and light to all around you. These qualities should be hallmarks of ours as men and women of faith. No doubt Jesus laughed a lot, and happiness and joy were at the heart of how He lived.

Jesus knew great sorrow and great pain, but I often think that if we were to meet Him in the flesh, part of what we would remember most would be His sense of fun and laughter. I like that.

I ALWAYS THINK THAT when we read the Old Testament it's a little bit like going into a dark room full of old furniture.

We stumble around a bit and have to feel our way. Gradually, as our hands pass over the sofas, chairs, and ornaments, we get a fuller sense of what's in the room. But it's still a bit vague, and it's only when the lights get turned on that we finally see exactly what's inside.

The New Testament is that light switch. Jesus reveals the Old Testament in ways we cannot understand when reading it by itself. To paraphrase Saint Augustine, "In the Old the New is concealed, in the New the Old is revealed."[8]

Jesus is the climax of God's great plan for the world. That's why Paul wrote, "My task is to bring out in the open and make plain what God, who created all this in the first place, has been doing in secret and behind the scenes all along" (Ephesians 3:8–9 MSG).

In the Greek, Paul used the word *photisai*, which means "to turn the light on so that people can see."

Jesus changes everything. Now we not only can approach God but we are also united with each other in new ways. We are "members together of one body, and sharers together in the promise in Christ Jesus" (Ephesians 3:6).

You've got questions about God? We all do. You're unsure about things, feeling a little in the dark? Join the club. That's all okay. Just keep reaching for the light. Christ is with us and is here to deliver us. That's what His name actually means.

23 THE POWER OF THE POOR

MOTHER TERESA WAS SO right when she said, "The poor people are very great people. They can teach us so many beautiful things. We must know them, there are very loveable people, they are great people, they are Jesus in the distressing disguise."[9]

Love for the poor is not optional. It is at the heart of what it means to know Christ.

"Blessed are the merciful," said Jesus, "for they will be shown mercy" (Matthew 5:7). When we allow our compassion to move us and show love to others, we're on the right track. And when we spot someone showing love to others who are on the outside—like Mother Teresa did—it's evidence of living faith.

Her words echo Jesus in Matthew 25 when He said, "Whatever you did for one of the least of these brothers and sisters of mine, you did for me" (v. 40).

When you read the stories about Jesus, it's good to notice where He is and who He's with. There are a few temples and religious leaders in there, but much of the time He's with the outcasts, the poor, the overlooked, and the down-trodden. He's with the people everybody knows are messing up.

If you want to see Him at work today, go join with others who are showing His love to ones the rest of the world so often overlooks.

24 LOVE WILL TRIUMPH

IT WAS A CRIME to practice Christianity in Reverand Fang-Chen's native country. That's why he was in jail. He had been horrifically tortured, but he refused to tell the authorities the names of his fellow believers. One day he was taken for yet more questioning and shown his mother—beaten, chained, and weak.

"I have heard," said the officer, "that you Christians have Ten Commandments, given by God. Would you be so kind as to recite them?"

Gripped by fear, Cheng recited the commandments, but the officer stopped him when he got to "Honor your father and mother."

"I want to give you the chance to honor your mother right now. Tell me who your fellow Christians are, and I promise you that tonight you and your mother will be free. You will be able to give her care and honor. Show me how much you really believe in God and want to follow His commandments."

It was an impossible decision to make. "What shall I do?" Cheng cried out to his mother.

"I have taught you from childhood to love Christ and His holy church. Don't mind my suffering. Stay faithful to the Savior and His followers. If you betray them, you are no more my son."

Cheng never saw his mother again. But her faith and trust in God left a lasting impression on him.[10]

> The fire of love stops at nothing—
> > it sweeps everything before it.
> Flood waters can't drown love,
> > torrents of rain can't put it out. (Song of Solomon 8:6–7 MSG)

This is the truth about God's love. Nothing can put it out. It casts out fear. It trumps hatred. It lives forever. And in every situation Christ can be found. The Lord will not call you to do anything that He has not prepared you for, neither will He lead you to a place where He is not present (1 Thessalonians 5:24).

Those two brave souls are among many millions who have stood firm in their faith against terrifying situations—and I am certain their joy is now complete.

25 LIVE WITHIN HIS LOVE

JESUS REALLY WAS SUCH an amazing man.

Time magazine called Him "the most persistent symbol of purity, selflessness and love in the history of western humanity."[11] His life is the supreme example of love, and it was said of His time on earth that "all who touched [him] were healed" (Mark 6:56).

There's nothing we need that Jesus can't provide, no wound so deep that His love won't heal.

As the Holocaust survivor Corrie ten Boom said, "There is no pit so deep that God's love is not deeper still."[12] This statement from her is so powerful. This incredible lady, who lost everything in the Holocaust, who saw horrors beyond horrors, somehow knew the love of Christ was within her.

> "I have loved you even as the Father has loved me. Live within my love." (John 15:9 TLB)

This is the invitation that Jesus always shared: to live within His love—to soak it in, to share it with others the way it has been offered to us: freely without being forced, full of grace.

26 RISK MORE

FOR CANON ANDREW WHITE, taking risks and facing danger is a way of life. Known by many as the Vicar of Baghdad, he has devoted himself to serving the people of the Iraqi capital.

Even when ISIS threatened to overtake the city and Andrew was forced by his clergy boss as well as the security forces to leave, he went only as far as Jordan, in order to be able to continue to serve those Iraqis living as refugees.

A medic by training, Andrew's initial career plans did not involve bullet-proof vests and security details. But once he started out on this journey of faith and love, everything about his attitude to life changed.

"I tell people not to take care but to take risks," he said. "It is difficult to learn how to do it though, and it is not something people gain overnight. It has to be an ongoing process."[13]

That process of embracing risk and finding courage relies on our making a daily choice to say yes to the opportunities God places in front of us. It's about taking small steps as we learn to listen to, and trust, God's voice.

Paul knew all about a life of risk and danger as well. "What, then, shall we say in response to these things? If God is for us, who can be against us?" (Romans 8:31).

The only real risk is refusing to be held by Christ. That's where we become weak and in danger. But under His wing, our lives and futures will always be assured.

27 GOD MADE US ALL

KOKO WAS FORTY-SIX WHEN she died in her sleep. It was not a dramatic death, but it was reported around the world. You see, Koko was a gorilla—and a very unusual one at that.

When Penny Patterson, a PhD student, told her tutor that she wanted to see whether gorillas could learn sign language, she was told that it was unlikely. She decided to try anyhow.

Even though Koko started slowly, learning just three words in four years, she finally got going. Eventually she learned more than one thousand words of sign language and could understand almost two thousand spoken words. She combined words when she needed to—calling a ring a "finger bracelet" and nectarine yogurt "orange flower sauce."

But the best signing she ever did was when a journalist asked her for the meaning of life.

"People be polite," she signed. "People have goodness."[14]

I love Koko's explanation of the meaning of life—and it seems a lot like the greatest commandment Jesus gave us: to love the Lord your God with all your heart and to love your neighbor as yourself (Matthew 22:36–39). Be polite. Have goodness. It's funny how so much of science and the natural world is intertwined with humanity, instinctively working in harmony.

Look at what the Bible says:

> But ask the animals, and they will teach you,
>> or the birds in the sky, and they will tell you. . . .
> In his hand is the life of every creature
>> and the breath of all mankind. (Job 12:7–10)

We're not alone in this universe. We're not on some pointless mission that makes no sense and has no destination. We're known and loved and invited into a relationship with the very Creator of the universe.

God made us all. The animals, the stars, the whole world. But we humans, His children, have always been the apple of His eye.

SOMETIMES, WHEN WE FEEL lost, it takes something truly dramatic to bring us back. But it's not the only way. Sometimes it is the quiet whisper in our hearts that leads us home.

Jesus says He is the way back to life, and we read in the Bible that Jesus "brings us right into the presence of God" (Hebrews 7:19 MSG). He says He is the One through which all life's true essentials—forgiveness, love, and power—are made possible.

So keep on seeking, keep on asking, keep on reaching out in your heart. He will be there. That's His promise. That's grace.

Do that, and "we see it taking shape day after day—a holy temple built by God, all of us built into it, a temple in which God is quite at home" (Ephesians 2:19–22 MSG).

A temple built on solid foundations. Built by Him, in you.

> SOMETIMES IT IS THE QUIET WHISPER IN
> OUR HEARTS THAT LEADS US HOME.

I HAVE DECIDED

INDIA IN THE NINETEENTH century was a dangerous place to travel. But that didn't put off the many missionaries who left the valleys of Wales with the goal of introducing people to faith. As they started preaching throughout Assam, India, many of them caused and got into serious trouble.

When one particular Indian family turned its back on the traditional religion and decided to follow Christ, the local chief went into a rage.

But however much the chief ranted, the family wouldn't take it back. They had found something special. Instead, the father carried on sharing the good news about this relationship he had found with the living God. Even more people in the community started to seek God's presence in their lives.

The chief went so far as to threaten to kill the family members if they wouldn't repent. But none of them would. Instead, the father poured out these simple words:

"I have decided to follow Jesus. No turning back, no turning back."

Eventually all the family members were tragically killed.

The chief was troubled, though. How had they shown such courage? What was it about this Christ that was worth laying down their lives for? What power was found in this strange God? The chief had seen so much death in his life—but never deaths like these. It broke him, and he fell to his knees. The chief, and the rest of the village too, started to follow Christ.[15]

> If you suffer as a Christian, do not be ashamed, but praise God that you bear that name. (1 Peter 4:16)

So much bad stuff went on in those days, and I am not saying we should be converting foreign lands left, right, and center. Likewise, let's hope that you and I never have to pay the kind of price that those brave martyrs endured.

But what if we lived with the strength that comes from knowing that Christ is always beside us, however hard the road of life becomes? What if we loved with the courage that comes from knowing that God will never leave us?

30 THE INVISIBLE PRESENCE

IT IS HARD TO believe in something we cannot see. And to believe in a God of love is a big statement—unless the evidence is beyond compelling.

Like the wind and electricity, just because we can't see God, it doesn't mean He doesn't exist. And like the wind and electricity, when we see the effects of God on human lives, it can knock us clean off our feet. Jesus described this as "the invisible moving the visible" (John 3:5–6 MSG).

God makes a clear promise to everyone who chooses to trust Him: "If we believe . . . we'll experience that state of resting" (Hebrews 4:3 MSG). It's a great place to be, that state of resting, but like many of God's gifts, it's internal. We don't physically see it. It's deep within us that God restores, renews, and revives.

God promises that His presence won't always be invisible. He says that there's a day coming when "the mountains will drip new wine, and the hills will flow with milk; all the ravines of Judah will run with water. A fountain will flow out of the LORD's house" (Joel 3:18). That time will be amazing. No pain, fear, evil, or illness. Heaven will be full of love and goodness and plenty of laughter.

Until then, let's stand tall and believe. Know His invisible presence with you. Trust God and allow your soul and spirit to be refreshed by Him today as you go about your business. That's faith.

HOPE

IN THE SUMMER OF 1996, I spent a month helping out on a game farm in the northern Transvaal in South Africa, advising on how to keep poachers at bay. I decided to head north to Zimbabwe for some fun before heading home to the UK. For me back then, fun meant skydiving with good friends, with cool drinks in the evening.

Life was all good.

The flight to fifteen thousand feet was uneventful. Soon I stood in the cargo area of the plane and looked down. I took a familiar deep breath, then slid off the step. The clouds felt damp on my face as I fell through them. How I loved that feeling of falling through whiteout. At four thousand feet I pulled the ripcord and heard the canopy open with a reassuring crack. My 130-mph free fall quickly slowed down to 25 mph, just as it always did.

But when I looked up I realized something was wrong—very wrong. Instead of a smooth rectangular shape above me, I had a very deformed-looking tangle of chute, which meant the whole parachute would be a nightmare to try to control. I pulled hard on both steering toggles to see if that would help me.

It didn't.

I kept trying to control it, but I was burning through time and altitude fast. It wasn't getting any better. Within seconds I was too low to use my reserve chute, and the ground was coming up fast. I flared the chute too high and too hard. This jerked my body up horizontally, then I dropped away and smashed into the desert floor, landing on my back, right on top of the tightly packed reserve chute that formed a rock-hard square shape in the middle of the pack.

I couldn't stand up; I could only roll over and moan on the dusty earth. I was biting the ground in agony.

I didn't know the extent of the damage at the time, that I had shattered three key vertebrae in my back and would go on to spend months in and out of military rehabilitation back in the UK, strapped into braces and unable to move freely. But in those first few minutes as I lay there, one thing I did know was that my life had just changed forever.

Sometimes it isn't until we get knocked down that we find which way is up. Sometimes it isn't until the sky clouds over that we notice the light. And sometimes it isn't until we lie in the gutter that we begin to see the stars.

The light of God has been the greatest source of hope this world has ever known. We can never be so far away that the light won't reach us. Sometimes it is good to be reminded of that. Hope will always win and the light of Christ reaches everywhere.

1 HEART AND EYES

JESUS OFTEN TOLD US that what goes on in our heart is what really matters. And our eyes are one of the gatekeepers to our hearts, to the inner life. That is why what you look at matters so much.

> "Your eye is a lamp, lighting up your whole body. If you live wide-eyed in wonder and belief, your body fills up with light. If you live squinty-eyed in greed and distrust, your body is a dank cellar. Keep your eyes open, your lamp burning, so you don't get musty and murky. Keep your life as well-lighted as your best-lighted room." (Luke 11:34–36 MSG)

Today, let's ask God to forgive when we have looked at things that we know and feel instinctively are wrong and to forgive the parts of us that are unkind or selfish. Let's guard what we look at and let into our hearts. Let's look to Christ to fill our hearts with His love, that our eyes would shine His light, mercy, and goodness.

2 FOUND IN CHRIST

WE ALL WANT TO find our purpose in something. It's just the way we're made. Look around and you can see the different places that people go searching for meaning for their lives. Some hunt down more wealth; others crave power or influence.

But our real nature is never determined by this kind of "success." The only way we truly know why we're here (and the only true source of real and lasting hope in this life) is in knowing to whom we belong and how precious we are to the Almighty.

Those who put their hope in Jesus "can no longer die; for they are like the angels. They are God's children, since they are children of the resurrection" (Luke 20:36).

I have experienced that incredible sense of purpose of being found in Christ, and it changes everything. We know we are truly loved; we find home, peace, and strength; we draw on His resources; and we reach out in love to all those we come into contact with.

That's a purpose that can follow us all through our lives and that will lead us to glory.

3 | FLAWED BUT FOUND

IT IS SOMETIMES TEMPTING to think of Paul as some sort of saint. But read this passage below. I find it so heartening. In it there is no presence of being all sorted out and together. Instead, there is a raw honesty about his failings and struggles. I like him all the more for this.

> What I don't understand about myself is that I decide one way, but then I act another, doing things I absolutely despise. . . . It happens so regularly that it's predictable. The moment I decide to do good, sin is there to trip me up. I truly delight in God's commands, but it's pretty obvious that not all of me joins in that delight. Parts of me covertly rebel, and just when I least expect it, they take charge. (Romans 7:15, 21–23 MSG)

These honest words remind me that we must never be conned into acting all spiritual and too together. We need to aim for honesty and a raw, simple dependence on Jesus. The rest will follow. He will help us to walk in His ways from here. God said, "Stop trusting in mere humans, who have but a breath in their nostrils. Why hold them in esteem?" (Isaiah 2:22).

We can stop trying to impress others; we need only have eyes and hearts for Christ. We are all flawed, but in Him we are found.

4 HOPE IS FOR EVERYONE

CHARLES HADDON SPURGEON WAS one of the greatest and most influential preachers of the nineteenth century, but he wasn't always a man of faith.

It was only when he was a teenager that he heard a speaker say something that made him think: "Look to Jesus Christ. Look! Look! Look! You have nothing to do but to look and live."

Writing years later, he described his reaction to these words: "Like as when the brazen serpent was lifted up, the people only looked and were healed, so it was with me. . . . When I heard that word, 'Look!' what a charming word it seemed to me! Oh! I looked until I could almost have looked my eyes away."[16]

It isn't complicated, and we certainly don't have to make it religious. Hope is a gift that is offered to everyone.

> The eternal God is your refuge,
> and underneath are the everlasting arms. (Deuteronomy 33:27)

All it takes is the humility to look, kneel, and accept.

5 DIFFERENT BUT THE SAME

In some ways Jesus and John the Baptist were so different. John, with his wild look and crazy diet, appeared to be an outsider. Jesus grew up like a regular guy with a steady job.* Yet they were the best of friends and 100 percent rooted in the same hope.

Neither of them acted the way they did because they wanted to impress people or win affirmation. They did it because they were true to their calling, true to their character, and true to each other. Above all, they had learned to put their hope in God alone.

> Since you are my rock and my fortress,
>> for the sake of your name lead and guide me. (Psalm 31:3)

So today, let's live like John the Baptist and Jesus, knowing where our home always is and rooted in God's love.

This is how to be empowered, to live fully, and to live kindly: always staying close to the source. This is key to life.

---

* I love it when Jesus replied to the criticisms of the religious elite by saying, "For John the Baptist came neither eating bread nor drinking wine, and you say, 'He has a demon.' The Son of Man came eating and drinking, and you say, 'Here is a glutton and a drunkard, a friend of tax collectors and sinners'" (Luke 7:33–34). So ironic. The elite accused John of having a demon and Jesus of being a glutton and a drunkard! Some people will never see truth, and you can only love them and smile.

6   NO CONDEMNATION

IT IS OKAY TO stop trying so hard to be good, because we aren't and we can't be. We are flawed and broken. But here is the clincher: it is only when we know our failings that we can find true strength. When we know that nothing we can do will "earn" us heaven, when we are honest about our failings, then we are brought to our knees and seek His mercy. It is then that we can be lifted up and restored by His presence and His love.

This is the way to power.

Look at what Jesus said to a woman who had been caught in adultery:

"Then neither do I condemn you," Jesus declared. (John 8:11)

There is *no* condemnation in Christ. He came to free us and save us, to love us and strengthen us. That's all. No catch. When we live like this—free and lifted up in our hearts—then we can love and do many good things. But we do it from a place of overflowing rather than from trying to earn anything.

Today let's live in God's overflowing goodness, showered down on us, to spread around to all we meet.

7   LIVES MADE WHOLE

A LOT OF PEOPLE get caught in the trap that if they act or look the right way, they'll somehow be more acceptable to God. Likewise, from the Old Testament times right up to today, people have thought that being really religious was somehow key to winning favor with God.

Jesus spoke against this again and again. Religion and good deeds can't earn our way to heaven. Our best deeds, Isaiah said, are like dirty rags to God. Jesus came instead to save us—often from ourselves and our superstitions and vain attempts at being good or finding confidence. Jesus came to end all that "religion" and hypocrisy, to end pretenses and to remove our false veneers. He came to free us from those sort of restraints and impossible expectations.

> You prepare a table before me
>> in the presence of my enemies.
> You anoint my head with oil;
>> my cup overflows.
> Surely your goodness and love will follow me
>> all the days of my life,
> and I will dwell in the house of the LORD
>> forever. (Psalm 23:5–6)

He came to forgive us, to restore us, to free us, to win us. Our lives are made whole when we truly encounter that unending, undeserved love for us. It is this love that brings with it courage, confidence, integrity, and strength, because it isn't ours—it is His.

8 THE PURSUIT OF HAPPINESS

SO MANY PEOPLE IN the world today are desperately searching for happiness. We look in all kinds of places: fulfilling relationships, a great job, a nice boat, becoming president, becoming a billionaire, or simply enjoying a good wine. None of these things are wrong. But on their own they won't lead us to lasting happiness.

In fact, the pursuit of these things can be one giant dead end and distraction in our pursuit of happiness. I have seen more misery from power, wealth, and fame than from any other corner of society. None of us want to spend our whole lives hunting down happiness in all the wrong places.

Christ said that happiness is found in closeness to Him:

"Whoever believes in me, as Scripture has said, rivers of living water will flow from within them." (John 7:38)

It is okay to want to live rich lives—that is natural. But the Bible says that the whole point of Jesus' coming to earth was so that we might "become rich" (2 Corinthians 8:9).

We become rich in blessings, in spirit, in happiness, in peace. We become rich in purpose and character. The Bible reminds us that the way of true riches is "the fear of the LORD," and that this brings "riches and honor and life" (Proverbs 22:4).

The happiest people I know have found it within, not without. This can take us a lifetime to figure out.

9 HOPE FOR YOU AND ME

HOWEVER DIFFICULT OUR SITUATIONS may be—however much trouble we are facing in life—there can always be hope. Hope transcends everything: every pain, sorrow, fear, and loss. Hope is what sets us apart as children of God. Hope is the light to the dark, the comfort to the pain.

Hope comes from knowing God's love for you. We might not feel very hopeful of anything, but His hope is out there—close. Just look for it. Trust it.

Even a tiny glimmer is enough. Great fires are started from tiny embers. Just hold on and look up.

Hope through the pain and through the doubts. Have faith, and know that faith and doubt are simply two sides of the same coin. You will have many doubts. Don't worry. Accept them and know that faith must be close by. Whatever we face, He faces it beside us. He will never desert us.

> The LORD is close to the brokenhearted
>> and saves those who are crushed in spirit. (Psalm 34:18)

Take heart. All will be well.

10 HEARTS AND FEET

I SOMETIMES REALLY STRUGGLE with going to church and organized religion as such—I think maybe it makes me feel too flawed, too judged, too broken. But church isn't a building or an institution. Church is the people of God. Church is any of us who want to cling to His robes and live in His strength, love, and light—together, with others who need His help. That's church.

I love how God said this:

> I can't stand your religious meetings.
>> I'm fed up with your conferences and conventions.
> I want nothing to do with your religion projects,
>> your pretentious slogans and goals.
> I'm sick of your fund-raising schemes,
>> your public relations and image making.

I've had all I can take of your noisy ego-music.
When was the last time you sang to *me*?
Do you know what I want?
I want justice—oceans of it.
I want fairness—rivers of it.
That's what I want. That's *all* I want. (Amos 5:21–24 MSG)

Forget the rituals; be kind. Forget the religion; love people. Be fair; be just. Love. Love. Love.

But it's not just the problem with religion and ritual that God is pointing out here. It's the fact that we develop hard hearts and soft feet. God wants us to have the opposite: soft hearts and hard feet. We should have hearts of love for the unloved and feet that are toughened by going where others fear to tread, wherever that might lead.

11 REACH OUT TO THE HEALER

I'VE GOT A GOOD number of physical scars from various adventures over the years. I don't mind them too much. As for my feet, well, they are just a mess. If I am honest, there are also a few emotional scars lurking about as well. They're the ones that take a lot longer to heal.

Joyce Meyer wrote that emotional "healing does not come easily and can be quite painful. Sometimes we have wounds that are still infected, and before we can be thoroughly healed, those wounds must be opened and the infection removed. Only God knows how to do this properly. As you seek God for the healing from your hurts, . . . spend time with God in His Word and wait in His presence. I guarantee you will find healing there!"[17]

Instead of being ashamed of our wounds, maybe it's okay to admit they exist. Maybe being aware that we need healing is a really good way to keep us holding on tight to our faith in God. Time and experience have taught me that there is nothing quite like the healing presence of Christ.

> Then the woman, seeing that she could not go unnoticed, came trembling and fell at his feet. In the presence of all the people, she told why she had touched him and how she had been instantly healed. Then he said to her, "Daughter, your faith has healed you. Go in peace." (Luke 8:47–48)

That's how we get healed. Reach out to the Healer.

12 YOU NEED ONLY BE STILL

MANKIND HAS ALWAYS GONE to such lengths to find hope, but the truth is that it's closer than the air we breathe. Finding hope can be like a child reaching for the outstretched hand of a loving parent.

It's natural but sometimes hard. It takes courage and faith, and life often beats those qualities out of us. Our job is to rediscover both courage and faith in order to find hope.

Writing in the fourteenth century, Thomas à Kempis knew just how close that hope is: "Father, let me hold your hand, and like a child walk with you down all my days, secure in your love and strength."[18]

When we place our hand in God's, we connect with the greatest power the universe has ever known. We find ourselves on the winning side. We are protected.

> The LORD will fight for you; you need only to be still. (Exodus 14:14)

This is what our great hope is—being found in His love and mercy.

13 ASK. BELIEVE. TRUST.

I LOVE THE EXPRESSION "to err is human; to forgive is divine."

The Bible is full of stories of people who lost their way. We all have moments when trusting God is hard. We all fall down. But what makes the difference is being able to reach out our hands and let God pick us back up again. This is what sets the Christian faith apart—the hand of forgiveness that asks for nothing in return.

So when doubt starts to rise up within us and faith grows faint, remember that it's normal. Many great men and women of faith have experienced much worse—and fallen much farther.

Trust Jesus to do what He came to do: to forgive, restore, and strengthen us. That is the beating heart of a vibrant faith. Know that Christ is good and wants good things for us. It all hinges on quiet trust and humble faith.

Jesus said that if you believe, you will receive whatever you ask for in prayer:

> "If you embrace this kingdom life and don't doubt God, you'll not only do minor feats like I did to the fig tree, but also triumph over huge obstacles. . . . Absolutely everything, ranging from small to large, as you make it a part of your believing prayer, gets included as you lay hold of God." (Matthew 21:21–22 MSG)

Ask. Believe. Trust God. Develop a childlike dependence and trust that Christ will provide and always be beside you. It is the hallmark of a champion.

WEALTH. EDUCATION. REPUTATION. IT is easy to base our self-esteem on things like these. But being confident because of what we possess or how we look isn't a good long-term strategy for life.

The writer of Proverbs has some advice that still works today: "The LORD will be your confidence" (3:26 ESV). When we look to Him for affirmation, so much goodness follows:

- Wisdom—"The wise will inherit honor, but fools get disgrace" (v. 35 ESV). Wisdom, good judgment, and discernment all follow when we trust God.
- Peace—"If you lie down, you will not be afraid; when you lie down, your sleep will be sweet. Do not be afraid of sudden terror or of the ruin of the wicked" (vv. 24–25 ESV). Success at work, wealth, and fame are of little value if you do not have peace. And peace comes from having a right relationship with God.
- Love—"Do not withhold good from those to whom it is due, when it is in your power to do it" (v. 27 ESV). We become better people when God is our guide.
- Intimacy—"The upright are in his confidence" (v. 32 ESV). The more we trust God, the closer we get to Him.
- Humility—"Toward the scorners he is scornful, but to the humble he gives favor" (v. 34 ESV). When we look to God for affirmation, we get a right view of ourselves: humble yet confident in His power and love.

People of love and faith don't always get it right; we fall down a lot. But let's fix our eyes on God and put our confidence in Christ.

15 FORTRESS FROM FAILURE

AT SOME POINT IN your life, you're going to fail big-time, especially if you set for yourself significant goals or follow your calling toward some big old mountains. Failure will be part of your journey. Don't fear it; embrace it. Failure means you are making progress. It is one of the many doorways you must pass through on your route to success. But failure, rejection, mockery, and humiliation hurt.

At times like these, it's good to remember the words of people like David, a guy who failed spectacularly and regularly. He was indeed a man who knew all about God's redemption, love, and grace.

> When I said, "My foot is slipping,"
>> your unfailing love, LORD, supported me.
> When anxiety was great within me,
>> your consolation brought me joy. . . .
> But the LORD has become my fortress,
>> and my God the rock in whom I take refuge. (Psalm 94:18–19, 22)

We can always turn to God for help and comfort in our failures. The power of failure evaporates in His presence. The love of Christ never runs out, and it always encourages us. Our well of resolve is limitless when we have Him as our cup.

16 THE TRUE SOURCE

SUCCESS IN LIFE ISN'T about being the strongest, the richest, the one who towers above all others. In God's eyes, true success means something else completely.

Mother Teresa wrote, "[God] is everything to me—and—His own little one—so helpless—so empty—so small."[19]

Paul expressed this dependence when he wrote about the "thorn in his flesh." Three times he pleaded with the Lord to take it away. But God said to him, "My grace is sufficient for you, for my power is made perfect in weakness" (2 Corinthians 12:9). Being aware of our failings and weakness can help us connect to the only true Source of power in this life.

> Abuse, accidents, opposition, bad breaks. I just let Christ take over! And so the weaker I get, the stronger I become. (2 Corinthians 12:10 MSG)

That's why the way of faith is so beautifully topsy-turvy to society's values. In our weakness we become strong. True success starts with humility and ends with plugging into a source greater than ourselves.

17 ▌ CASTING OUT FEAR

FEAR IS TOXIC TO happiness. It can destroy our enjoyment of the present and suffocate any hope we have for the future. But it doesn't have to be this way. God promises to rescue you "from hidden traps, [he] shields you from deadly hazards. His huge outstretched arms protect you—under them you're perfectly safe; his arms fend off all harm" (Psalm 91:3–4 MSG).

The psalmist told us to "fear nothing" (v. 5 MSG), and he went on to describe the kind of fearlessness we can all hope for: "You will not fear the terror of night, nor the arrow that flies by day, nor the pestilence that stalks in the darkness, nor the plague that destroys at midday" (vv. 5–6).

How do we get there? Perfect love casts out fear. When we are rooted in the love of God—the presence, strength, and peace of God—we see beyond the fear. The closer we are to God, the weaker fear's grip becomes on us. As the psalmist wrote,

GOD, you're my refuge. I trust in you and I'm safe! (v. 2 MSG)

Fear doesn't have to have the last word or be the loudest voice within us. And it is God's love that always drives it away.

18 ▌ IN THE MIDST OF THE STORM

THE STORM ON THE Sea of Galilee didn't just whip up the wind and the waves; it sent everyone in the boat into a panic. Even the hardened fishermen among them who would have been used to bad weather were reduced to terrified children. Well, almost everyone.

As the disciples panicked and prayed, Jesus stayed asleep. The disciples were only too aware of the danger and the risk. They knew that waves of that size could overturn their boat and take their lives.

Jesus stayed asleep.

Two thousand years later, we are still so often found panicking in the boat. When life gets tough we can spend a lot of time and energy wondering when Jesus is going to wake up and do something! In times like this, our faith is being tested.

Eventually Jesus acted, and the storm was silenced as quickly as it came. He calmed the wild sea that was raging around and within the disciples.

"Quiet! Be still!" (Mark 4:39)

He's still the same Lord, and He's still got the same power to calm the winds, the waves, and the panic within us. He still has the power to take a story that begins with fear and end it with faith.

As crisis tests your faith, remember that Christ is strengthening you: He wants you to learn to look to Him, to trust Him even in the middle of the fiercest of life's storms. And like a muscle, as we work it, it gets ever stronger. This is how men and women of faith are made: they live in the knowledge that God protects them.

19 LIGHT TO A DARK PATH

WE ALL GO THROUGH times when we feel as though we're in a desert. It's simply part of life, and it's nothing to hide from. If you are in the badlands right now, hold on to these truths below. I hope they help you as much as they've helped me.

God says, "Don't be afraid. . . . You're mine. When you're in over your head, I'll be there with you. . . . It won't be a dead end" (Isaiah 43:1–2 MSG).

I am GOD, your personal God. . . .
I paid a huge price for you. . . .
    That's how much I love you!
I'd sell off the whole world to get you back,
    trade the creation just for you. (vv. 3–4 MSG)

You are precious and valued because He loves you. So often we fail to understand quite how valuable we are to God. We're worth the price He paid: the death of His own Son, Jesus.

In all the struggles and difficulties of life, God has a good plan for your future. He said, "I'm about to do something brand-new. . . . I'm making a road through the desert, rivers in the badlands" (v. 19 MSG).

Just because we can't see or feel God close to us, it doesn't mean that He isn't there, and it doesn't mean that His plans have failed. The hope we have in Him is much bigger than anything we currently feel in simply our emotions. To many great men and women through the ages, Christ has been light to a dark path, strength to a failing body, and hope to a struggling mind.

20 | LOVE SO AMAZING

PAUL WAS A MAN who suffered greatly. He endured beatings, near drownings, starvation, rejection, imprisonment, and so many other hardships. In fact, it is said he was disfigured beyond recognition through torture.[20] But he said that these sufferings cannot come close to comparing to the glory we will see one day. There is no comparison "between the present hard times and the coming good times" (Romans 8:18 MSG).

That's courage, trust, and faith in action, a faith forged and tested through the fire of life—and pain. Through it all, Paul knew the truth. He had seen it on the road to Damascus. Here is that truth—and we can build our life on it: "Nothing will ever be able to separate us from the love of God demonstrated by our Lord Jesus Christ when he died for us" (Romans 8:39 TLB).

Hymn writer Isaac Watts wrote, "Love so amazing, so divine, demands my soul, my life, my all."[21] How will we all now live, knowing that nothing can ever separate us from God's love? This love is the source of all true courage.

21 HOSTILES

IN AUSTRALIA THEY CALL it "tall poppy syndrome": the idea that the public wants to "cut down to size" anyone who they think has excelled in some aspect of life. It's not just Down Under. All over the world people find that the higher the profile they have, the greater criticism they receive.

People of all faiths have faced opposition. The Israelites were under constant threat, and nearly all the leaders of the early Christian church were murdered for their beliefs. A life of faith isn't meant to be easy.

"Don't think I've come to make life cozy," said Jesus. (Matthew 10:34 MSG)

How we react to criticism is crucial. We don't need to be defensive or go on the attack. Instead, we are called to break the cycle of retaliation. We are called to be peacemakers, to know that whatever storms rage around us, we can hold tight to God's truths.

We have this hope as an anchor for the soul, firm and secure. It enters the inner sanctuary behind the curtain. (Hebrews 6:19)

So develop broad shoulders and don't let the critics hold power over your heart. Instead place your trust in God and walk on. He's the One strong enough to see you through and to hold you firm.

Our value isn't in man's empty praise. Our value is in being a son or daughter of the Almighty, treasured and protected. Trust in that alone.

22 OUR LIFE WORK

I USED TO THINK that following Christ meant going to church and obeying rules, and neither sounded like much fun. Luckily, I was wrong.

Here is what a life of faith is really about: being free, being loved, being forgiven, and then giving kindness, goodness, and the love of Christ to all. That's the calling. What we do here on earth has eternal consequences. The Bible says that one day we will all have to give account for what we've done with our lives.

At her coronation Queen Elizabeth II was handed a copy of the Bible inscribed with these words: "We present you with this book, the most valuable thing that this world affords." It's a powerful reminder of our responsibility before God to share the love and truth that the Bible reveals. But we don't do it alone. We are serving an all-powerful God who encourages us at every turn:

"I'm on your side, taking up your cause." (Jeremiah 51:36 MSG)

So let's never give up. Let's make sharing the love of Christ our life work.

23 STEWARDS OF HOPE

HOPE IS A STRANGE word, and we don't all know just how much we need it until it is gone. But hope is so desperately needed in our world. And where we find it really matters.

We all see so many dead-end "miracle" solutions around us that all too often lead us nowhere. I remember once hearing an old man say, "Choose wisely where you find your hope, as it will shape your life and future."

This verse is where I choose to find real hope today: "The LORD will guide you always; he will satisfy your needs in a sun-scorched land and will strengthen your frame" (Isaiah 58:11).

Trusting in Christ makes us His sons and daughters, His stewards of hope.

A pastor friend of mine once wrote, "We steward the only message on planet earth that can give people what their hearts need most, which is hope. Hope that sins can be forgiven. Hope that prayers can be answered. Hope that the doors of opportunity, that seemed locked, can be opened. Hope that broken relationships can be reconciled. Hope that diseased bodies can be healed. Hope that damaged trust can be restored."[22]

This hope of ours is powerful stuff, and we get to live it and radiate it out to others. That's pretty amazing.

24 THE THREE SISTERS

WE ALL FACE TIMES when faith feels hard to find. When troubles line up in front of us, it can seem like trusting God is crazy, and love and kindness get us nowhere. And as for hope, well, we *hope* things will improve soon, but that's about it!

But faith, hope, and love form the three great theological virtues. And hope is a lot stronger than we might think.

As Raniero Cantalamessa wrote, these great virtues of faith, hope, and love "are like three sisters. Two of them are grown and the other is a small child. They go forward together hand in hand with the child hope in the middle. Looking at them it would seem that the bigger ones are pulling the child, but it is the other way around; it is the little girl who is pulling the two bigger ones. It is hope that pulls faith and [love]. Without hope everything would stop."[23]

So never underestimate the power of hope, however small that hope feels. Sometimes in survival, in life, and in faith, an ember is all we need.

> In his great mercy he has given us new birth into a living hope through the resurrection of Jesus Christ from the dead. (1 Peter 1:3)

Whatever you're facing, you are not alone. Let whatever small bit of hope you can find inside lead you on. Ask for God's presence, and put your hand into His. Faith and love will flow from that.

Remember: Christ beside us, Christ within us, Christ to win us.

25 WHERE HOPE COMES FROM

WHENEVER WE FIND OURSELVES wondering how we're going to get through the tough times in life, the answer is found in where we look for our hope. Being hopeful is much more than mere wishful thinking. Because of what Christ did for us, we have total confidence in being full of hopefulness. And because of the way the Holy Spirit works, there's a constant source of hope being nurtured and tended deep inside us.

This hope is the driving force for our day-to-day living. As Erwin McManus commented, hope "lifts us out of the rubble of our failures, our pain and our fear to rise above what at one point seemed insurmountable. Our ability to endure, to persevere, to overcome is fueled by this one seemingly innocuous ingredient called hope."[24]

> May the God of hope fill you with all joy and peace as you trust in him, so that you may overflow with hope by the power of the Holy Spirit. (Romans 15:13)

Now that's a prayer to start our day.

26 DISTINGUISHING FEATURES

A HOLLYWOOD MAGAZINE EDITOR once commented on how many times I must have broken my nose, then offered to "straighten" it for the cover image of his magazine. It made me smile. I'm actually okay with my bent nose, just like I'm okay with my wrinkles. They tell a story, and together they remind me of the many adventures that life has taken me on.

I love the description of Paul found in a second-century document called the *Acts of Paul and Thecla*: "A man little of stature, thin-haired upon the head, crooked in the legs, of good state of body, with eyebrows joining, and nose somewhat hooked, full of grace: for sometimes he appeared like a man, and sometimes he had the face of an angel."[25] That is the part that really distinguished him: not his crooked legs or nose but his face shining bright like an angel.

The physical quirks that we all have don't really matter. They pass. What matters is how we live, because that endures. Let's make sure our lives are ones that reflect the peace, love, and light of Christ.

Jesus came and stood among them and said, "Peace be with you!" (John 20:19)

This is what He brings: lasting peace through His love-fueled presence. That's how to be distinguished.

Taste and see that the LORD is good;
blessed is the one who takes refuge in him. (Psalm 34:8)

This is what I would like on my tombstone—not that I had a crooked nose but that I tasted and saw that the Lord was good, that I was blessed because I took refuge in Him.

27 IT WILL ALL BE OKAY IN THE END

KING DAVID HAD IT rough at times. He was captured by the Philistines in Gath and was abused and beaten. Yet it wasn't the end for him.

Hard times aren't the end of our story. We all go through tough moments. Life can beat us all up. Maybe it is severe and you are persecuted, tortured, and killed. Still, that would not be the end of your story. Our futures are assured in Christ. As Jesus said to the thief on the cross next to Him,

"Truly I tell you, today you will be with me in paradise." (Luke 23:42)

Our role, as Paul said, is to "keep your eyes open, hold tight to your convictions, give it all you've got, be resolute, and love without stopping" (1 Corinthians 16:13–14 MSG).

We are on the right side of history. Love will always be the winning team.

Voltaire, an eighteenth-century philosopher and critic of Christianity, said, "Within a hundred years the Bible will be obsolete and will have gone out of circulation altogether."[26] A hundred years later the Bible was more popular than ever. It still is the highest-selling book of all time. Yet the book itself is but a pale reflection of the character of Jesus Himself. Christ will always be number one in the world. When people encounter Christ, He changes them for the better.

Whether in the life of Emperor Constantine, who heard the truth of Jesus and changed the entire Roman Empire, or of a broken prisoner in modern-day Syria, the presence of Christ changes human hearts. It is happening every day. He changes us and is leading us all home. Our job is to let Him.

28 GOD–CONFIDENCE

PEOPLE TALK ABOUT WANTING self-confidence. But this has its flaws. If all we trust in is ourselves, we will fail. Human history tells us this repeatedly. Man is fallible.

Instead of self-confidence, let's develop God-confidence. Be confident in Him and in these fundamental truths:

- You are precious to God. (Jeremiah 31:3)
- Your salvation was bought at a great price—Jesus hung on a cross alone for you and me. (1 Corinthians 6:20)
- He loves you unconditionally, no strings attached. (1 John 4:19)
- He will never leave you or let you down. (Deuteronomy 31:8)
- He will strengthen you and bring you His peace. (Colossians 1:11–20)
- He gives you His courage, His wisdom, and His humility. (Micah 6:8)
- "Nothing will be impossible with God." (Luke 1:37 ESV)

Make these truths your source of confidence. Trust in the Almighty for your strength and power. The great men and women of faith throughout history have always relied on Him alone. That has been their key.

29 THE SOLDIER'S PRAYER

AFTER MY DAD DIED, I found a copy of "The Soldier's Prayer" among his papers. It was a thin, worn-out bit of paper, tucked into the side of his diary. In my father's semi-illegible scrawl were written these simple words: "Lord, I know what I must do this day. If I forget you, do not forget me. Amen."

It was a humble reminder not only of his time serving as a commando but also of the faithful journey with Christ that my late father had traveled.

When we embark on this adventure of faith, we don't just have a future inheritance when we get to heaven. We get to enjoy the first tastes of heaven right here on earth:

> Our offering to God is this: We are the sweet smell of Christ among those who are being saved and among those who are being lost. (2 Corinthians 2:15 EXB)

The longer we spend with Him as our guide, the more our lives change. Day by day, we find ourselves overflowing with the things that really matter in life: "love, joy, peace, forbearance, kindness, goodness, faithfulness, gentleness and self-control" (Galatians 5:22–23).

I saw this in my dad, and I see it in the lives of friends who quietly, humbly, and faithfully bow their knee and follow Christ and His way of love. We don't need to settle for second best—we can have it all. Let's aim to be full of the Holy Spirit, to overflowing, and receive our inheritance here on earth today.

WHAT IS THE MEANING of life? According to Richard Nixon, "Life is one crisis after another."[27]

John Lennon sang, "Life is what happens to you while you're busy making other plans."[28] But plenty of other public figures have said that the meaning and purpose of life was to be found in Jesus Christ. What does this mean, and what does it bring to our lives?

I see it as six beautiful things.

First, believers have forgiveness. Marghanita Laski, a well-known atheist, made a powerful statement on television once: "What I envy most about you Christians is your forgiveness." She added, "I have nobody to forgive me."[29]

Second, we have freedom. We're a free people—free of the penalties and punishment chalked up by all our misdeeds. And not just barely free either. "*Abundantly* free!" as the Bible says (Ephesians 1:8 MSG).

Next, we are indwelt by the Holy Spirit: "When you believed, you were marked in him with a seal, the promised Holy Spirit" (Ephesians 1:13). The Holy Spirit has come to live within us. When a package was dispatched in the ancient world, a seal was placed on it to indicate where it had come from and to whom it belonged. Your life has been sealed with the Holy Spirit.

We also have hope for the future. Our inheritance is guaranteed. We have "the riches of his glorious inheritance in his holy people" (Ephesians 1:18).

We are then entrusted with power and position: God's "incomparably great power for us who believe" is in you (Ephesians 1:19). Power belongs to God, but He has come to live within you and to give you "endless energy, boundless strength!" (v. 19 MSG).

Finally, we are called to love each other. The whole law is summed up in these words: love God and love each other (Mark 12:30–31).

PURPOSE

AS A KID I had no real idea what climbing the highest mountain in the world would require, but that didn't change the fact that it was an all-consuming dream of mine. My father and I would spend many a day scrambling up the chalk cliff faces near where I was brought up on the Isle of Wight in the UK. He'd climb beside me, encouraging and guiding me all the way to the top. They were special times together, and I believed there wasn't a mountain in the world I couldn't summit as long as my dad was there beside me.

When I broke my back all those years later while I was serving with the British Special Forces, the Everest dream that I had always held on to lay shattered too. Lying in recovery in that military hospital, I encountered some of the darkest, most doubt-filled times of my life. I lost not only my strength, movement, and ability to walk properly but also my confidence, sparkle, and spirit—and I felt so lost.

In those dark nights of the soul in that rehabilitation center, it was the dream of one day getting strong enough again to attempt to climb Everest that drove me on. It became the whole focus of my recovery. Do or die.

If I could make it, I would become one of the youngest climbers ever to reach the summit, but the real reason I wanted to attempt it was the feeling that life had given me a precious second chance, and I needed to make use of that.

I had smashed my back in three places, but miraculously I hadn't been paralyzed. I had survived for a reason, and however low and lacking I felt at the time, I would get stronger. I felt life calling me to grab it and to live it: to throw myself in feetfirst, 120 percent; to get out there and take risks; to fail and get back up; to laugh at the setbacks and at myself; to explore; to try to never give up. After all, I had come so close to losing it all, right?

Everything ahead of me was a gift—now what was I going to do with it? With a sense that nothing was impossible, I felt a tiny tingle returning inside of my spirit. God works through the storms of our lives, and tough times so often mean fresh beginnings.

1 NO ACCIDENT

THERE ARE MORE THAN 25,000 varieties of orchid, and the orchid is just one of 270,000 different flower species. There are more than 100 billion stars like our sun within our galaxy, and our galaxy is one of more than 100 billion other galaxies. It's said that for every grain of sand there are a million stars. I love the fact that it almost feels like a throwaway line in Genesis when the writer tells us, "He also made the stars" (Genesis 1:16). Clearly God does not do things by halves. God operates on the most massive scale, a scale too big for us to get our heads around.

But there's something even more mind-blowing than the size and detail of creation. It's the fact that God knows each one of us by name. He knows everything about us, and He loves us.

> You know me inside and out,
> > you know every bone in my body;
> you know exactly how I was made, bit by bit,
> > how I was sculpted from nothing into something. (Psalm
> > 139:13 MSG)

You weren't a mistake, and you're not overlooked. You're known and loved by the most powerful force in the universe.

GOD DOES NOT DO THINGS BY HALVES.

2 TACKLING LIFE

HOW CAN WE TACKLE huge projects without getting overwhelmed? How can we face even the smallest of tasks when often we just don't feel able?

Chosen by God to be a military leader, Gideon faced some monumental struggles. His response was very human: he was riddled with fear.

> Gideon replied, "but how can I save Israel? My clan is the weakest in Manasseh, and I am the least in my family."
>
> The LORD answered, "I will be with you." (Judges 6:15–16)

The same promise that God made to Gideon is repeated by Jesus to us:

> "And surely I am with you always, to the very end of the age." (Matthew 28:20)*

If we want empowered lives, we have to start with the knowledge and trust that He is with us, ready to guide and strengthen our steps each day. Be confident in that simple life-changing truth, because it changes everything.

> **IF WE WANT EMPOWERED LIVES, WE HAVE TO START WITH THE KNOWLEDGE AND TRUST THAT HE IS WITH US.**

---

* I had this verse engraved on the inside of Shara's wedding ring when we were first married. It's a good 'un.

3 BROKEN POTS

A WATER BEARER IN India had two large pots, both hung on the ends of a pole that was slung across his neck. One of the pots was perfect and always delivered a full portion of water. The other was cracked. At the end of the long walk from the stream to the house, the cracked pot always arrived half full.

The broken pot was embarrassed and miserable. One day, while the water bearer was filling it up at the stream, the pot spoke: "I am ashamed of myself, and I want to apologize to you. I have only been able to deliver half of what you give me because of this crack in my side. I leak all the way back to your house, making extra work for you."

The water bearer smiled. "Haven't you noticed the flowers that are growing on only your side of the path? I've always known about your crack, and so I planted flower seeds on your side of the path, not the other. You've watered them every day without realizing it."[30]

You don't need to be perfect for God to use you. You just need to be available.

> Therefore I will boast all the more gladly about my weaknesses, so that Christ's power may rest on me. . . . For when I am weak, then I am strong. (2 Corinthians 12:9–10)

With less false dependence of our own worthiness (less of us) and a greater awareness of our need for His help and presence (more of Him), we create space to receive the light of God. Our flaws and hurts allow Christ to shine through us, and they become a way for His love to reach others.

THE PATH TO SUCCESS

EVERYBODY STRUGGLES. BUT WE don't have to struggle on our own. We have a never-ending source of support and energy that can work so powerfully within us. All we need to do is remember how dependent we are on God's help and power for each and every task we face. And then we need to ask for His help.

That's why I try to start every day the same way: on my knees quietly, reminding myself that I desperately need the presence of Christ with me. I ask for His forgiveness, His confidence, His strength, His wisdom (which, by the way, is one of the select things that God always promised to provide us with when we ask). I ask Him to protect my family, to bless my day, and to guard my encounters, words, attitudes, and actions. I ask Him to take away my fears and give me His peace, and I thank Him for the many blessings.

And God has never let me down. He's always been there. I've never been alone with anything I've faced. Nothing has been too impossible for Him. There's nothing He can't help me through, no cave too dark or mountain too steep. He is Lord of it all.

> The LORD was with Joseph and gave him success in whatever he did. (Genesis 39:23)

This is the way God works—the way He has always worked. He draws us to our knees so He can draw us closer to Him. He blesses us so that we can bless others. Be His ambassador on earth today. That's our calling.

5 BE THE GLOVE

AT SOME POINT IN our lives, we will all reach a point where we feel broken, weak, and at the end of our ropes. For some of us, it'll happen a lot more than once.

However often we find ourselves facing these tough times, the best response we can give will be to stay calm, to keep trusting God, to remain full of faith, and to ask for help. Like the wise saying goes, "Calm is trust in action."

You might not be in the middle of a tough time right now, but all of us can practice our response to challenge every day. With every obstacle we meet, try not to rush into action. Look up first. Be still. Plug into the source. Learn to look to God first, then act in calm faith and assurance.

It's not always easy, but Jesus made this promise:

"Be sure of this—that I am with you always, even to the end of the world." (Matthew 28:20 TLB)

Let Him lead today. Kneel and invite Him in. Give Him permission to lead you, to take the reins of your heart and life. Be the glove to His hand. He knows the best way for your life, better than you. Trust Him in all circumstances. His way is good, and His plan for your future is secure.

6 YOUR CONFIDENCE

WHEN YOU FACE SOME of your greatest challenges, you have to trust the systems put in place. This doesn't just apply to bungees and Boeing 747s. The Bible is full of the kind of truth that you can build your life on.

Proverbs 3 tells us it's foolish to put our trust in ourselves and wise to trust God (v. 35). It explains that success at work, wealth, and fame are of little value if we do not have peace—and that true peace comes from a right relationship with God (vv. 24–25). When we live like this, trusting God, He pulls us closer (v. 32), "shows favor to the humble" (v. 34), and unloads so many good things on our life (vv. 33–35).

The LORD will be your confidence. (Proverbs 3:26 AMP)

We can trust the natural order of the universe. We can trust the Creator who made us, the Son who came to heal us, and the Spirit who moves within us. Trusting God—putting our confidence in Him—isn't such a strange thing. It's natural, it's in our DNA, and it's what we're made to do.

7 CALLED TO LOVE

AT THIRTY-FIVE YEARS OLD, Martin Luther King Jr. was the youngest person ever to receive the Nobel Peace Prize. Four years later he was dead. Though his remarkable life was short, he lived long enough to see society transformed. One week after his death, the Civil Rights Act came into law. But his influence spread even wider, and his dream of equality and justice captivated the whole world.

Martin Luther King Jr. was a man who followed Christ. The agenda he served was God's own—caring for individuals and bringing about the transformation of society. The mission is still the same. We're called to love people, all people, with kindness and generosity. And the Bible tells us how:

> GOD hates cheating in the marketplace;
>> he loves it when business is aboveboard. . . .
> GOD can't stand deceivers,
>> but oh how he relishes integrity. . . .

The one who blesses others is abundantly blessed;
>   those who help others are helped. (Proverbs 11:1, 20, 25 MSG)

When we treat people fairly, when we live with honesty, when we give away not just the scraps but the best that we can, then lives get healed and people are blessed—us included.

8 | HERE TO LOVE

WHEN LIFE IS AT its toughest and we're wondering what the point of it all is, love is often the first thing to go out the window. We stop being kind to others. We stop being kind to ourselves. And we stop looking to God to remind us that everything's still okay. But there is great power when we actively choose God in the tough times and when we actively choose love.

As Joyce Meyer wrote, we need to "stir up love in your life—towards your spouse and towards your family, friends, neighbours and co-workers. Reach out to others who are hurting and in need. Pray for people and bless them."[31]

Love knows no limits. There's not a square meter on this earth that can't be reached by God's touch.

> For great is your love, reaching to the heavens;
>   your faithfulness reaches to the skies. (Psalm 57:10)

This is where it all starts, even when we feel at our worst. Choosing love as our focus of everything is the smart way to live.

Take those moments to say yes to His presence, His help, His strength, His way. Deep in your heart know that love is always the answer. Know that He will never leave you and that He will always equip you when you ask.

9 CONTROL

HERE ARE FOUR HABITS I've found helpful to focus on in order to try to live a more faithful, love-filled, productive life:

Try to control what you think about. The life you lead will flow from your heart. Try to concentrate on good things, the sort that bring life and health. "Above all else, guard your heart," says Proverbs 4:23, "for everything you do flows from it."

Try to control what you say. Your words are powerful, so use them carefully. Before you speak, ask these three questions: Is it true? Is it kind? Is it necessary?

Try to control what you look at, as difficult as it is sometimes. In the age we live in, you've got to be careful about what you look at. Porn is messing up so many people's view of sex and relationships. Alternatively, what we look at can help us. You know the good stuff: inspiring films, mountaintops, books, music gigs, and so on. As Jesus said, "If your eyes are healthy, your whole body will be full of light" (Matthew 6:22).

Try to control where you go. There are a ton of shortcuts out there, but if we decide to "run with perseverance the race marked out for us, fixing our eyes on Jesus," He will "make level paths for [our] feet" (Hebrews 12:1–2, 13). The easy path is rarely the right path.

All this trying should be underpinned by the central truth that our efforts are not linked to our salvation. We all fail, and we fail often. But these guides will help keep you rooted in love and heading in the right direction.

10 INHERIT THE EARTH

A MUSTARD SEED NEEDS to be planted in the ground if it's going to start growing. Once planted, the growth is so strong it can even break through concrete. That's how it is with God. His power can transform anything.

Jesus unpacked this in His most famous sermon. "Blessed are the meek," He said, "for they will inherit the earth" (Matthew 5:5). *Meek* does not mean weak, spineless, or feeble. It's the word used to describe Moses (Numbers 12:3 RSV) and the word that Jesus chose to describe Himself (Matthew 11:29 KJV). It's used to describe a horse that has been tamed; it means strength under control, being gentle, considerate, and protective of those around us.

This can be very countercultural. After all, the world sometimes seems to reward the brash and the boastful. But God plays by different rules. He "chose the foolish things of the world to shame the wise; God chose the weak things of the world to shame the strong" (1 Corinthians 1:27).

The lesson is simple: when we are meek, we receive His power; when we are weak, He will be our strength.

11 BEING MADE WHOLE

"THE *TITANIC* IS A metaphor of life," said James Cameron, director of the movie about the infamous ship that went down with 1,513 people in 1912. "We are all on the *Titanic*."[32]

In many ways he's right. The *Titanic* was declared unsinkable because it was constructed using a new technology that divided the ship's hull into sixteen watertight compartments. As many as four of these separate compartments could be damaged or even flooded, and still the ship would float.

For years people believed that it sank because five of its watertight compartments had been ruptured in a collision with an iceberg. But on September 1, 1985, when the wreck of the *Titanic* was found lying upright on the ocean floor, there was no sign of any long gash on the ship's hull. Only one of the watertight compartments had been damaged in the collision. But it was enough to affect all the rest.

I used to think I could divide my life into different compartments. I thought what I did in one area of my life would not affect the rest. It's a classic *Titanic*-style mistake to make.

For everything, absolutely everything, above and below, visible and invisible, rank after rank after rank of angels—*everything* got started in him and finds its purpose in him. (Colossians 1:15–17 MSG)

It is all linked: our choices and our hopes, our encounters and the angels, the life of Jesus and our future, our triumphs and our failures. God doesn't do compartments. He wants us to be made whole. And when we invite Him into every part of our lives, He can begin mending the hurts, healing the damage, linking the good together, and turning our stories into something beautiful.

Trust Him to do His job, and you will see Him in action.

12 THE KEYS

WHETHER WE'RE IN PAIN, in debt, or just in over our heads, we can often feel powerless. But whatever we're facing, we do have power. We often just can't see it.

I love the story of Jesus telling Peter that He was giving him the keys of the kingdom, giving Peter access to the same power that Jesus Himself had. It was a promise that didn't die with the disciple. The whole church—all of us—from that day on has been given huge power and authority. Like all keys, these come with both privilege and responsibility:

> You will have complete and free access to God's kingdom, keys to open any and every door: no more barriers between heaven and earth, earth and heaven. A yes on earth is yes in heaven. A no on earth is no in heaven. (Matthew 16:19 MSG)

When we're weak and worried, it can be hard to believe that we've got this kind of power. But isn't that just like God to turn upside down our ideas about what power and strength actually look like? After all, He's the one who sent His Son to rescue earth as a tiny baby, born under scandal to a young, tired, and fragile refugee couple. When it comes to God and power, the normal rules just don't apply.

13 KNEELING DOWN, LOOKING UP

WHEN YOU BEGIN TO have a sense of purpose, the way you face opposition changes. As our minds become set on the path ahead and we start to move to God's rhythm, criticism loses some of its sting. People of love and faith have known and lived this truth for centuries. I love the story of how Paul and Barnabas reacted to the criticism they faced in Antioch:

> The word of the Lord spread through the whole region. But the Jewish leaders incited the God-fearing women of high standing and the leading men of the city. They stirred up persecution against Paul and Barnabas, and expelled them from their region. So they shook

the dust off their feet as a warning to them and went to Iconium. And the disciples were filled with joy and with the Holy Spirit. (Acts 13:49–52)

It's the last bit that gets me. Instead of taking the criticism to heart or overreacting or allowing themselves to be "stirred up," they dusted off their feet and kept going, full of joy. It's completely upside down—and so typical of a life rich in love, faith, and light. They found their purpose and peace away from trying to impress others or becoming important. They found it by kneeling down and looking up.

When we have Christ beside us and within us every day, we find great freedom. It's our great gift, so today let's live it and enjoy it.

14 MEASURING SUCCESS

IT IS SO EASY to link our worldly status to our significance: if we are wealthy, with the right car and "perfect" family, the ideal career or the movie star body, then we are "successful."

But real success doesn't work like that. The smart person stores up for the long term, not the short term. Chasing gratification only for the self and ego in this life is the ultimate short-termism. And ego always leads to unhappiness because whatever you get is never enough.

God calls us to live by a different set of values, to store up for the long term through faithful, daily actions of kindness and care to the broken. That is how Christ measures success: in service and love to others. It turns the values of the world on their head, but it leads to life and happiness. It is how to be truly significant.

We are all a work in progress, and the verses below are a challenge to us all, but let's make them a focus and learn to listen to our hearts in how we see people and how we give of our time and resources:

> So here's what I want you to do, God helping you: Take your everyday, ordinary life—your sleeping, eating, going-to-work, and walking-around life—and place it before God as an offering. (Romans 12:1 MSG)

> Whoever oppresses the poor shows contempt for their Maker,
>   but whoever is kind to the needy honors God. (Proverbs 14:31)

When we use these words as our compass and guide, we'll find ourselves on the path to life.

15 OUR WHY AND OUR HOW

A MAN OR WOMAN with purpose is a powerful thing, but discovering our purpose can be so hard. We often chase goals that lead us in directions that are counter to what we are really meant to be doing, or we get dazzled by the bright lights that can seduce the best of us. Having a true, God-given sense of purpose in life matters so much more than our profile, property, or possessions. Having enough to live *with* is a poor comparison for having something to live *for*.

It has been said that the two greatest days of your life are the day you were born and the day you find out why. And when we know our *why*, the *how* will fall into place.

This is the purpose God puts before His children, and it leads to a life rich in love and fulfillment:

To act justly and to love mercy
  and to walk humbly with your God. (Micah 6:8)

I try to remind myself of this verse often. It keeps the goals of life simple and gives me a purpose and a direction in which to travel.

16 HE'S GOT YOU

WHEN YOU'RE HANGING FROM a rope, halfway down a mountain, it's easy to let fear build up and overwhelm you. I have felt this many times. We are all human. But our response to fear is what sets people apart.

Paul knew this, which is why his letters often reminded people of the fact that they can have faith and assurance because of who Jesus is. Paul continually reminds us that the Jesus he had spent so much of his own life persecuting was undeniably divine, that Jesus died and was buried but came back to life. Paul wanted to make it clear that the resurrection was rooted in facts, grounded in Scripture, and confirmed by experience.

But the truth is that Christ *has* been raised up, the first in a long legacy of those who are going to leave the cemeteries. . . . And why do you think I keep risking my neck in this dangerous work? . . . It's resurrection, resurrection, always resurrection, that undergirds what I do and say, the way I live. (1 Corinthians 15:20, 30, 32 MSG)

You and I can now see through different eyes. Aware that the antidote to fear is knowing that Jesus is who He said He was. And that means He's got you—that you are truly loved, forgiven, freed, empowered, and accepted. That's the truth that casts out our fears today and forever.

17 THE FRONT LINE

I KNOW A WONDERFUL Catholic priest named Raniero Cantalamessa, who described life as being a battle against a "triple alliance . . . the world, the flesh and the devil; the enemy around us, the enemy within us and the enemy above us."[33]

His words echo Paul's: "Our struggle is not against flesh and blood, but against the rulers, against the authorities, against the powers of this dark world and against the spiritual forces of evil in the heavenly realms" (Ephesians 6:12).

It's good to rely on God, but that doesn't mean we should be passive. We should be prepared to fight, but with nonconventional weapons: humility, prayer, kindness, and courage. We fight darkness by leaning on His strength, His presence, His faithfulness, and His promises. He will never fail us.

We are part of the only army where the safest place to be is on the front line—standing strong in His love and mercy and sheltered under His arms.

18 STICK WITH LOVE

OVER THE YEARS, I have heard many remarkable, transformational stories of hate-filled people being set free by love. Because hate is an unbearable burden, that ultimately suffocates life. Only love has the power to truly transform us for the better.

This radical truth runs through every page of the story of Jesus. The words of Jesus contain the answer to the greatest longing of the world today. In all our searching for significance, for affirmation, for status, what we're really chasing is love.

Conversely, fear is something everybody wants to get rid of. It is all too easy for us to live lives full of fear, not love. But fear and love are like oil and water, repelling each other. Where there is love, fear melts away.

Perfect love drives out fear. (1 John 4:18)

And remember:

Cast all your anxiety on him because he cares for you. (1 Peter 5:7)

19 WORD MADE FLESH

"YOU STUDY THE SCRIPTURES diligently because you think that in them you have eternal life. . . . Yet you refuse to come to me" (John 5:39–40). These are incredibly powerful and poignant words from Jesus to the Pharisees. The religious elite were so steeped in "religion" and looking for salvation and rescue in the physical, historical Scriptures that they missed the living incarnation of that rescue standing before them.

"Let anyone who is thirsty come to me and drink," said Jesus. (John 7:37)

As the author C. S. Lewis explained, "It is Christ Himself, not the Bible, who is the true word of God. The Bible, read in the right spirit and with the guidance of good teachers, will bring us to Him. We must not use the Bible as a sort of encyclopedia out of which texts can be taken for use as weapons."[34]

Christ is all you need to find hope, life, salvation, and healing. We mustn't treat the physical Bible as sacred. People and the way of love and forgiveness are sacred. It is your relationship with Christ in your heart that is sacred.

"I will put my law in their minds
and write it on their hearts.
I will be their God,
and they will be my people." (Jeremiah 31:33)

If you want to protect, respect, and revere anything, make it Christ in your heart.

20 LIFE, NOT RELIGION

THE PHARISEES, WHO WERE deeply religious, had become corrupted, legalistic, and rigid. They criticized Jesus because a man paralyzed for thirty-eight years had carried his bed on the Sabbath. But Jesus was about life and healing, not religion.

"I have come that they may have life, and have it to the full." (John 10:10)

His words are powerful—and certainly not the words of simply a good teacher. Good teachers don't claim to be God. But if He is God, then surely this is how we all hope God to be: loving, forgiving, understanding, and breaking through all barriers to reach us.

Look at what the Pharisees said about Him: "He was even calling God his own Father, making himself equal with God" (John 5:18). And when Jesus was interrogated, He was clear: "Truly I tell you, the Son can do nothing by himself; he can do only what he sees his Father doing, because whatever the Father does the Son also does" (v. 19).

Jesus' healing a man on the Sabbath is reflective of His nature: smashing through conventions to reach us and heal us. The same applies to us today.

Sometimes people think of God as a person in the sky who is distant and uncaring. Jesus is the opposite. He was clear in His purpose. He said, "For the Son of Man came to seek and to save the lost" (Luke 19:10). He spoke clearly about who He was and how He would do this. And then He did it.

So you and I never need get "religious." We just need to look up quietly and trust Jesus' promises for our lives: life, not religion.

21 OUR PURPOSE

SOMETIMES IT CAN SEEM as if everyone else is in on the party while we're locked outside. Everywhere you look people appear happier, more successful, wealthier, healthier, stronger, and more assured.

But if we spend our lives wanting to be someone else, we will always be a pale version of who we are made to be. Comparison is the thief of joy. Lining ourselves up against other people is a one-way route to anxiety and failure.

Thankfully, there's a better way. We're called to see ourselves as strangers here on earth with a clear calling for our lives. We're not here to worry about how well we measure up to others, but we are here to live with the full assurance that we are loved and that the light of Christ is within us.

> Go out into the world uncorrupted, a breath of fresh air in this squalid and polluted society. Provide people with a glimpse of good living and of the living God. Carry the light-giving Message into the night. (Philippians 2:15 MSG)

Live a life of integrity, power, calm, and love. Give your strength to the weak. Support the sick. Bind up the injured. Bring back the strays. Search for the lost, and show all people kindness. This is how we should live today. This is our purpose.

22 LISTEN

THE BIBLE IS FULL of stories of the Israelites getting into trouble. Sometimes they were taken as slaves, sometimes they were facing grinding poverty, sometimes they were invaded by a hostile force. Whatever the consequence, the root cause always seemed to be the same: they stopped listening to God.

Jesus said the key to life is to listen to Him and believe: "Very truly I tell you, whoever hears my word and believes him who sent me has eternal life and will not be judged but has crossed over from death to life" (John 5:24).

The Bible doesn't just tell the story of the failure of people to listen. Again and again it shows how they put things right:

They cried out to the LORD for help. (Judges 6:6)

For you and me, just like the Israelites thousands of years ago, the turning point is often the same: we admit that we can't do it on our own, and we go running back to Him. Then we can begin to access His blessing.

I am so grateful for the many times in my life when God has answered my cry for help and restored me.

> THE TURNING POINT IS OFTEN THE SAME: WE
> ADMIT THAT WE CAN'T DO IT ON OUR OWN,
> AND WE GO RUNNING BACK TO HIM.

23 | CREATED FOR GOOD WORKS

WHEN A JOURNEY DOESN'T unfold the way we planned, we often start wondering, *Have I strayed too far from my original course? Am I headed in the wrong direction?*

Sometimes it's good to stop and check, especially on the journey of faith. From time to time we all need to be reminded of the fact that we are human—we stray off course and we fall down. But life is about being willing to humble ourselves; it's about acknowledging our failing and then standing back up, leaning on His strength and His supply. And then, as the Scouts say, do your best.

When we do this, good things follow.

God never forces Himself into our lives. He works where there are willing, available hearts. He isn't looking for strong hearts, but willing hearts—hearts and lives that are open to Him coming alongside and leading us into life and light.

For we are his workmanship, created in Christ Jesus for good works, which God prepared beforehand, that we should walk in them. (Ephesians 2:10 ESV)

Once we put our heart and hand into His, then He can lead. And where He leads is always good—it's not always easy, but it is always good. That's faith and trust, and both are the source of all great power.

24 FAITHFUL IN ADVERSITY

HAVE YOU EVER WONDERED what difference your life might make? How can you change the world for the better? If we want to live a life that really counts, we need to stay faithful to the way of love and to the truths of Christ, in good times and bad.

Almost every book of the Bible tells the story of faithfulness in adversity. We see it in Abraham's fears about seeing his family line dying out, as well as in Joseph's capture, slavery, and imprisonment. They stayed faithful.

Moses and Gideon knew they were totally ill-equipped for the challenges they faced, while the story of Job describes how one man's trust in God was tested to the absolute limit. Yet they stayed on course.

Peter, Paul, and so many others in the New Testament tasted endless failure and opposition, but they stuck firm to Christ—all the way.

These humbling stories can help put all our problems into perspective, and they remind us that we don't have to pretend that everything is always rosy. When life sucks, it is okay to feel downhearted. But don't wallow in it long. Look up, not in. Know that there's always a bigger picture: God is with us in the tough moments, right beside us, calming us and strengthening us.

Let's try to be like Paul:

Sorrowful, yet always rejoicing; poor, yet making many rich; having nothing, and yet possessing everything. (2 Corinthians 6:10)

This is how it works with the topsy-turvy King and the way of grace. Christ turns everything on its head for the better.

25 DON'T GO IT ALONE

WE ALL HAVE DAYS when we feel as though we don't match up to other people. We all experience times when we're unsure what move to make next, and none of us will go through life without experiencing fear at some time.

Gideon faced all of this. Thankfully, it didn't matter that he was lacking in self-confidence. He had God-confidence instead. In fact, just to make sure he didn't try to find confidence anywhere else, God reduced Gideon's army from twenty-two thousand men to just three hundred!

It's a vital lesson to take on. If we put our hearts and trust and confidence in God, He will work through us powerfully—just as He did through Gideon. God does not need large numbers. He just needs willing hearts. When we give that, we gain the greatest power:

The Spirit of the LORD came on [him]. (Judges 6:34)

Whatever today holds for us, we all need the light and love of God to enrich us and our relationships and encounters. We need Him to give us the power to fulfill the calling He has for us. We can't go it alone, and we're not designed to. Stay in the power zone: less of our frail attempts; more of His strength in everything we do.

26 IT'S ALL ABOUT TIMING

THERE'S AN ART TO waiting well. Whether we're stuck in traffic or waiting at a remote jungle landing strip for the clouds to clear, the principle is the same. We have to relax, accept what we can't control, and focus positively on what we can.

It's the same with life, faith, and God, only those things can be way harder. That's because "with the Lord a day is like a thousand years, and a thousand years are like a day" (2 Peter 3:8). His timescales are eternal. Ours aren't. Much of the time we want things fixed yesterday. But God's timing is perfect. He's never early and He's never late. He is never in a hurry, but He is always on time. If we can get over ourselves and learn to relax and trust God when the waiting seems like it's lasting for ages, there's huge comfort and strength to be drawn from this.

> He placed his right hand on me and said: "Do not be afraid. I am the First and the Last." (Revelation 1:17)

Next time we're wondering why this painful season is lasting so long, let's remember this: everything is in hand. God's timing is better than ours, there is always a positive purpose to the storms, and our future is assured.

FOR YEARS HANNAH HAD been trying to get pregnant. Along with the pain and sadness, she'd had to put up with ridicule, shame, and cruelty from people around her. But she kept quiet, refused to retaliate, and allowed all her turmoil to drive her closer to God.

When she finally—miraculously—got pregnant, her first reaction was not to go bragging to her detractors. Nor did she retreat in fear, worried that everything was going to go wrong. Instead, the Bible says that Hannah gave thanks to God: "My heart rejoices in the LORD," she said (1 Samuel 2:1).

She was so excited to be pregnant, but what shone through was that the ultimate source of her joy was even greater than her child: it was God Himself.

I'm walking on air. . . . GOD brings life. . . . He rekindles burned-out lives with fresh hope, restoring dignity and respect to their lives. (vv. 1, 6, 8 MSG)

It's not always easy, but when we put it all on God—all our hope, all our joy, all our trust—we find ourselves drawn deeper and deeper into the greatest relationship we can ever have: the relationship we were all made for.

Let's remember this—whether we are celebrating or mourning, whether feeling feel joy or pain—the greatest thing we possess is our friendship with Christ. It's a relationship that improves everything else in our life. The more we prioritize it, the more this truth comes into play.

28 BE A BLESSING MACHINE

PURPOSE MATTERS, AND EVERYONE is after it. We want to know that our life has meaning beyond just survival—beyond food, water, shelter, and procreation. As children of Christ we are called to spread goodness and light, to bless people. A friend of mine often describes it as being a "blessing machine." I love that.

But how do we do this? First, we need to receive in order to give. And the more we can connect to the infinite source of love, light, and power, the more we can give to others. When our own lives are overflowing with goodness, we can be more effective "blessing machines."

As the pastor Nicky Gumbel said, "It is God's blessing on your life that enables you to make a difference to the lives of others. God is the source of all blessing. He loves to bless you."[35]

What God wants for your life is good. It will not necessarily be easy, but you will not be able to improve on God's plan for you. He has known the intricacies of your life from long ago, and He will ultimately make all our lives beautiful. His promise is that He will always give you the energy you need to bless others: "That energy is *God's* energy, an energy deep within you" (Philippians 2:13 MSG).

Let's draw on this and never tire of doing good in words, deeds, actions, and attitudes. Together, let's daily fire up that blessing machine.

RESTLESS FOR A REASON

SAINT AUGUSTINE WROTE, "[GOD,] you have made us for yourself, and our hearts are restless until they rest in you."[36]

In the Psalms, David marveled at the fact that human beings are the pinnacle of God's creation—a masterpiece—made in His image. God not only loves you and cares about you but has given you extraordinary privileges:

> You made them rulers over the works of your hands;
>> you put everything under their feet. (Psalm 8:6)

We have been put in charge of everything God has made. That's an incredible privilege. But it's also a powerful responsibility. Knowing this, we should be at the forefront of the protection, preservation, and care of God's amazing creation. And that means the earth, the animals, and all people.

How do we do that? Start by always knowing where our power comes from: closeness to Christ and dependence on His strength, His goodness, and His peace. When we walk away from this, let's be aware of that restlessness within that is acting like a magnet, edging us ever back to the shadow of His wings.

> Under his wings you will find refuge. (Psalm 91:4)

TIME TO REST

SOMETIMES WE GET SO caught up in the busyness of life that we never stop to either enjoy the moment or rest or soak up the powerful energy all around us. We all live busy lives, and that's okay. But it hurts us when we fail to take enough time for ourselves among the madness.

This can be hard as a single mom or as a soldier. It is tough to take time out when we are up against deadlines and pressures on all sides. But God reminds us that it is important for our all-round health—especially our mental health—to put aside time to rest. That's why on the seventh day, God rested. That's why we have weekends. (Or at least Sundays!) We need time to recharge and to reconnect with the good stuff in our lives. Sometimes gratitude needs time to be discovered.

And let's not kid ourselves that the world will stop without us, that we can't afford to take a break, or that there is too much to do. There always is. Get over it, because the world will be okay without you. Take the time to rest and recover. Go for a hike, a swim, a snooze on the grass or under a tree. Those are good things, and Jesus did them all.

Remember: "Christ is the same yesterday and today and forever" (Hebrews 13:8). He "laid the foundations of the earth, and the heavens are the work of [his] hands" (Hebrews 1:10). Everything is in hand. So take a little regular time to rest. It will always allow us to return stronger and more effective come tomorrow. God knows that, and He designed us that way. Come Monday we are ready to go!

DETERMINATION

I WAS CRAZY NERVOUS when I first applied to attempt Selection for the British Special Forces. But I will always remember the first SAS officer I ever met saying to me, "Everyone who attempts Selection has the basic mark-one body: two arms, two legs, one head, and one pumping set of lungs. What makes the difference between those who make it and those who don't is what goes on in here," he said, touching his chest. "Heart . . . that is what makes the big difference. Only you know if you have got what it takes."

The only qualification I needed was beating inside that chest of mine. It is also called the fire inside, grit, guts, or spirit.

In the months that followed I had plenty of time to find out just how much of that I had. Selection starts with a series of intense physical tests to weed out those who shouldn't have even applied: the long day and night marches across the mountains—carrying heavy backpack, webbing, and weapon—always against the clock, the weather, the terrain, and your own doubts.

The two-minute, no-holds-barred boxing rounds; the endless pull-ups and press-ups; and the lung-busting hill runs—often carrying another recruit in a fireman's lift—pushed us so hard we often puked. Worst of all, I will never forget the dawn "bergan-bashes," which were fast runs through the mountain forestry tracks in full kit and packs (our bergans) when we were already exhausted, tired, soaking wet, and riddled with blisters.

You were only safe if you gave 150 percent, stayed near the front, and never gave up.

It didn't get easier. If I wanted to make the grade, I had to push myself harder every week. But gradually something inside me changed; I was learning to get used to the pain. I was learning what determination looked and felt like. I learned to ignore the temporary pain and to focus on the long-term gain and goal.

Years later, I'm grateful for those lessons, and I'm still learning. But to keep going in your own strength will always be finite and flawed. The key to enduring for me was knowing that I had a reservoir of refreshing living water to draw on inside: the knowledge that however tired or lacking in self-belief I felt, there was a Presence beside and within me that was edging me on, helping me stand, keeping me moving.

This Presence asks nothing in return. It is strong and good and rooted in love, like a parent to a small child, cheering us on and guiding and protecting our steps.

I always knew that this Presence was there, and it has never left me. Some call it God; some call it this universal force of power and love. Jesus lived in this force and shared it all day, every day. He said He *was* this force: "I am the way and the truth and the life" (John 14:6), and I have learned through a lifetime of adventure that His promises for our lives and our future always hold true.

How we respond to the promises of Christ over our lives changes everything. It doesn't have to be religious or loud. In fact, it is the opposite. Real faith is often raw, honest, shines brightest in our struggles and failings, and will never let us down.

Take heart. Our journey of faith is just getting going, and we have the ultimate power and friend within us.

1 LET GO

SO MANY TIMES THE struggles in my life have come from wanting to be in control, but the truth is that power comes from relinquishing control. It happens when we understand that God knows better than we do what is best for our lives, and that takes courage and faith.

But remember who He is. He's the same powerful force that placed "his right foot on the sea and his left foot on land, then called out thunderously, a lion roar" (Revelation 10:2 MSG).

God rewarded trust in the Bible time and time again. Think of young Mary when she was told she was carrying the Messiah child or of Daniel in the lions' den. Think of Joseph in prison or Moses as he led the Israelites away from Egypt. We're in strong hands.

The power comes when we relinquish control and trust Him with our lives, with our future, and for our daily bread. He loves us and will lead us into light and life, if we let Him.

2 THE LIGHT

I AM SURE THAT you have gone through a few dark times in life. Saint John of the Cross spoke of the "dark night of the soul."[37] It's a good description because those times can be both frightening and isolating.

There were so many dark days for the people of God in both the Old and New Testament times, and the history of the church is full of periods when the outlook has appeared bleak.

But the light of the gospel has never gone out. Never.

It is a light that "shines in the darkness, and the darkness has not overcome it" (John 1:5).

The amazing truth is that we have that light within us from the Holy Spirit. Wherever we go, we bring a light greater than the darkness. That's a powerful truth.

Wherever we go, we can bring love and kindness and blessing. We're a blessing machine.

3 GOD WITH US

IT CAN TAKE A lot to stand up and defend yourself—a lot of courage and a lot of risk. But one thing we don't always need when we're speaking up for ourselves is a lot of words.

When Jesus stood before Pilate, He was the perfect example of calm assurance. Even though He had to deal with so much abuse—lies and unjust criticism, mockeries, humiliations, and torture—He kept His cool.

When Pilate asked Jesus, "Are you the king of the Jews?" (Matthew 27:11a), Jesus' reply was brief: "You have said so" (v. 11b). No false modesty. Just clear honesty.

How did He manage it? Even though He stood and faced His accusers on His own, Jesus was never alone. As He said, "I and My Father are one" (John 10:30 NKJV). That's a bold statement. But if it is true, it changes everything.

Ultimately Jesus' quiet assurance came from knowing who He was.

You and I aren't gods, but we have God inside of us. Jesus repeatedly told us that we are His sons and daughters and that He came down to die in our place, to pay the price of our sin and mistakes. That is what the name *Jesus* actually means: "the one who saves." Jesus came ultimately to die, to be separated from heaven, so that we never need be alone again. The more deeply we know this huge love that He has for us, the easier it is to stand in the face of opposition. "If God be for us, who can be against us?" (Romans 8:31 KJV).

Whatever you're facing today, remember that you will never face it alone. God is always with you. As Isaiah prophesied, "[They] will call him Immanuel" (Isaiah 7:14, literally meaning "God with us").

4 DO NOT FEAR

THERE ARE MOMENTS IN any journey when we can all get a little discouraged. Even if we've been feeling great, when we become tired and stressed and feel fear rise within us, we can quickly lose hold of our positive outlook.

It's the same with faith. Sometimes we can forget that God is on our side, that He is for us and beside us. That's why we do well to heed the advice of Moses:

> Do not be terrified; do not be afraid of them. The LORD your God, who is going before you, will fight for you. (Deuteronomy 1:29–30)

> The LORD our God is near us whenever we pray to him. (Deuteronomy 4:7)

It's so easy to struggle when things start to go wrong, but don't allow opposition to put you off. Often it is a sign that you are doing something right!

It is in these battles of life that we can show our faith in action. So when opposition strikes, do not retreat and do not fear. Focus on His presence. He indeed is for us, beside us, within us, to win us.

5 | SHELTER

FAITH DOES NOT KEEP you from trouble. It's better than that: it helps you get *through* trouble. It's hard, but try not to focus on your problems. Focus instead on the One who carries you through them.

That's why I love this psalm. It's God-focused, optimistic, and so full of fuel for life:

> I lift up my eyes to the mountains—
>> where does my help come from?
> My help comes from the LORD,
>> the Maker of heaven and earth.
> He will not let your foot slip—
>> he who watches over you will not slumber;
> indeed, he who watches over Israel
>> will neither slumber nor sleep.
> The LORD watches over you—
>> the LORD is your shade at your right hand;
> the sun will not harm you by day,
>> nor the moon by night.
> The LORD will keep you from all harm—
>> he will watch over your life;
> the LORD will watch over your coming and going
>> both now and forevermore. (Psalm 121)

Wherever we are and whatever we're facing, we should always stay under His wing. We do that through an attitude of calm trust, passing any glory on to Him, because when we are sheltered under that wing, God gets the glory and God takes the flack.

Shelter with God. Be close to Him and trust Him to lead because He is good.

6 | LET LOVE BE YOUR HALLMARK

WHEN I REACH THE end of my life, I hope I have done three things: fought the fight, finished the race, and kept the faith.

None of these are small things, and they impact every aspect of life, from family to friends to work. I need as much help with them as possible.

These verses give us just the kind of fuel we need:

> GOD's your Guardian,
>> right at your side to protect you. . . .
> GOD guards you from every evil,
>> he guards your very life.
> He guards you when you leave and when you return,
>> he guards you now, he guards you always. (Psalm 121:5,
>> 7–8 MSG)

Keep your eyes fixed on Christ. Trust His promises, lean on Him, draw your strength from Him, see others with His eyes, and let love be your hallmark. This is the way of true power and purpose.

7 | LIMPS AND THORNS

GOD DOES NOT MAKE us superhuman. He allows us to live with our weaknesses because in them there is room for His power to work.

Jacob was a pretty cool guy, but after wrestling with God—literally—he walked with a limp. Paul in the New Testament was similar. Three times he asked God to heal him from an unnamed physical condition that he called his "thorn in my flesh" (2 Corinthians 12:7). Both men seem to have carried their wounds right through to the end of their lives.

A wise lady once said, "I never trust anyone who doesn't walk with a limp." The limp shows we are real and honest. But know that our weaknesses and vulnerabilities do not stop God from using us. In fact, it is often the opposite. God uses our weaknesses just as much as our strengths. Paul understood that God's power is "made perfect in weakness" (2 Corinthians 12:9).

Perhaps you feel you have a "thorn in the flesh." Maybe you know you're "walking with a limp." Join the club. Neither is a barrier to God. Those wounds might just be the very thing that keeps you walking in the light all your days.

> "You're blessed when you're at the end of your rope. With less of you there is more of God." (Matthew 5:3 MSG)

8 THIS IS NOT THE END

I HEARD A STORY once about a one-year-old boy who fell down a flight of stairs, shattering his back in the process. He spent his entire childhood and his teenage years in and out of the hospital. To many people, his story was one of heartbreaking tragedy.

But when he was interviewed one day, the boy said something that stunned people.

"God is fair," he said.

"How old are you?" asked the man who was interviewing him.

"Seventeen."

"And how many years have you spent in the hospital?"

"Thirteen."

"Do you think that is fair?" said the interviewer.

The boy paused and smiled. "God has got all of eternity to make it up to me."

This brave young man saw beyond his current suffering.

Suffering is not part of God's original created order. There was no suffering when the world began, and there will be no suffering when God creates a new heaven and a new earth (Revelation 21:3–4).

> "He will wipe every tear from their eyes. There will be no more death" or mourning or crying or pain, for the old order of things has passed away. (v. 4)

Understanding this gives us the most amazing perspective on our life and any hardships we encounter today. Understanding where we're going helps us persevere when times are tough. This is not the end, so hold tight, and all will be renewed. Trust the long game.

9 TRUST IN THE TROUBLES

NO ONE CAN GO through life without facing troubles. If David's example is anything to go by, anyone in a position of leadership will face more than most. David's also a great example of how to handle ourselves when we're in trouble. Even when he was facing great spiritual, mental, and physical challenges, he stayed firm in his trust in God. In Psalm 31, he was up against it all—distress, sorrow, grief, anguish, groaning, affliction, illness, enemies, contempt, terror—but still he chose to trust God.

> My times are in your hands;
>> deliver me from the hands of my enemies. . . .
>> Save me in your unfailing love. (Psalm 31:15–16)

It is in the tough times that the object in which we trust is really put to the test. And if we want to get better, then just as with any skill, the best way to improve is to practice. Put yourself in places where you have to trust God. Ask Him for help and expect Him to answer. Let Him lead you into the challenges He has in store. God always shows up in our lives when we look to Him for help rather than plowing on and trying to do it all on our own.

Great leaders always know how to bend the knee in both the good times and the tough times.

10 DO NOT BE AFRAID

"LIFE IS JUST ONE . . . thing after another." Whether Mark Twain first wrote this or not, there's something true about it. We're all in a battle. Life is full of struggle. Hard times are never far away.

Raniero Cantalamessa, a Catholic priest, offered some deeper insight on how we can approach these times:

> In the tales of medieval battles, there always comes a moment when the orderly ranks of archers and cavalry and all the rest are broken and the fighting concentrates around the king. That is where the final outcome of the battle will be decided. For us too, the battle today is taking place around the King: the person of Jesus Christ himself.[38]

By turning our attention to God, we gain real perspective and hear the essential instructions He's been handing out since the time of Moses: "Do not be afraid" (Numbers 21:34).

God doesn't always take the difficulties away, but He does help us through the struggles. We have no more need to be afraid. Instead, all we have to do is ask, trust, be patient, and keep moving forward, always acting in love.

11 HOLD TIGHT

WHEN WE'RE FACING SOME of life's toughest storms, we have a choice. We can either let fear take hold or we can look to a greater source. It's not always an easy thing to do. But many brave men and women, world leaders and great warriors, have been in that place before:

> *O joy that seekest me through pain,*
> *I cannot close my heart to thee;*
> *I trace the rainbow through the rain,*
> *and feel the promise is not vain*
> *that morn shall tearless be.*[39]

These old lyrics articulate a powerful truth: troubles do not have the last word.

We can see plenty of this in the Bible. "My soul is downcast within me," said King David. But he never gave up. "Therefore I will remember you. . . . Deep calls to deep" (Psalm 42:6–7). Often it's in the times of our greatest difficulty that we put down the deepest roots—that's when "deep calls to deep."

Our hardest times can bring about some of our greatest moments, especially if we're determined and do all we can to trust that in all things "God works for the good of those who love him, who have been called according to his purpose" (Romans 8:28).

When we find ourselves slipping down beneath the weight of fear, God is never out of our reach. In fact, it is then that He is closer than we ever dare imagine. Remember Jesus' final words: "Surely I am with you always, to the very end of the age" (Matthew 28:20).

12 WORRY MATTERS

"WORRY," AS CORRIE TEN Boom wrote, "does not empty tomorrow of its sorrow. It empties today of its strength."[40] Life is so much harder to face when we worry. The answer is not trying to find a problem-free life. No one goes through life without facing problems, battles, and causes for worry. What matters is how we deal with them.

David faced many difficulties in his life, and he wrote about them in Psalm 55. He described being betrayed by a close friend—a man with whom he had shared his secrets and trusted deeply. So David had a choice. Should he worry, or should he turn to God?

> As for me, I call to God,
>> and the LORD saves me.
> Evening, morning and noon
>> I cry out in distress,
>> and he hears my voice. (Psalm 55:16–17)

If you are involved in a confrontation with a close friend or family member, turn to God for wisdom, comfort, and strength. Always do your best to forgive and to show grace. Those elements change so much and strip confrontation of its negative power. Whenever you feel the worry begin to build up, kneel down and lift it to Him. We have a Father in heaven who cares.

Trust this promise:

> Cast your cares on the LORD
>> and he will sustain you. (Psalm 55:22)

That's a key secret to living well and to finding peace.

13 THE ROD AND STAFF

DETERMINATION MATTERS SO MUCH in so many situations. But it can be incredibly hard to source when we are feeling beat up. If it were easy to persevere, then no one would ever give up. So where can we source real, deep-rooted determination and perseverance? The Bible says there's one all-powerful source that gives us the strength we need to keep going through the darkest valley and up the highest mountain: God's Spirit inside you.

> Even though I walk
> > through the darkest valley,
> I will fear no evil,
> > for you are with me;
> your rod and your staff,
> > they comfort me. (Psalm 23:4)

This is a promise. He is with us. Claim this truth. It is a gift of God to empower you.

The rod and staff are Christ, and He keeps us standing. He is the weapon with which to protect ourselves. We need not fear; we just need to walk on with Christ beside us.

14 THE DEEP, CALM WATERS

LIFE IS FULL OF turbulent waters—maybe even more so once you start living in light and faith. Being set apart can lead to conflict sometimes. But even though a life of love, kindness, forgiveness, and courageous faith isn't easy street, for so many heroes of the past it has proved the right street.

As Father Raniero Cantalamessa put it, "A Christian in whom the Holy Spirit dwells is not exempt from having to experience struggle, temptations, disorderly desires, rebellious feelings." But while these troubles are on the surface, there is a "peace in the depth of the heart. That is like a deep-ocean current, always flowing steadily, regardless of the wind and waves on the surface."[41]

I don't believe we were designed or made to travel through this life all alone.

> "I, your GOD,
>
>> have a firm grip on you and I'm not letting go.
>
> I'm telling you, 'Don't panic.
>
>> I'm right here to help you.'" (Isaiah 41:13 MSG)

On this journey, claim the peace that God offers. Draw on His strength to keep walking in the light, and never give up the good fight.

15 THE BATTLE

THE APOSTLE PAUL WROTE, "Our struggle is not against flesh and blood, but against . . . the spiritual forces of evil" (Ephesians 6:12). I don't want to get weird here, but it is good to remember that the Bible says we're caught up in a spiritual battle. That means a battle for our hearts.

So today let's stay alert and keep on our guard against darker forces pulling us to disharmony in our lives. We often get attacked in the areas of ambitions, relationships, and temptations. Knowledge is power, so watch across those areas especially.

But above all, remember that God's power in you is always so much greater than any dark forces. We are already conquerors. It's the great promise of protection and redemption that we have in Christ.

He won all these battles long ago on a cross: alone, forgotten, despised. The sky darkened, and the giant temple curtain that had always separated people from the holiest part of the temple altar was suddenly ripped in two. It was His battle, and He won it for us.

Whatever we're facing today, if we reach out to Him and ask for His presence and protection, we can be assured that the ultimate victory is already secured. Then walk humbly and confidently in His light, because love always wins.

16 N.G.U.

SMITH WIGGLESWORTH WAS ONE of the great nineteenth-century preachers. Drawing from his experience of a tough upbringing in a poor farming community in Yorkshire, UK, he once said, "Great faith is a product of great fights. Great testimonies are the outcome of great tests. Great triumphs can only come out of great trials."[42]

We live in a hard, fallen world. Not everything is perfect, not by a long shot. Everyone goes through tough times, and we often find ourselves fighting battles on all fronts, whether it be finances, justice, health, or relationships. Many people find themselves in circumstances that make life hard all the time. The key is holding on to what is most valuable to us in our lives. It is in Christ that we find true resilience. In Christ we find our hope, our life, our purpose, our peace, and our future.

Take heart that the presence of the Almighty is with us in the battles.

Even to your old age and grey hairs
  I am he, I am he who will sustain you.
I have made you and I will carry you;
  I will sustain you and I will rescue you. (Isaiah 46:4)

There is always a light at the end of the tunnel, and the dawn so often comes after the darkest hour. But don't let go. Christ will never let go of you. Know that, and hold on to Him too. Ultimately what matters is never giving up. N.G.U. Hold firm—stay faithful. Jesus said, "The one who stands firm to the end will be saved" (Matthew 24:13).

17 DO YOUR BEST

SOMETIMES GIVING OUR ALL is hard. We can get tired, discouraged, and fed up. At times like these, determination can be hard to come by. But if there's one thing that helps when you're battling through a difficult challenge, it's having someone beside you to cheer you on and offer encouragement. And that's exactly what God offers through passages like this one:

> "'You are my servant';
>> I have chosen you and have not rejected you.
> So do not fear, for I am with you;
>> do not be dismayed, for I am your God.
> I will strengthen you and help you;
>> I will uphold you with my righteous right hand." (Isaiah 41:9–10)

When I was a soldier on Special Forces Selection, I used to repeat this line often to myself under my breath: "I will strengthen you and help you." As I struggled across the mountains carrying huge weights against the clock, those words had power, and His presence was always with me.

God tells us that He is "our refuge and strength, an ever-present help in trouble" (Psalm 46:1). He's by our side, and that changes everything. On our own, doing our best is hard. But with God beside us, a whole world of possibilities opens up.

18 NEVER GIVE UP

SIR WINSTON CHURCHILL HAS been described as Britain's greatest leader ever. He lived a long, heroic life and rallied a nation with his inspiring leadership. But life wasn't always easy for him, and he was certainly no stranger to failure. One of his fateful decisions led to the disaster of the Dardanelles campaign of World War I, causing huge human suffering and losses. As a result, he had to resign from the government. But that failure taught him a vital lesson that would stay with him for the rest of his life.

There's a story that once, when he returned to his old school to address the boys, the pupils assembled to listen to his words of wisdom. The great man arose and started to speak: "Never give in, never give in, never, never, never, never—in nothing, great or small, large or petty—never give in except to convictions of honour and good sense."[43]

That was all he was reported as saying. The entire speech had supposedly lasted only a few seconds, yet no one present ever forgot his words.

Jesus is the ultimate master and supreme king of never giving up! There's no greater example of determination than when He returned to Jerusalem in the final week of His life on earth. He knew He was going to be mocked and spat on, and He knew He was going to be tortured to death. Yet He was utterly resolute. He did not give up.

Paul encouraged the church at Galatia, "Let us not become weary in doing good, for at the proper time we will reap a harvest if we do not give up" (Galatians 6:9).

Churchill, Jesus, and millions of others down through history have known these words to be true. When we do what's right and stick to it, victory—in the end—will follow.

19 PATIENCE, CHILD, PATIENCE

THE INTERNET, BAGGAGE CLAIM, the big break you've spent years hoping for. When things go slower than we want them to, waiting is hard. But if you're waiting for God to bring His plans into fruition, you're not alone. Abraham waited twenty-five years for God to fulfill His promise that he would become a father. Joseph waited thirteen years before his dream came true and he stood before Pharaoh. Moses waited forty years in the wilderness. And Jesus waited thirty years before He went public. If God is making you wait, you're in good company.

> And we know that in all things God works for the good of those who love him, who have been called according to his purpose. (Romans 8:28)

God is always at work on your behalf, but we don't always get to see what He's doing. Yet we can trust Him, every step of the way, like a child—patient, trusting, always faithful. When we are faithful in the little things, we are trusted with even more.

20 FIGHT FOR THE VULNERABLE

GENERAL WILLIAM BOOTH, FOUNDER of the Salvation Army, was a great example of determination. He chose to fight for others, and he refused to give up.

This is what he once said: "While women weep as they do now, I'll fight; while children go hungry, as they do now, I'll fight; while men go to prison, in and out, in and out, as they do now; while there is a poor lost girl upon the streets, I'll fight; while there remains one dark soul without the light of God, I'll fight, I'll fight to the very end!"[44]

You and I are called into the same battle that Booth fought. We're called to fight for good, for justice, for those who can't fight for themselves. But we never do it alone: we fight with the Creator of the universe by our side and within us. We fight with His strength, not ours.

The LORD will go before you,
the God of Israel will be your rear guard. (Isaiah 52:12)

Be on your guard; stand firm in the faith; be courageous; be strong.
(1 Corinthians 16:13)

His weapons are love and mercy, kindness and generosity, and all the fruits of the Spirit. It's the only army in the world where the safest place to be is on the front line, making ground, in the thick of the fight, totally committed!

21 WHAT TO AVOID

IF WE'RE DETERMINED TO live the right way, the writer of Proverbs has some sound advice for us:

- Avoid laziness—it never gets us anywhere. "A farmer too lazy to plant in the spring has nothing to harvest in the fall" (Proverbs 20:4 MSG).
- Avoid cynicism—it's common to mock people today, but talking people down only weakens community and damages relationships. "Get rid of all bitterness, rage and anger, brawling and slander, along with every form of malice. Be kind and compassionate to one another, forgiving each other, just as in Christ God forgave you" (Ephesians 4:31–32).
- Avoid lying—dishonesty will only ever lead us into trouble. "The LORD

detests lying lips, but he delights in people who are trustworthy" (Proverbs 12:22).

- Avoid quarrelling—being argumentative is just a shortcut to even more problems. "It is to one's honor to avoid strife, but every fool is quick to quarrel" (Proverbs 20:3).

The advice might sound old-fashioned, but there's a universal truth within it that is undeniable. Avoid lying, cynicism, quarrelling, and laziness; instead, give positive energy, courage, kindness, and commitment to the day.

When we learn to carry ourselves the way God intends, we find that "the LORD lifts up those who are bowed down" (Psalm 146:8). Let's start every day humbly before God, because it's the place of maximum power.

22 STRUGGLES DEVELOP STRENGTH

AT NO TIME DID Jesus ever offer us a trouble-free life. Far from it. He actually went out of His way to explain that anyone living according to God's way of kindness, love, and mercy will face "tribulation *and* distress *and* suffering" (John 16:33 AMP). So it's not surprising that apart from John, who spent his final years in captivity, every one of the apostles was brutally killed for his faith.

But a life of trial and trouble wasn't the only promise Jesus made to His followers. He promised them peace and confidence, help and rescue.

"I will not leave you as orphans; I will come to you." (John 14:18)

Those same promises are made to you and me today. They are the promises that have inspired and helped brave men and women shine the light of Christ in many a dark place. The light always defeats the dark, and a life of struggle is a beautiful thing when it is coupled with friendship with the Almighty and assurance of a bright future.

"Be strong and courageous. Do not be afraid or terrified because of them, for the LORD your God goes with you; he will never leave you" (Deuteronomy 31:6). And remember that the struggle also develops our strength.

23 STARTING OVER . . . AGAIN

WE'RE ALL GOING TO make mistakes at some point in our lives. Some of us will make many. What matters most is that we can admit when we've gotten ourselves into trouble, have the humility to say we are sorry, and then summon the determination required to start again.

The psalmist King David found himself in trouble on multiple occasions. "As for me, my feet had almost slipped; I had nearly lost my foothold. For I envied the arrogant when I saw the prosperity of the wicked" (Psalm 73:2–3). But he also recognized when he slipped up. And time and time again, he found himself kneeling before God, humbly saying he was sorry. From this position, he realized how unbelievably blessed he was:

> Yet I am always with you;
>> you hold me by my right hand.
> You guide me with your counsel,
>> and afterward you will take me into glory. (Psalm 73:23–24)

Nothing compares to a strong relationship with God, rooted in forgiveness. When we rely on His guidance and strength, we have the power to overcome any obstacle—including all our failures and our pride.

24 ☰ LISTEN TO UNDERSTAND

WE ALL KNOW THAT good communication is at the root of all positive relationships and that the converse is also true. But less understood is the key role that listening plays in our friendships, our marriages, our faith, and almost all the battles that we find ourselves fighting. Listening is the unsung, potent weapon in our arsenal, but it is much underused.

General George Marshall said, "Formula for handling people: listen to the other person's story. Listen to the other person's full story. Listen to the other person's full story first."[45] As Marshall knew, it is not listening in order to respond; it is listening to truly understand.

The Bible makes it clear what happens when people don't listen. Throughout the book of Kings we see time and again the consequences of not listening. "They would not listen. . . . They would not listen" (2 Kings 17:14, 40). Every one of the kings of Israel is described as doing "evil in the eyes of the LORD" (2 Kings 17:2), and it led to the early destruction of the kingdom.

The kings of Judah were better. Some of them actually listened to God, and under those kings Judah flourished. Jesus made it even clearer, putting this instruction at the heart of His manifesto:

"Blessed rather are those who hear the word of God and obey it." (Luke 11:28)

When we speak, we learn nothing. When we listen, we learn much. It takes effort, humility, and patience to listen properly, but it leads to much fruit. And the blessings that follow are worth it: those we love will grow ever closer, and those we are in conflict with will often lose their anger.

25 IS IT WORTH IT?

DO YOU EVER HEAR an Olympic gold medalist complain that the training wasn't worth it? Even if the race is over in a matter of seconds, the years of hard work and determined preparation are a small price to pay for the ultimate prize.

Paul understood this too. "You've all been to the stadium and seen the athletes race. Everyone runs; one wins. Run to win. All good athletes train hard. They do it for a gold medal that tarnishes and fades. You're after one that's gold eternally" (1 Corinthians 9:24–25 MSG).

If sporting glories fade, how much more should we train and work hard for the prize of life? Paul wrote, "I don't know about you, but I'm running hard for the finish line. I'm giving it everything I've got. No sloppy living for me! I'm staying alert and in top condition" (1 Corinthians 9:26 MSG).

But if there's one massive difference between athletes and us, as those who know Christ, it is this: this race is not won with our own strength and abilities.

> It is God who arms me with strength
> and keeps my way secure. (2 Samuel 22:33)

This race is one that has already been won. Our job is to hold on and ride the train to glory and never give up.

26 BEATING THE RAT RACE

EVEN THOUGH IT CAN sometimes feel this way, life is not a competition. God doesn't judge us by our wins, and we have no need to be held back by our losses. Life need not be a rat race. It is about more than that. It is about relationship.

This is the way of Christ, and it is different, richer, and better than a life of struggling for power. It is more lasting and more fulfilling. He invites us all to know Him. This offer that He makes to every one of us is both a huge privilege and a life-enhancing opportunity. God has trusted us with gifts and abilities, and He wants us to use them or lose them.

I love the fact that if we do the very best with what we have, God will give us more. He'll say, "Well done, good and faithful servant! You have been faithful with a few things; I will put you in charge of many things" (Matthew 25:21).

In any relationship, communication is vital. We need to talk and we need to listen. It's called prayer. The God-centered life is a life of consistent prayer. Jesus taught His disciples to "always pray and not give up" (Luke 18:1). There it is again: never give up! But the more we do this—communicating with Christ— the deeper we go, the more productive we will be, and the happier we will feel.

27 OUR WOUNDS

WE ALL HAVE WOUNDS, and not just the physical kind. Each of us carries a few emotional scars we've picked up over the years. The truth about wounds— both physical and emotional—is that it helps to get them treated. If we don't, they can easily get infected. When that happens, the rest of our lives start to suffer. Some of my past wounds have needed more care than others. But for all of them, the treatment has been the same:

> He heals the brokenhearted
> and binds up their wounds. (Psalm 147:3)

Looking to the love of God to treat our wounds is the best thing we can do, and most of the time we have to keep on going back to Him day after day. We need to rely on Him, trust Him, and allow Him the time and space in our lives to put us back the way He intended us to be.

Love heals all. Sometimes it is fast and dramatic, sometimes slow and painful. But letting Him into our damaged areas to soothe the wounds is always worth it.

28 LOOK CLOSER

FRANCIS COLLINS, DIRECTOR OF the Human Genome Project, led a team of more than two thousand scientists who collaborated to determine the three billion letters in the human genome—our own DNA instruction book.

After years of painstaking research and dedication, one of the world's foremost scientists reached this startling conclusion about the origins of life on earth: "I cannot see how nature could have created itself. Only a supernatural force that is outside of space and time could have done that."[46] I love that all his knowledge and study led him to see something beautiful through all the data. That statement must have taken great courage, but it also showed incredible insight.

> The heavens declare the glory of God;
>> the skies proclaim the work of his hands.
> Day after day they pour forth speech;
>> night after night they reveal knowledge. (Psalm 19:1–2)

Faith should never be blind. Yes, sometimes faith involves a brave leap into the dark, but we don't have to be unthinking or unquestioning in order to believe in the Almighty. God invites us to look, to search, to question— and to meet Christ in new and surprising ways along the way.

Science shouldn't be a stumbling block to faith. It should be a window.

Our hunger for the truth shouldn't prevent us from asking questions. We are designed to explore, probe, and seek knowledge. It is beautiful and heartening when we do so, and our conclusions bring us back to what we naturally feel in our hearts. For me, it is that God is love and God is good.

29 STAY HUMBLE

JUST AFTER HE'D GIVEN Moses the Ten Commandments, God outlined some key details to His people for the journey ahead. Good things were about to happen, and the former slaves were on their way to the promised land.

But God was crystal clear in His instructions:

> Understand, then, that it is not because of your righteousness that the LORD your God is giving you this good land to possess, for you are a stiff-necked people. (Deuteronomy 9:6)

Three times God repeated the message in the passage, and the warning could not be more plain. They were free by God's grace, not because of their goodness. They must remember that—and always stay humble.

Humility is one of the most magnetic but rare qualities in human beings, and when we see it, it is beautiful. Staying humble is about knowing that we have been forgiven much. It is about letting others shine and considering them greater than ourselves. It is thinking less about self and more about those around us. Such humility is the hallmark of great men and women and the signature of truly great leaders.

That's why God gives clear instructions to us, as He did to Moses.

> Seek GOD, all you quietly disciplined people
> who live by GOD's justice.

Seek GOD's right ways. Seek a quiet and disciplined life. (Zephaniah
2:3 MSG)

Justice, right ways, and a quiet, disciplined life. These are all positive signposts to help keep us on track.

30 WHO YOU ARE

HOW WE SEE OURSELVES when the lights are up, the music has stopped,
and the rose-tinted spectacles are put down determines so much in our lives. It
is easy to think either too little of ourselves or too much. Both result in a dis-
torted truth and a negative outcome. Knowing our true worth and identity is
key to success, and this verse is very clear:

The LORD has chosen you to be his treasured possession. (Deuteronomy
14:2)

Those are powerful words—powerful enough to transform our lives and
how we see ourselves. This truth never should lead to us being big-headed and
arrogant. It's the reverse. When we know our worth, we stop having to promote
ourselves or impress others.

Instead, we can draw on the resources of heaven, calm and assured in our
status as a child of God, and we can love and build up others. That's how we are
meant to live.

I love these words of Jesus: "If you walk around with your nose in the air,
you're going to end up flat on your face. But if you're content to be simply yourself, you will become more than yourself" (Luke 14:11 MSG).

More than just yourself. That's the journey of life.

RELATIONSHIPS

GOOD RELATIONSHIPS ARE AT the heart of all success. Nobody can fully achieve what they were created for without strong relationships at the center of their life.

Relationships are so vital to a healthy, satisfying life that you can measure your real wealth in terms of the quality of those relationships. Strip away all the money and possessions and what have any of us got left? You can't truly call yourself rich if you've got a billion in the bank but no friends or family who love you.

Relationships cover every aspect of our lives—work, home, and play. They matter, and they affect our lives in every way. For example, one of the strongest motivations for me to do my best work is the team I work with, especially the filming crew. We're like brothers and sisters. We've grown up together, seen each other get married, have children, and juggle the game of life, family, work, and risk, all together. We know each others' frailties and vulnerabilities, whether that's time away from home, the fear of jumping out of a plane, or just finding it really hard to keep going after we've been working in the rain for a long time. I like to see us as a crew of fallible warriors who always have each others' backs.

The best relationships, whether with family, friends, or work buddies, are the ones where you don't have to hide the cracks and the flaws. You love those people not because they're brilliant but because of who they are and what you've been through together. It is so often the quirks and foibles that make relationships special.

But sometimes I wonder whether as a society we're missing some of this vulnerability in a lot of our relationships. We can get so caught up with appearing the right way, doing the right job, and generally looking like we've got a handle on life that we forget the power that vulnerability has to unite and bond us. Giving the impression of being "too sorted" simply creates distance between people.

Without good, honest, vulnerable relationships, humans grow anxious. If we don't allow others to know us with all our failings, we'll look in the mirror and only see the "behind the scenes" version of ourselves in all its mess. And when we look at other people all we will see is their "show reel" of highlights. This destroys self-worth and the positive power of relationship.

God's way is different. We can be as raw and broken and honest with Him as we dare. When we find love and acceptance in Christ, we don't need to try to impress others with our lives. We can be vulnerable and real. That in turn creates and strengthens bonds with those around us. As men and women of faith, we can love the unlovable in each other. We can forgive because we have been forgiven. We protect, give, help, and support because we have found all that and more in the Almighty.

In short, faith should make us great at relationships because we are rooted in an abundant source of love, forgiveness, and kindness. God loves relationship. He wants to bless our marriages, our friendships, and our work relationships. And He summed it all up in the words of Jesus:

"Love each other as I have loved you." (John 15:12)

THE POWER OF WORDS

OUR WORDS ARE POWERFUL. They can harm in an instant. Sometimes the damage can last a lifetime.

"The mouth of the wicked is a dark cave of abuse," says Proverbs 10:11 (MSG). "Sin is not ended by multiplying words, but the prudent hold their tongues" (v. 19).

It's vital that we learn to control our words, especially in this digital age when the damage they do can be even greater and travel so much further than ever before. As Abraham Lincoln said, "It is better to be silent and thought a fool, than to speak and remove all doubt!"[47]

But our words can build as well as destroy. With kind and encouraging words, you can change a person's day—or even their entire life. Your words have the power to bring great blessing: "The mouth of a good person is a deep, life-giving well. . . . Love pulls a quilt over the bickering" (Proverbs 10:11–12 MSG).

Speak well of people and to people. Use your words to spread kindness and love, and if you can't think of something good to say about someone, say nothing. People will know and appreciate you for this positive quality of discretion.

FRIEND OF GOD

FRIENDSHIPS ENRICH OUR LIVES and strengthen us in the face of hardships. Now imagine having the almighty Creator of the universe as your closest friend, the one who has your back through thick and thin. His promise is that you and I can be His friend. The same promise that God made to Moses—"My Presence will go with you, and I will give you rest" (Exodus 33:14)—extends to us too. Be grateful with all your heart for this gift, and know it is all grace.

Clothe yourselves with humility toward one another, because,

> "God opposes the proud
> but shows favor to the humble." (1 Peter 5:5)

When we really think about the way God keeps on pouring out His love and mercy on us, despite our failings, humility makes sense. Humility doesn't mean that we have to feel bad about ourselves. As Rick Warren put it, "True humility is not thinking less of yourself. It is thinking of yourself less."[48] When we are surrounded by the love of God, our eyes lift off ourselves and our hearts look up with love and gratitude. That's humility.

3 SIDE BY SIDE

LORD RADSTOCK, THE MISSIONARY who played a part in the Great Russian Awakening, was once staying in a hotel in Norway. He heard someone playing the piano badly downstairs in the hallway and went to investigate. He found a little girl hammering the keys, unaware that her tuneless melody was driving Radstock mad.

As he watched, Radstock saw a man approach the piano and sit down on the stool beside the girl. She carried on playing the same dud notes, but the man filled in the gaps. To Radstock's amazement, the pair produced the most beautiful music. It was only later that he discovered that the man was the girl's father, Alexander Borodin, composer of the opera *Prince Igor*.[49]

So much of our journey of faith and love is like this too—it's a relationship where our tuneless notes, our mess, our attempts to do our best only come to life when Christ stands beside us and touches our hearts. It takes Him edging us on toward love and light, into kindnesses and hidden good works, into doing bold, brilliant things with our life. With His touch we can in turn touch lives all around us. Hand in hand, every day, never looking too far ahead or behind, with His presence our lives come to life.

And just like that father with the little girl, God is always close:

> The moment we get tired in the waiting, God's Spirit is right alongside helping us along. (Romans 8:28 MSG)

4 BEAUTIFUL FEET

PEOPLE OFTEN ASK THE writer Shane Claiborne what Mother Teresa was really like in person. In his book *The Irresistible Revolution*, Shane explained that while some people wondered whether she had an angelic glow about her, the reality was much more mundane. He described her as a pretty standard, beautiful old granny: short, wrinkly, perhaps a little grouchy from time to time.

But one thing he said he'd never forget were her deformed feet. He'd stare at them and wonder whether perhaps she'd contracted leprosy. One day he discovered the truth: whenever shoes were donated, Mother Teresa never wanted anyone to get stuck with the worst pair. She'd always dig through the pile and make sure she was the one who got the really broken, beaten-up shoes. After years of living like this—loving her neighbor as herself—her feet were deformed.[50]

That's grace. That's sacrificial love in action. Selflessly putting others first. That's humility.

> How beautiful are the feet of those who bring good news! (Romans 10:15)

This is how, as men and women of faith, we stand out. We put others first, and with Christ inside us, we go the extra mile for people. We try to be

Christlike. That's what Mother Teresa was doing: shining and sharing the light and love of Christ to people, always through her actions. Her feet reflected her heart—broken for the poor yet beautiful through her kindness.

Today, we ask Christ that our hearts and feet be instruments of love and courage in how we live.

5 DOING LIFE TOGETHER

IT GOES AGAINST THE grain, but the key to winning your battles is not to rely on your own strength. King David learned the hard way that the only way forward is to put your trust in God. At the end of the day, human strength and power are not enough:

> No king succeeds with a big army alone,
>> no warrior wins by brute strength.
> Horsepower is not the answer;
>> no one gets by on muscle alone. (Psalm 33:16–17 MSG)

God gives victory to those who trust Him:

> Watch this: God's eye is on those who respect him,
>> the ones who are looking for his love.
> He's ready to come to their rescue in bad times;
>> in lean times he keeps body and soul together.
> (Psalm 33:18–19 MSG)

As humans, from birth, we are taught to be self-reliant, but that will only ever take us so far. Real power comes from relinquishing that power and plugging into something greater than ourselves. It comes from kneeling and looking up. God has everything we need, so trust Him. Like David. Like Joseph. Like Moses and Joshua. Like John the Baptist. Like Peter. Like Paul.

So instead of initiating our own plans and asking God to bless them, let God lead your heart. Let Him direct and empower your steps and bless your journey together. That's His greatest wish: to do life with you.

6 FRIENDSHIP MATTERS

"FRIENDSHIP," WROTE C. S. Lewis, is the "crown of life and school of virtue."[51] To have great friends—the kind who you consider to be soulmates—is an incredible gift. Friendship multiplies joy and divides sorrow, and the Bible is full of amazing examples to follow.

David and Jonathan, Moses and Aaron, Naomi and Ruth, Elijah and Elisha—they all stood beside each other in tough times and laughed together in the good.

> Two are better than one,
>> because they have a good return for their labor:
> If either of them falls down,
>> one can help the other up. (Ecclesiastes 4:9–10)

This great verse is often used to illustrate the importance of friendship and unity in marriage, but the original context of this verse is actually that of friendship.

In another respect, friendship is even more important than marriage: marriage is temporary; friendship is eternal.

So we need more good partnerships today. There are great reasons why Jesus sent His disciples out two by two. There are times when life, work, and our mission can get really tough and a little lonely. Going out in pairs can make all the difference.

So be loyal to your friends, especially when they're not with you. Be the kind of friend who makes the laughter last longer and the tears ease sooner. Encourage them by words and deeds, by text, by email. Build each other up. Have their backs and speak well of them to others. Each of those deeds is another solid brick in the wall for a friendship that will be eternal.

7 HUMILITY, LOVE, AND TOLERANCE

EVEN BEFORE JESUS HAD physically left the earth and given the disciples the job of establishing the church, they were arguing. In fact, Jesus' work had barely even begun when the disciples started disagreeing about who was going to be the greatest among them.

So Jesus gave them (and us) some vital lessons on how to keep friendships strong.

Choose Humility

It's natural to want to compare ourselves, but envy and rivalry are toxic to relationships. Jesus told the disciples not to compete with each other, unless it's to get the last place: "Anyone who wants to be first must be the very last, and the servant of all" (Mark 9:35).

Choose Love

Picking up a child, Jesus said, "Whoever welcomes one of these little children in my name welcomes me" (Mark 9:37). We are called to love and welcome everyone, especially those who are unable to do anything for us.

Choose Tolerance

Sometimes we find it easy to put up with the mess in our own lives but are intolerant toward other people who make mistakes. Jesus taught us to be gracious toward others but to be vigilant and intolerant about sin in our own lives: "And if your eye causes you to stumble, pluck it out" (Mark 9:47; a metaphor, I hasten to add!).

When we act like this consistently, we build the kind of friendships that last through life's fiercest storms.

8   PEACE, PEACE, PEACE

PEACE IS AT THE heart of everything good in this world. If you want to live right, prioritize peace in these three key areas:

With God

When we live right with God and show Him proper respect, peace is an unstoppable outcome. "The Fear-of-GOD builds up confidence, and makes a world safe for your children. The Fear-of-GOD is a spring of living water" (Proverbs 14:26–27 MSG).

With Others

"As far as it depends on you, live at peace with everyone" (Romans 12:18). Patience, kindness, and generosity all help strengthen our relationships. Besides, "when you're kind to the poor, you honor God" (Proverbs 14:31 MSG).

With Ourselves

A lot of us struggle with this one. Our minds can be anything but peaceful. But you and I can know a true and lasting peace through Christ's presence in our hearts: "A calm *and* peaceful *and* tranquil heart is life *and* health to the body" (Proverbs 14:30 AMP).

Anger, lack of forgiveness, envy, and jealousy all leave a trail of destruction—not only in our communities and relationships, but also in our relationship with God. Pursuing peace is always the answer. Peace. Peace. Peace. Know His calming presence in your heart.

9 GOD NOW HERE

IF YOU LOVE SOMEBODY, what you long for more than anything else is that person's presence. Photos are a comfort. Telephone calls, emails, and texts are nice. Letters are good. Skype and FaceTime are great ways to communicate. But nothing can compare to actually spending time with them in person.

The moment Adam and Eve turned their backs on God, they lost something precious: their genuine connection with Him.

Later, the Israelites saw the temple not mainly as a place of sacrifice but as a place of God's presence. Whenever they were captured and hauled off by some foreign power, the hardest part for many of them was being away from God's presence.

For us all, the moment Jesus was resurrected from the dead changed everything. It means that every divine claim He made about Himself was true. It means He is not some dead historical figure. Instead, He fulfilled His destiny.

Throughout the Old Testament we see signposts to Jesus: prophecy after prophecy fulfilled in this carpenter from Nazareth, who lived as God among us. Through His life, death, and resurrection, we can experience God's presence with us. The words that were written about Jesus before He was born remain true for all of us today:

"My Spirit, who is on you, will not depart from you." (Isaiah 59:21)

God is not nowhere. God is now here.

10 THE GOOD SOIL

IF WE WANT TO have great relationships, we have to treat the other person with respect. It's the same for spouses, close friends, or parents and children. Closeness and trust can thrive only when people are thoughtful, kind, honest, and loving.

It's also true when it comes to us and God. The way we respond to Him has an influence on how close we get. We can ignore Him, choose not to respect Him, and live our lives heading away from Him, and He'll seem a million miles away. (By the way, the irony is that even then He is close at hand. But our hearts will often ache and feel alone.)

But if we look for Him with honesty, humility, and respect, then everything can change. Our lives will thrive in ways we might never anticipate:

> "Still other seed fell on good soil. It came up and yielded a crop, a hundred times more than was sown." (Luke 8:8)

There's a beautiful paradox at the heart of this life of faith and love. We are not His equal, yet God involves us in His plans, as precious sons and daughters. He could do it all on His own, but He chooses to involve us, to invite us closer to Him. He gives us total freedom, yet He remains in perfect control.

All of us have things that are wrong in our lives, but if we are willing to say a tentative yes to God, He works with us, just where we are. Our hearts become fertile soil, and He uses us and blesses us.

11 CONFRONTATION NAILED

CONFRONTATION IS SIMPLY A part of life. It's not always easy to handle and sometimes incredibly painful, but how we deal with it can make or break so much.

Jesus was the master at dealing with confrontation (and He never confused confrontation with condemnation). He never shied away from confrontation, and He never acted out of any motive but love.

Nicodemus was a very powerful man. He was a moral and upright Pharisee and a member of the Jewish ruling council. Jesus was undaunted by his position. He lovingly confronted Nicodemus with his need to lose the "religion" and to start anew, leaving behind past hurts, habits, and ways. Jesus shared His message of transformation clearly, kindly, and with nothing but love.

And what does love look like?

> Love is patient, love is kind. It does not envy, it does not boast, it is not proud. It does not dishonor others, it is not self-seeking, it is not easily angered, it keeps no record of wrongs. Love does not delight in evil but rejoices with the truth. It always protects, always trusts, always hopes, always perseveres. Love never fails. (1 Corinthians 13:4–8)

Speak the truth in love. That's how we deal with confrontation, no matter who we're facing.

It can take a lifetime to learn how to handle confrontation effectively, but looking at how Jesus did it, whether with Nicodemus, Pontius Pilate, or the traders in the temple, sets the perfect example. It is part of the reason that people all through time, whether believers or not, have so often held up Jesus as the ultimate benchmark of a leader and an example of perfect love and unending wisdom.

12 REAP AND SOW

JESUS WAS CONSTANTLY SURROUNDED by people, which means the stories about His life are full of great insight for how to navigate relationships, especially when it came to the disciples. If you wanted to create the longest-lasting, most influential faith community in mankind's history, you wouldn't have picked this lot. They were a mess. They were like you and me. They got it wrong more often than they got it right. They argued and fought, and they forgot plenty of what Jesus taught them. But Jesus was patient and kind, and He knew that eventually they'd come good and be the ones to build His church. He shows that same kind of faith in us.

Jesus knew that in relationships three fundamental truths apply:

- You reap what you sow.
- You reap later than you sow.
- You reap more than you sow.

These truths apply to every aspect of our journey of faith. As the apostle Paul wrote,

> Remember this: Whoever sows sparingly will also reap sparingly, and whoever sows generously will also reap generously. (2 Corinthians 9:6)

If you want to live a full, rich, rewarding life, keep giving. Make it your aim to be the most generous person you know. Be generous with your kindnesses, your enthusiasm, your positivity, your money and possessions, your time, and your love.

Life is really very simple: what we put in is what we get out.

13 MAKING A DIFFERENCE

DO YOU WANT YOUR life to make a difference? Do you want to make an impact? You can, every single day. All you've got to do is let God work through you. "The fruit of the righteous is a tree of life," said the writer of Proverbs 11:30.

It's true: when we live with the Almighty beside us, we find that all kinds of good things flow out from that. Galatians 5:22–23 lists those good things: love, joy, peace, patience, kindness, goodness, faithfulness, gentleness, and self-control.

If we want to make a difference to the world around us, we must allow God to make a difference within us, then let that goodness and grace flow to everyone we meet.

> Now we look inside, and what we see is that anyone united with the Messiah gets a fresh start, is created new. The old life is gone; a new life burgeons! Look at it! All this comes from the God who settled the relationship between us and him, and then called us to settle our relationships with each other. (2 Corinthians 5:17–18 MSG)

That's powerful and good news. Through His presence and the resource of the Holy Spirit, we can truly make a positive difference wherever we go. And of that resource there is no limit.

"THE FRUIT OF THE RIGHTEOUS IS A TREE OF LIFE," SAYS THE WRITER OF PROVERBS 11:30.

14 ▌KINDNESS, KINDNESS, KINDNESS

EVERYONE WE MEET IS fighting a battle of some sort. It is good to remember this when we think that someone is being particularly difficult or obstructive. I can bet you that they are having a tough time in another aspect of their life that is making them that way. When we remember this, it changes how we see people. So always be kind, as Plato said, for everyone indeed is fighting a hard battle.

When we release kindness into the world around us, it creates a ripple of goodness. Healthy relationships are created, connections are nourished, and people in turn become inspired to do what they can to spread that kindness further. Kindness changes us as well as others. And it is the unexpected kindnesses that are the most powerful.

I love the story of David with Mephibosheth, a man who was crippled and described himself as a "dead dog." "Don't be afraid," said David, "for I will surely show you kindness. . . . I will restore to you all the land . . . and you will always eat at my table" (2 Samuel 9:7). Mephibosheth spent the rest of his life living in the palace in Jerusalem. David's kindness changed everything for him, and we are discussing it to this day.

Kindness. Kindness. Kindness. Write it in your heart. Kindness is king.

> **WHEN WE RELEASE KINDNESS INTO THE WORLD AROUND US, IT CREATES A RIPPLE OF GOODNESS.**

15 THE GREAT LIES

WE ALL GET TEMPTED. Leading a life of integrity in relationships is not easy. There are temptations all around, and at times the pull can get really strong, especially when it comes to sex, money, and power. It's nothing new. The Bible has plenty of stories of people who were tempted to cheat on their partners. Plenty of them gave in too. Plenty of them believed lies like this: "Stolen water is sweet; food eaten in secret is delicious!" (Proverbs 9:17).

It's such a deception, though. Stolen water is never sweet for long, and food eaten in secret is empty. The cold reality is that sin drags us away from freedom and light. Ask someone who has been through the experience of drugs, affairs, or deception. The buzz lasts but a minute. The dark sense of being manipulated by sensations leads to fear and shame—and the shame is always the hard part.

> But little do they know that the dead are there,
>> that her guests are in the realm of the dead. (Proverbs 9:18)

That's why Peter's words are so important to us:

> Whoever would love life
>> and see good days
> must keep their tongue from evil
>> and their lips from deceitful speech.
> They must turn from evil and do good;
>> they must seek peace and pursue it. (1 Peter 3:10–11)

God is on your side. He knows what it is to be tempted and what it takes to resist. His promise is that we will never be tempted beyond what He can help us resist. Focus on the truth, on the long game, on the value of fidelity. It will be a struggle and we might fail. His arms of forgiveness will never falter or fail, but sin damages us.

So if we have been given the tools and the power of God to resist, then claim that and stand firm. Every little victory makes us stronger. And like a muscle, the more often we resist and win, the stronger that resilience becomes.

16 SCARS

WE ALL CARRY A few scars and injuries as we get older. It's part of life, and they are reminders of many an adventure. Some I don't mind; others I do. I feel embarrassed about the state of my feet, for example. One of them is especially wonky and misshapen. (I can remember exactly the fall that caused that!) But the truth is that I shouldn't be ashamed of damage or brokenness. They are signs of being in the battle—and of having survived. Deformed feet and scars can be so beautiful. They show dignity and courage.

Jesus knew this all too well. It was only through His scars, through being punished in our place, that He could truly reach us. His scars are our gateway to life.

> But he was pierced for our transgressions,
>   he was crushed for our iniquities;
> the punishment that brought us peace was on him,
>   and by his wounds we are healed. (Isaiah 53:5)

So instead of seeking perfection (which doesn't even exist in this life), let's embrace the misshapen and the scars, because it is in the broken parts of our lives that the mercy and tenderness of Christ shines brightest. That's His nature. And His presence is always good and always healing.

17 | GUARD YOUR WORDS

WE ALL GET ANGRY sometimes, and we all say things we later regret. But be under no illusion, the words we say can cause a great deal of trouble. So be careful.

> A perverse person stirs up conflict,
>> and a gossip separates close friends. (Proverbs 16:28)

(By the way, if you're ever unsure whether you're gossiping or not, ask yourself this: Will the person you are speaking to think less or worse of the person you are speaking about? If the answer's yes, then it's gossip, and leave it out.)

But our words can also heal: "A gentle response defuses anger" (Proverbs 15:1 MSG), "Kind words heal and help" (v. 4 MSG), and "The soothing tongue is a tree of life" (v. 4). If we offer genuine encouragement to people, we're offering verbal sunshine, the sort of truth that can make people's day, even change their lives.

Ultimately, how you speak about others speaks loudest about yourself. (My mum taught me that.) So always guard your words and know their power to build or destroy.

18 | LOYALTY LASTS

LOYALTY IS SUCH A precious quality that it is underrated in society today, yet it is something we all need in this world. Without it our families, businesses and communities, politics, and even nations start to crumble.

Loyalty is built on such a beautifully simple concept: it declares that I am going to stick by you whether you are wrong or right, but I will tell you when you are wrong and help you get it right. I love friendships like that. I love it when people have my back and they let me have theirs. And I love the fact that Jesus always has my back. When I fall, stumble, trip, and fail, His presence and forgiving arms help me to my feet and encourage me on.

Perseverance takes on new meaning when we have power beyond ourselves inside of us. Christ is always with us. I have depended on this truth every day of my life of faith.

> I lift up my eyes to the mountains—
>> where does my help come from?
> My help comes from the LORD,
>> the Maker of heaven and earth. (Psalm 121:1–2)

When we trust God and look to Him for the help we need in life, things get put right. Life starts to work the way it was supposed to. We have access to power we never knew before. Finally, we start to live freely, lightly, and effectively. It all starts and ends with loyalty: loyalty from us, loyalty from Him. Through good and bad, thick and thin, we are together. This is the foundation of all great relationships.

19 WHAT IS WORSHIP?

IN SOME CHURCHES, A lot of time is spent doing something called worship. At some point the band will start playing and people will stand up, sing a few songs, raise their arms, and then all sit down again. I used to find it a bit weird. (Although throughout the Bible there was often a lot of raising of arms, and it is a strong physical expression of devotion. Singing love and gratitude to

God—I like that.) Don't get me wrong, I love the singing sometimes, and there are some amazing songs and writers out there! But is that all worship is?

Jago Wynne wrote, "Worship is about what I say with my tongue. It's about what I watch . . . what I think . . . where I go with my feet."[52] Worship can involve singing, but it can't just be about singing. It's got to be about something more. Worship is about honoring God. We do that in how we live. Every kind deed we do, every act of mercy, every moment of humility, selflessness, and generosity makes God smile. That's worship.

That's why Paul encourages us to pay attention to how we're living—to our relationships. And his advice is brilliantly practical:

> Share with the Lord's people who are in need. Practice hospitality. Bless those who persecute you; bless and do not curse. Rejoice with those who rejoice; mourn with those who mourn. Live in harmony with one another. (Romans 12:13–16)

That's true worship.

20 LOVE DOESN'T JUDGE

IT IS SO EASY to be critical, especially of people who don't see the world the way we do. But our instructions are clear: we're not to judge, especially not people whose beliefs are different from ours. Leave justice to God and focus instead on our role, which is to love and be kind. Paul gave some perfectly clear advice:

> Welcome with open arms . . . [those] who don't see things the way you do. . . . Eventually, we're all going to end up kneeling side by side in the place of judgment, facing God. (Romans 14:1, 10 MSG)

All of us—whatever beliefs we hold here on earth—will one day end up on our knees before the Almighty. Tolerance is always at the heart of love, and maybe our ways aren't the only ways. There are so many divisive, difficult issues in the world of faith. And who really knows the answers to all of them?

What we can know and trust is that love is the way—it is patient, respectful, tolerant, and kind. We can know that love puts relationships and unity before always having to be "right." So don't judge or criticize.

As Jesus said,

"Don't pick on people, jump on their failures, criticize their faults—unless, of course, you want the same treatment. That critical spirit has a way of boomeranging. It's easy to see a smudge on your neighbor's face and be oblivious to the ugly sneer on your own." (Matthew 7:1–3 MSG)

Love transcends all beliefs and always sees the best.

21 LONELINESS

THERE IS SO MUCH loneliness in our society, probably more than at any point in human history, and people are suffering across the generations. Young people have fewer safe places to process their growing pains, parents are struggling to raise families alone, and the elderly are marginalized and isolated. We turn to what we hope will help us deal with isolation, but too often these "solutions" only make things worse.

We are not intended to be alone. God created us all for community—one that's as close and as interdependent as the various parts of the human body. And like a body that's made up of different parts, we belong to one another. You might think that a kidney is less important than an arm, but you would be wrong.

On the contrary, those parts of the body that seem to be weaker are indispensable. (1 Corinthians 12:22)

We all desperately need each other—we are inextricably linked.

Let us consider how we may spur one another on toward love and good deeds, not giving up meeting together, as some are in the habit of doing, but encouraging one another—and all the more as you see the Day approaching. (Hebrews 10:24–25)

So when you see someone isolated, alone, or struggling, bring them into the fold. We are a family, each and every human being: wonderfully made and created to be with God and each other.

22 LABELS

THE MORE DIVERSITY THERE is in the world, the more we need each other to work together effectively.

That's why maybe it's time to drop the labels—to stop describing ourselves or others as a particular type of Christian. Labels all too often lead to division.

Most of all, let love guide your life, for then the whole church will stay together in perfect harmony. (Colossians 3:14 TLB)

Like a body, we are different but of one. As chief ambassador to World Scouting, I see two hundred countries of diverse cultures, looks, and languages, all bound together by a common set of positive life values. It works brilliantly because love, respect, and tolerance are the very foundations of what it means to be a Scout.

So when we encounter someone different on this journey of faith, let's remember how God sees them: as His unique, precious jewels. Let's treasure diversity, value our differences, dwell on what unites us rather than what separates us, and focus always on love. This is how God intended His family to be, and every encounter is a chance to show and share His love.

23 START WITH THE CLOSEST

OUR WORDS, ACTIONS, AND attitudes have the power to transform lives for the better. They can bring healing to people, communities, and even nations. Our lives should be guided by Jesus' Golden Rule: "Do to others what you would have them do to you" (Matthew 7:12).

As John Wesley said, we should work hard to "do all the good you can, by all the means you can, in all the ways you can, in all the places you can, at all the times you can, to all the people you can, as long as you can."[53]

So how do we do this? It seems an impossible task. Well, we don't do it alone. The burden does not rest on our shoulders. That's why God sent us His Helper, the Holy Spirit.

> He gave us a good bath, and we came out of it new people, washed inside and out by the Holy Spirit. Our Savior Jesus poured out new life so generously. God's gift has restored our relationship with him and given us back our lives. (Titus 3:5–7 MSG)

We don't achieve much impact on our own. But when we have the humility to kneel before the Almighty, He gives us all the power we need to change our world for the better. And where do we begin? Always with those closest to us.

24 RISK AND REWARD

AS RICK WARREN HAS pointed out, "Criticism is the cost of influence. As long as you don't influence anybody, nobody's going to say a peep about you. But the greater your influence . . . the more critics you are going to have."[54]

This doesn't just apply to leaders and people with upfront influence. We all have influence over people. In our marriages and friendships, with colleagues, even with those we simply meet day to day. Therefore, in a sense, all of us are leaders.

Sociologists tell us that even the most introverted individual will influence ten thousand other people during his or her lifetime. That means we will all be open to criticism, hurt, and loss. It's the price of relationships and influence.

When Jesus met the rich young ruler and invited him to join Him, He said, "Come, follow me" (Mark 10:21). He didn't offer him investment advice; He offered him a relationship, with all the associated risk. The same heart-thumping, painful, inspiring, costly relationship He offers us today.

It was too much for the rich young ruler. He walked away from Jesus. And we also get to say no and walk away if that's what we choose. But the gain will always be greater than the loss.

"Everyone who has left houses or brothers or sisters or father or mother or wife or children or fields for my sake will receive a hundred times as much and will inherit eternal life." (Matthew 19:29)

As a leader and person of faith you will have hard times and no doubt some criticism. Embrace it as part of the journey and the cost. Just keep your eyes always on the prize and the Prize-giver.

25 9,100 FEET UP

MOUNT HERMON IS VAST. If you're in northern Israel and look north, you'll see it. It sits way up on the border between Syria and Lebanon and reaches 9,100 feet, which means that most of the year there's snow on the peaks. The streams and rivers that flow from it, including the River Jordan, irrigate the land for miles and miles around.

So when the Bible describes unity as being like "the dew on Mount Hermon" (Psalm 133:2 MSG), it's a powerful image, and its influence is clear to see. God loves unity. I have seen the positive results of unity so many times in marriages and families, in teams and communities, and even in nations.

> How wonderful, how beautiful,
> when brothers and sisters get along! (Psalm 133:1 MSG)

Just like the water that collects on the slopes of Mount Hermon, unity has the power to sustain life. If people like you and me choose to unite (and maybe at times to swallow our pride), we inherit God's blessing. Unity paves the way for His power to flow from one to the next, with no broken connections.

Let's be people who unite rather than divide. Then the blessing of God will fall on us.

> No one has ever seen God; but if we love one another, God lives in us and his love is made complete in us. (1 John 4:12)

ON THE MOORS IN the Welsh highlands, two ministers once met a young shepherd boy who had impaired hearing and was illiterate. They carefully explained that Jesus wanted to be his shepherd, that He would always look after him, in much the same as the boy looked after his sheep.

They taught the boy to remember five simple words: "The LORD is my shepherd" (Psalm 23:1). Using the thumb and fingers of his right hand to help him, they repeated the words slowly, over and over. And each time they got to the fourth word, *my*, they'd pause and remind the boy that the psalm was meant for him.

Some years later, one of them was passing through that same village and asked about the shepherd boy. He was told that the previous winter there had been terrible storms and the boy had died on the hills, buried in a snowdrift. The villager who was telling the story said, "There was one thing, however, that we didn't understand. When his body was discovered he was holding the fourth finger of his right hand."[55]

Many people today think of God as some great impersonal force, but with Jesus it is different. His relationship with us is personal. As Paul wrote, He is "the Son of God, who loved me and gave himself for me" (Galatians 2:20).

He is "my God" (Philippians 4:19), and He is yours. This truth brings with it a power, intimacy, and strength that is beyond anything our world knows.

STARTING STRONG, STAYING TOGETHER

EACH DAY I TRY my best to start out on my knees. I remind myself to tackle the day with Christ first—that I am the glove and He is the hand; I try to listen and be still; then I read a little bit of the Bible, say thanks for all the good, and ask for help with all ahead. It takes me ten minutes or less, but it is where I get my soul fuel for the day and tasks ahead.

Wherever I am in the world, I also know that one of my closest friends, Jim, will be doing the same thing. He, like me, is a busy guy, but he never misses a day. We do this together every single day, Christmas included. And each year, we commit to going again. We read the same verses and then send each other an email with any thoughts, struggles, and feelings. This brotherhood is a source of lasting strength for us both. Accountability, friendship, and growth all belong together.

As the Proverbs say,

> As iron sharpens iron,
> so a friend sharpens a friend. (27:17 NLT)

We're not wired to live in isolation. We are designed to live in communities where love and friendship flow freely, where people of peace try to strengthen and support each other every day. This is how we grow and build strong foundations in our lives: through honest friendships, accountability, challenge, shared courage, and enduring commitment. Thank you, Jim.

NO MORE BARRIERS

APARTHEID. RACISM. DISCRIMINATION. ALL of these should be over by now. And certainly the sexes should not be at war. As Pope Benedict XVI put it, "In Christ the rivalry, enmity and violence which disfigured the relationship between men and women can be overcome and have been overcome."[56]

Two thousand years ago, Jesus showed us how we should respond to the kind of hate-driven barriers that oppress people who are different. He chose a Samaritan—a despised and powerless minority of no perceived value. "Jews in those days wouldn't be caught dead talking to Samaritans" (John 4:9 MSG).

To make His point even clearer, Jesus chose a Samaritan woman. And not just any woman: one with such a wretched history of broken relationships that even her own people treated her as a social outcast. She drew water alone at midday, and that's where Jesus met her and asked for a drink. There's no hint of Him patronizing her or lecturing her. He simply asked her for help. And instead of running away in fear or shame, she stayed. And everything changed as she realized the truth of His claim that the water He gives "will be an artesian spring within, gushing fountains of endless life" (John 4:14 MSG). Jesus was about bringing life in equal measure for all.

> There is neither Jew nor Gentile, neither slave nor free, nor is there male and female, for you are all one in Christ Jesus. (Galatians 3:28)

God loves us regardless of our color, creed, race, gender, previous life, or present lifestyle.

That's grace.

29 ENOUGH

THE POP STAR ROBBIE Williams once went on a shopping spree in Los Angeles and bought seven cars, including a brand-new Ferrari, a brand-new Porsche, and a brand-new Mercedes. Within a week he wished he had not bought any of them.

In his song "Feel," he sings about the gap inside him—a gap that can be filled only by love.

You've got to admire Robbie Williams's openness about himself. He's been ruthlessly honest about his addictions to drink, drugs, and himself. But he's not the first person to feel that ache inside. There's a need and an ache in every one of us. It's not a design flaw or a glitch. It's God-made, implanted by Him. God created that desire "to feel real love." He built me with a "hole in my soul," just as He built you with a hole in your soul too.

But it cannot be filled by cars, wealth, success, or drugs. It is a God-shaped hole. The French philosopher Blaise Pascal knew it too: Loosely paraphrased, "There is a God shaped vacuum in the heart of each man which cannot be satisfied by any created thing but only by God the Creator, made known through Jesus Christ."[57]

Jesus speaks straight to that ache in us all: "Let anyone who is thirsty come to me and drink" (John 7:37). What Jesus gives is an eternal fountain of life, love, freedom, and mercy. It pours down from the cross, from His open hands, into the hearts of men and women.

I have seen many things in my life, but the living water found in Christ is the only thing I have ever known that truly answers that deep ache. And it is for us all, given anew, every day.

30 BE RESTORED

EVEN GREAT PEOPLE OF God experience times of great discouragement. Look at the great leader Elijah. Having killed all four hundred of those prophets of Baal, you would think he could take on anything. For a while it looked as if he could, as he outran King Ahab's horse and chariot. But eventually the exhaustion caught up with Elijah. Extreme tiredness gave way to fear and anxiety, and soon he ended up depressed.

After we've taken on a bunch of emotional, spiritual, and physical risks, we all need replenishing. Elijah's recovery was no different. He needed sleep, food, exercise, friends, and God's healing, restoring presence. He needed to know that God had him.

God . . . is not far from any one of us. (Acts 17:27)

Are you feeling tired? Worn out? Exhausted? Be disciplined in making sure you rest properly. Give yourself a break and know that God is close by, ready to reinvigorate you in His own perfect way.

Whoever dwells in the shelter of the Most High
will rest in the shadow of the Almighty.
I will say of the LORD, "He is my refuge and my fortress,
my God, in whom I trust." (Psalm 91:1–2)

Claim it. Soak it in. As He was with Elijah, so God is with you.

VISION

THERE WAS A TIME a few years ago when things were tough at work. We were out there trying to find our way, earn a living, and do something good that felt in line with faith. But when we got to season three of *Man vs. Wild*, there was a whole spate of negative press, and we came really close to the show being canceled. But in the end Discovery Channel chose to invest in the show rather than kill it. Though it was difficult for a while, it ended up being the point from which it all started to accelerate dramatically.

A great friend of mine—a guy I've always respected and who has helped me a lot in my faith—once told me that God's calling always has a birth, a death, and a resurrection.

Sometimes when you're doing what's on your heart and going where your competency is, something catastrophic happens. You think that's the end of it. But actually that's precisely the time for you to have vision and hold on. That's your time to dig deep and trust that God will bless the plans He set in motion.

It's easy to have vision when the days are clear and the going is smooth. But vision counts most when a storm hits and you can't see through the wind and debris. That's when you learn to depend on God and not your own strength.

By the way, whether or not we feel we are working in our earthly calling, it is important also to remember that ultimately the only vision that really matters is the one that puts our lives into the hands of Christ. Our earthy calling is about our journey on this earth and the positive effect we hope to have—after all, we want to do something good, right? It's important, but it really doesn't matter as much as the single vision of being with Christ.

In terms of my earthly calling, I am hopefully still on that path, as is our team, doing our best and helping empower other people's adventures through TV, books, and so on. But what I do know is that today I can look back at the time when the TV show's future was so precarious and know that it was a key turning point. It was the moment when I had to have the courage to hold firm, to not panic, to not give up, and to trust God in it all. It was the moment I discovered what part of the vision for my life was God-given.

Vision is holding firm when everything is less clear. It's doing the thing you said you'd do long after the clear 20/20 has gone.

1 WIDE-ANGLE LENS

WHEN YOU WORRY THAT you're facing too many obstacles or that the storms you're going through will never pass, remember that God's perspective is not like ours.

We see what's happening now and fear that it will never change, but God knows otherwise. He knows that "his favor lasts a lifetime; weeping may stay for the night, but rejoicing comes in the morning" (Psalm 30:5). We don't have to get stuck in fear, and we don't have to live with a clouded vision of the future. The life-changing truth is that the Almighty is at work in our lives.

> "I know the plans I have for you," declares the LORD, "plans to prosper you and not to harm you, plans to give you hope and a future." (Jeremiah 29:11)

Hold on to this truth in the storms, and know that your life is in His hands. His plans are good and His hands are safe.

2 A VISION OF INTEGRITY

FORMER US PRESIDENT DWIGHT Eisenhower, Supreme Commander of the Allied Forces in Western Europe during World War II, once said, "The supreme quality for leadership is unquestionably integrity. Without it, no real success is possible, no matter whether it is . . . on a football field, in an army, or in an office."[58]

Integrity is the opposite of hypocrisy. The word's Latin root means "whole," and it describes an undivided life. It means your interior life and your exterior life are aligned.

People said of Jesus, "We know that you are a man of integrity" (Mark 12:14). He was truth and love personified.

Closeness to Christ brings with it an awareness of our failings and our need for help. Closeness to Christ also brings peace, courage, and joy, and it leads us into a life of integrity. We have no need to pretend in anything. That's freedom.

People will always gravitate to real integrity. It has a raw power to it.

As General Norman Schwarzkopf, commander of the coalition forces in the Gulf War, said, "Leadership is a potent combination of strategy and character. But if you must be without one, be without the strategy."[59]

3 DOUBTS AND QUESTIONS

EVERYBODY DOUBTS FROM TIME to time. And it is right that we have questions, some of which will never be answered on this side of heaven. When we live a life of love and faith, there's no need to bury those doubts and questions or pretend they don't exist. Jesus' disciples certainly didn't.

Even at the Last Supper, as they took their final meal with Jesus and listened to Him give them their instructions before He was killed, the disciples were scratching their heads. Thomas had no idea that Jesus was really going back to heaven (John 14:5–6), and Philip didn't appear to understand Jesus' purpose (vv. 8–10).

After all that time they'd spent with Him, and after all they'd seen Him do and teach, the disciples were still clueless. But Jesus was patient and kind with them—just as He is with all of us who at times get confused, become lost, and stumble away.

After Jesus' resurrection, "he said to Thomas, 'Put your finger here; see my hands. Reach out your hand and put it into my side. Stop doubting and believe'" (John 20:27).

This is the journey, and doubts and questions are all part of life. But through them all, keep your eyes and your heart on Christ. Seek answers and ask those you respect for help.

But also know that you are neither alone nor the first to feel these doubts. Jesus understands. He consoles and strengthens. He whispers truth to our hearts through the Bible, through His Holy Spirit, and through others.

As my grandfather used to say, there is always music in the garden, but sometimes our hearts have to be very still to hear it. And each time we return with courage and faith to His presence, we grow in character, strength, and wisdom. This is the journey of faith.

4   WHY ME? PART 1

MOSES WAS A GREAT leader. He was a man of vision and courage who led a nation out of slavery and into freedom. But Moses was also a reluctant leader. He got scared and overwhelmed and made a ton of excuses as to why he should not do what God was calling him to do.

Moses told God that He had made a mistake in choosing him. "Who am I?" he said (Exodus 3:11). He felt inadequate, as though he was unable to match up to the task, both in worthiness and all-round courage.

God's reply is perfect: "I will be with you" (v. 12). That is all that ever matters.

At various points in my life I've been able to relate to Moses' fears of the unknown and of the challenges ahead. It's natural to experience moments of self-doubt and fear of failure. But those impostors are no match for God. Becoming a person of vision means allowing Him to lead us, to strengthen us.

All we need to do is trust—then walk on in faith, with love in our heart and steel in our backbones. He will provide all we need day to day.

5 WHY ME? PART 2

WHEN GOD REVEALED HIS plan to rescue the Israelites, Moses freaked. First of all, he began to wonder what would happen if people started to doubt him. Having talked calmly and rationally before, God then took a different approach. He performed a couple of supernatural signs—the sort that would leave most of us speechless. Not Moses. He saw his walking stick turn into a snake and then back again, and his arm was transformed from healthy to leprous and back. But Moses was still not convinced.

> Pardon your servant, Lord. I have never been eloquent. . . . I am slow of speech and tongue. (Exodus 4:10)

Yet God was kind and encouraging, telling Moses that He would help him always. But it still wasn't enough. Finally, Moses got to the heart of the matter: his belief that someone else would do it much better than he would. "Pardon your servant, Lord. Please send someone else" (v. 13).

And God's reply?

> "I . . . will teach you what to do." (v. 15)

We can all probably think of a load of reasons why God wouldn't want to use us. At the heart of most of them will be fear. But God loves to strengthen us so that we can walk through our fears with Him beside us. It is one of His many great promises.

The lesson of Moses is simple: God is with us always. He will teach us. He has a plan for us. It is good. It will be daunting at times, but if we trust Him and look to Him, we will prevail.

6 INVESTING FOR WEALTH

SOCIETY PLACES SUCH IMPORTANCE and worth on money. Yet history shows us over and over that money is dangerous and needs to be handled very carefully if we are to avoid damaging our relationships with it.

Of course money matters, but it is easy for us to place an excessive value on earning money over other important things in life. Where do we spend the best of our time, focus, and energy? If it is all about the accumulation of wealth, then the risk of damage to ourselves and those around us is high. It is an empty way to live.

Money cannot compensate for unkind marriages, broken friendships, or lost years. Jean Paul Getty, at one time America's richest man, once said, "I would gladly give all my millions for just one lasting marital success."[60] When we have good relationships, we are told we "[lack] nothing of value" (Proverbs 31:11).

We can learn more about relationships from farmers than we can from bankers. Farmers have to plant generously and then nurture and protect their crops. If you hold back and use only the minimum seeds, cheapest fertilizer, and tainted water, your crop isn't going to be impressive. But if you show care, love, time, and attention to your crops, come harvest time you'll be smiling.

A stingy planter gets a stingy crop; a lavish planter gets a lavish crop. (2 Corinthians 9:6 MSG)

Our relationship with God works the same way. When we give our time, our gifts, our ambitions, and our resources to Him, He multiplies them. Whatever we give, Christ blesses and transforms into more, often in ways we would never expect.

If you want real wealth in your life, invest in the things of lasting value: friendship, with each other and with God.

7   AS FAMOUS AS GOD

I ONCE READ THAT in a survey of millennials, 50 percent said that a major life goal was to become famous.

Madonna said, "I won't be happy until I am as famous as God."[61] Seeking fame or celebrity is a dead-end path to go down. Fame to the ambitious is like salt water to the thirsty: the more you get, the more you want.

King David was a kind of celebrity, but there's no sign that he tried to seek out glory for himself. He always pointed people toward God, encouraging them to live for the Almighty rather than themselves.

> My feet stand on level ground;
>   in the great congregation I will praise the Lord. (Psalm 26:12)

David shone, but he stood among his people. He humbled himself as king and sought only to reflect God's goodness and love. We too can follow King David's example: keep our feet grounded and our eyes on God. (After all, people wrapped up in themselves make very small packages!) In the kingdom of God, if we want to be a king, we simply need to be a servant.

So always give God the credit in your heart for any success, and the more success you taste, the more humble you must try to be. Fame is never the answer. Fame alone leaves hearts empty. But a life empowered by Christ allows us to soar like the eagles.

> Humble yourselves before the Lord, and he will lift you up. (James 4:10)

8 JOY FUEL

JESUS DIDN'T HAVE IT easy. A refugee at birth, He narrowly escaped a mass killing of infants in Bethlehem. As an adult He was misunderstood, falsely accused, and plotted against before He was brutally tortured and murdered. He did not turn away from the path laid out for Him. Yet He was joyful.

That joy came in a number of ways: Jesus was close to God and spent time with Him, He enjoyed good relationships with other people, and He enjoyed the world God had created. (No one enjoyed a good party like Jesus!)

When we live like this—enjoying the intimacy, freedom, and friendship that is found in Christ and loving other people and the world He created—we change. Our perspective on hard times, our hope for the future, our lives and impact on the world around us—they all change.

But it starts with being connected to the Source.

> May the God of hope fill you with all joy and peace as you trust in him,
> so that you may overflow with hope by the power of the Holy Spirit.
> (Romans 15:13)

Then we start to live in a way that we are designed for. Our joy isn't connected to circumstances; it's connected to who we are. We are found in Christ—and that brings power, freedom, and joy beyond anything the world can offer.

9 JUMP!

A STORY THAT PASTOR Nicky Gumbel once told took place during World War II, in the terrible days of the Blitz, when a father, holding his small son by the hand, ran from a building that had been struck by a bomb. In the front yard was a shell hole. Seeking shelter as quickly as possible, the father jumped into the hole and held up his arms for his son to follow. Terrified, yet hearing his father's voice telling him to jump, the boy replied, 'I can't see you!' The father called to the silhouette of his son, "But I can see you. Jump!' The boy jumped, because he trusted his father. In other words, he loved him, he believed in him, he trusted him and he had confidence in him.[62]

> That's right—he rescues you from hidden traps,
>   shields you from deadly hazards.
> His huge outstretched arms protect you—
>   under them you're perfectly safe;
>   his arms fend off all harm. (Psalm 91:3 MSG)

Trust your heavenly Father's promises for your life. Trust that He has you, that He is in control, and that your future is secure in Him. Knowing these truths leads to courage, calm, confidence, and power.

10 A GOD WORTH BELIEVING IN

WHEN WE LOOK AROUND and see all the pain, loneliness, and injustice in the world, it's easy to ask why God doesn't do something. The answer is that He has. He sent His only Son, Jesus, to reach and rescue us—to save, redeem, and restore us. The promise of Jesus on earth remains: "That everyone who believes may have eternal life in him" (John 3:15).

This life is a battleground, but it is not the end.

The answer to the pain and sorrow and cruelty on earth is found in the fact that Jesus understands suffering. He suffered for us, and He suffers alongside us.

I love the words of the novelist Anthony Burgess: "If God is like Jesus, God is worth believing in."[63]

Our task here on earth is much the same as that of Jesus' closest friend, John the Baptist, two thousand years ago. "He is the one," said John, "the straps of whose sandals I am not worthy to untie" (John 1:27). John's task and ours is to look away from ourselves and up to Christ—the Creator, the Light of the World, the transformer of lives and revealer of God.

The answer to all suffering and to our future is found in Him.

> **THIS LIFE IS A BATTLEGROUND,
> BUT IT IS NOT THE END.**

JESUS' WAY

THERE WAS A MOMENT when Jesus' fame was increasing and the Pharisees were keeping count of the baptisms He performed. When they declared that Jesus had baptized more than John, they had a clear aim: turn them into rivals.

It didn't work. As soon as Jesus heard what they were saying, "he left Judea and went back once more to Galilee" (John 4:3). Jesus was not interested in rivalry, fame, or competition. He wouldn't play by man's rules. He had a mission to accomplish:

> Jesus said . . . . "The Son of Man came to seek and to save the lost." (Luke 19:9–10)

If we're going to be people of vision who help others find light and happiness in their lives, we need to be led by God. Being a leader doesn't mean being top; it means caring for others and walking beside them toward truth. To be a support for others means that we first have to draw strength from Christ and remain humbly before Him.

> The LORD will guide you always;
>> he will satisfy your needs in a sun-scorched land
>> and will strengthen your frame.
> You will be like a well-watered garden,
>> like a spring whose waters never fail. (Isaiah 58:11)

God's ways are different. He's not scared off by our vulnerability or frustrated by our need for continual guidance. On the contrary, our weaknesses become His strength in us. "He must become greater; I must become less" (John 3:30).

12 JESUS IN DISGUISE

LORD LONGFORD WAS A controversial figure. He spent much of his life visiting prisoners, including many murderers. Despite the criticism he received, few can doubt his compassion and his faithfulness, both to God and to those he visited. When he died, former prisoners joined hundreds of mourners to say farewell to the man who had spent his life faithfully fighting for society's outcasts.

On his deathbed he asked his wife, "You know what the most important quotation from the Bible is?" With his last breath, he quoted the words of Jesus: "I was in prison and you came to visit me" (Matthew 25:36).[64] Lord Longford understood that when Jesus told His disciples to serve the poor, the oppressed, and the outcast, He was giving the clearest of instructions.

"Whatever you did for one of the least of these brothers and sisters of mine, you did for me." (Matthew 25:40)

The next time you wonder how you can use your gifts and talents wisely, remember these words of Mother Teresa: "The dying, the unwanted, the unloved—they are Jesus in disguise." When we have this attitude for how we see the vulnerable, it changes so many of our aspirations as to how we want to live and how we invest our time, love, and energy.

As we go about our days, let's keep our hearts and eyes wide open to the Jesuses in disguise who are all around us.

13 LIFE ETERNAL

JESUS MAKES AN AMAZING promise to every person who chooses to receive it: "I give them eternal life" (John 10:28). *Eternal* doesn't just mean a never-ending quantity of life—it's also about quality. Christ satisfies our spiritual hunger and thirst in ways that nothing here on earth can ever hope to satisfy.

When we dedicate ourselves to being His sons and daughters, close to Him, we find a profound and deep soul satisfaction that simply cannot be found anywhere else. Christ promises that this relationship with Him will go on forever, and it starts now. Once we're on board, what we've gained can never be lost.

As Jesus promises,

"No one will snatch them out of my hand." (John 10:28)

There will be many struggles along the way. There will be great temptations as well. But if you give your life to Christ, you're protected by the most powerful force that has ever existed in the universe. You and I might lose our jobs, our money, our family, our freedom, and even our lives, but we will never lose this gift of His eternal presence. Live in the confidence of this truth.

14 THE CHURCH WITHIN US

EVEN TWENTY YEARS FROM now, some of the trends, movements, and brands that occupy so much of our thinking will be gone. They will be mere phantoms, half remembered from the past. But communities of people who quietly know and love Christ in their hearts will still be here.

Such communities or churches have outlived great empires, philosophical systems, and totalitarian systems for one simple reason: this church isn't simply some building. The church is not an establishment or a set of rules. The church is within us—men and women, boys and girls living humbly a life of love and faith. It is rich in relationship and rooted in the freedom of Christ.

> Blessed are those who . . . walk in the light of your presence, LORD. . . .
> For you are their glory and strength. (Psalm 89:15–17)

However you feel about the buildings and the services that take place within them, make your number one priority living in this way of grace. It is a community, a church—with no walls, no set of standards that have to be reached, no limits, no exclusions, and no end. Christ came to earth to win us and to find us. All of us, from every corner and every background and every religion. We are His forever.

15 GOD WILLING

IT IS GOOD TO plan ahead, as long as we bear in mind this simple truth: "You don't know the first thing about tomorrow" (James 4:14 MSG). We're in the dark. We can plan and imagine and put in place good attitudes and a road map, but ultimately our tomorrows are totally dependent on God, and that's the way it should be.

The expression "God willing" is a good one to use when discussing plans and aspirations. It shows a humility and acceptance that we are not the ones running the show. "God willing" reminds us of our place—dependent on a perfect, loving Father who knows exactly what we need better than we do.

I love the way David described his single aim in life:

I'm asking GOD for one thing,
  only one thing:
To live with him in his house
  my whole life long.
I'll contemplate his beauty;
  I'll study at his feet. (Psalm 27:4 MSG)

David simply wanted to be close to his Creator. He knew that if he was a friend of God then the rest would take care of itself. Yes, David would do his part by being faithful, hard-working, wise, determined, and brave, but beyond that he would trust his future to the goodness of God. He would trust God to look after the plans and after himself.

If you want a direction for your life, be like David: Don't try to fit God into your plans. Live in His ways in terms of your words, actions, and attitudes. Then let Him lead your heart and what you do with your days. God so often works through our heart's desires.

16 PEACE, PERFECT PEACE

IN 1555, NICHOLAS RIDLEY, a former bishop of London, was burned at the stake in Oxford because of his faith. On the eve of Ridley's execution, his brother offered to stay with him in the prison cell so that he wouldn't spend his last night alone. Nicholas declined. Instead of staying awake all night, fearful of what the morning would bring, he said he planned on going to bed and getting the best night's sleep of his life.[65]

God's peace is a powerful force. The Hebrew word for peace, *shalom*, translated from the Greek word *eirene*, means far more than just the absence of war or hostility. God's peace means wholeness, soundness, well-being, oneness with Him—every kind of blessing and good thing. The world around us needs this kind of peace. We need this kind of peace every day, in the good times and in the battles. But in order to share it with others, we first need to find and hold on to it within ourselves.

God is our refuge and strength,
> an ever-present help in trouble.
Therefore we will not fear. (Psalm 46:1–2)

Fear robs us of peace, but in Christ we need not fear anything. His love casts out fear. And in its place we can know His presence and His peace.

Be a person of peace today. Ask God to fill you with wholeness, well-being, and unity with Him where you need it most. Look for opportunities to share it with others and know it in your heart.

17 NO MORE RELIGION

JESUS CAME TO DESTROY religion.

Some churches are great communities of God. But some aren't. When it goes bad, religion can feed off the worst of our impulses. A lot of damage gets done in the name of religion: corruption, division, abuse. Religion allows people to build great empires for themselves, whether through power, money, position, fame, reputation, or even just through a false front of respectability.

We can live a much freer, truer, more empowered way—outside of religion. There is no need for any of us ever to be religious: to do certain rituals, to act all nice and sanitized, like we have it all together, or to attend church out of a sense of trying to earn God's presence.

All those things are illusions. True faith allows us to be totally raw, brutally honest, and broken at times. True faith allows us to be quietly kind, to be free—to get down on our knees before Christ—always aware of how much we need His help and strength to lead us forward.

> The stuck-up fall flat on their faces,
>> but down-to-earth people stand firm. (Proverbs 11:2 MSG)

At the end of the day, it does not matter if our lives appear to have been a failure or if other people have built more impressive empires than we have. Those things are so transient. All that really matters is that we have searched for God with humility, openness, determination, love, and courage. When we do that, He always finds us.

18 WHEN NECESSARY, USE WORDS

SOCIAL MEDIA BRINGS WITH it so many pressures, such as perceived perfection or highly edited promises. So often these turn out to be lies. How often are we deceived by things that appear amazing but in the end offer us nothing but emptiness?

The French philosopher Simone Weil understood one of the most powerful truths in life: "Imaginary evil is romantic and varied; real evil is gloomy, monotonous, barren, boring. Imaginary good is boring; real good is always new, marvelous, intoxicating."[66]I want to fill my life with the light that comes from the real good, to run from those empty illusions that pull me toward the dark.

Here is how we do that:

> Your job is to speak out on the things that make for solid doctrine. . . .
> dignity, and wisdom . . . healthy faith, love, and endurance. . . . [to be

people who are] models of goodness. . . . virtuous and pure. . . . Then their good character will shine through their actions. . . . to take on a God-filled, God-honoring life. (Titus 2:1–3, 5, 10, 12 MSG)

So don't be deceived by the glitz and the gloss out there. Trust your instinct on what is good for you and those around you and about what isn't. Our hearts tend to have a pretty solid built-in moral compass. Listen to it.

When we pursue these positive qualities, it is such a powerful, counter-cultural way to be. When you live and love like this, with purpose and integrity, people will gravitate to you—they will want to know where the light they see comes from. That's evangelism.

19 MAKING IT COUNT

GOD PROMISES THAT HIS love for you will last forever, and He doesn't break His promises. There's no use-by date on the good things He offers each and every one of us.

God is not human, that he should lie,
　　not a human being, that he should change his mind.
Does he speak and then not act?
　　Does he promise and not fulfill? (Numbers 23:19)

Because of who Jesus is and what He did, you and I get to inherit all the blessings promised to His children. You are loved. You are forgiven. You are blessed. He will give you strength.

So let's not waste our lives; let's make the most of every moment and opportunity. Be bold; be kind; be determined and unafraid to fail. You have the greatest resource inside you—the Holy Spirit—and you have nothing to lose and nothing to prove. You have only good to give, love to share, and a "never give up" fire within.

That makes you a potent force.

Each day is God's gift. . . . Make the most of each one! (Ecclesiastes 9:7, 9 MSG)

20 UNLESS THE LORD . . .

WHEN OUR VISION IS to live and work for our own glory, and when we see success as the "be all and end all," the road can be lonely and the burden heavy. But when our vision is to serve God, it's a different story. As Victor Hugo wrote, "When you have accomplished your daily task, go to sleep in peace; God is awake."[67]

I try to view the work I do in this way: it isn't my work; it is God's work and He has included me in it. That is very freeing. We are called to do our part as best we can, with commitment and integrity and pride. But our work isn't our primary purpose on this earth.

The real purpose of my life is to be close to the light and love of Christ. That's where my true identity is found, not in work or skills or accolades.

Living with Christ as our purpose, guide, and helper changes how we approach life. Life is no longer about us, about what we can gain or accumulate for ourselves. There is a much more fulfilling path and a much less futile way to spend our days.

Unless the LORD builds the house,
    the builders labor in vain.

> Unless the LORD watches over the city,
>   the guards stand watch in vain.
> In vain you rise early
>   and stay up late. (Psalm 127:1–2)

Let's make sure we are working for a greater cause than ourselves. We won't always manage this, and we all get distracted from time to time. But there is huge power and freedom when we cease thinking of our work as "ours" and when we start to let God take the lead.

From experience, I know that He will always be better at being in charge. He sees it all, He can bless it all, and He can help with it all. Our job is just to keep going, faithfully, humbly onward.

> Be strong and do not give up, for your work will be rewarded. (2 Chronicles 15:7)

21 THE PATH OF LIFE

THE WARNING SIGNS THAT get posted on narrow mountain tracks are there to keep us safe. They're built out of care and love. It's the same with the Bible. The words of warning it contains are designed to keep us on the path that leads to life. As Jesus said, there is a path that leads to life as well as one that leads to destruction (Matthew 7:13–14).

God wants you and me to walk on His paths. That's why "He put your feet on a wonderful road that took you straight to a good place to live" (Psalm 107:7 MSG). He doesn't want us wandering for "years in the desert, looking but not finding a good place to live, half starved and parched with thirst, staggering and stumbling, on the brink of exhaustion" (vv. 4–5 MSG).

God says, "Your salvation requires you to turn back to me and stop your silly efforts to save yourselves. Your strength will come from settling down in complete dependence on me" (Isaiah 30:15 MSG). This was music to my ears and balm to my fears when I first understood it.

Remember that God is actively looking to bless us and be with us today, so let Him.

22 SELFLESS

TO A LOT OF us, it seems logical to take control and put in the maximum effort to make sure our plans come off well. But getting too caught up with our own plans for our lives, families, and careers is living with our eyes turned inward. And eyes turned inward lose their effective vision.

The Bible constantly reminds us that empowered, meaningful living is about trusting God and living and loving radically. We see it in the lives of everyone who has had lasting, historical, biblical impact: Noah and Abraham, Daniel, Esther and David, John the Baptist, Peter and Paul. They all lived differently yet were rooted in faith and stepped out in courage.

God wants to be involved in every area of our lives—to bless them and to increase our vision beyond ourselves. If we want our work to have lasting value, we need to make sure we are partnering with the Source of all light, love, and power—not proudly going it alone and in the wrong direction.

The LORD will fulfill his purpose for me. (Psalm 138:8 ESV)

He will. Christ is our ultimate resource, and He has a huge purpose for your life. Trust that promise, follow His ways, listen to His whispers—and He will take you on an adventure like no other.

23 HOW TO BE A GOOD LEADER: PART 1

IF YOU WANT YOUR life to impact others, there's no finer leadership example to follow than Jesus. Here are the first two of six of His character traits we should endeavor to embrace.

Be Authentic

On the occasions when Jesus had harsh words for people, He was usually attacking the hypocrisy of the religious leaders. He hated the way they used their position of power to weigh down people with the burden of guilt instead of lifting them up.

Being authentic means that we don't try to impress or oppress people. What matters is who we are when nobody is looking. Jesus speaks about your "secret" life with God (Matthew 6:6). Try to develop an authentic, honest, private life with God.

Be Humble

Jesus warns against loving titles and recognition. Prominent positions and public flattery are not good for some of us—we start believing our own hype when people treat us as special. Jesus warns us not to let people put us on a pedestal.

"For those who exalt themselves will be humbled, and those who humble themselves will be exalted." (Matthew 23:12)

Make it your goal to promote Christ, not yourself.

24 HOW TO BE A GOOD LEADER: PART 2

IN LOOKING AT THE life of Jesus, we see undeniably the most influential leader for good the world has ever known. Here are two more of His character traits that we can build into our lives for the better.

Be a Person with Vision

True leaders should have big visions. They aim for the stars and are never small-minded or timid. Jesus attacked the religious leaders of His day for exactly this, calling them "blind guides" (Matthew 23:16).

Ask that God would give you a vision of what He wants you to do—a vision so big that without Him it is impossible. Think of Noah and his ark or Moses and his staff.

Be a Person with Focus

Avoid getting caught up with excessive minutiae and having to lead on everything. Empower people to take charge and let them do their jobs. Then back them, support them, and trust them.

Jesus criticized the religious leaders of the day for getting into little turf wars and becoming legalistic and petty. Jesus encouraged us to focus on "the more important matters . . . justice, mercy and faithfulness" (Matthew 23:23).

True leaders concentrate on the things that really matter—the bigger picture. They fight against injustice, champion the poor, and demonstrate faithfulness in their relationships with family and others.

HOW TO BE A GOOD LEADER: PART 3

HERE ARE THE FINAL two lessons in leadership from the incredible life of Jesus. Can you imagine how much better the world would be if we all embraced these two?

Be Compassionate

Jesus ultimately showed what true, selfless compassion looked like when He let Himself be tortured and killed in our place on that cross. But history shows that His whole life was an example of such compassion, and He went out of His way to serve and show love to the outcasts and unwanted.

He also attacked the religious leaders for putting stumbling blocks in regular people's way. "You shut the door of the kingdom of heaven in people's faces," He said. "You yourselves do not enter, nor will you let those enter who are trying to" (Matthew 23:13).

Leaders need to do the opposite: to be open, welcoming, and servant-hearted to everyone—to encourage, embrace, and build up others. And it is in the quiet, unseen moments of simple kindness that we truly define ourselves. That's leadership.

Be Generous

Generosity is the opposite of greed and self-indulgence. It is an outward expression of the inner gratitude we feel for all that we have been given. Be generous in all things: time, talent, treasure. The more we give, the more we get. Leaders understand this.

"Keep open house; be generous with your lives. By opening up to others, you'll prompt people to open up with God, this generous Father in heaven." (Matthew 5:16 MSG)

"Giving is true having," said Charles Spurgeon. And true leaders always give of their love, their time, and themselves in order to serve others. That's what sets Jesus apart from other great world leaders: the scale on which He gave of Himself for us.

HOPE TO HOLD ON TO

THERE'S A LOT OF injustice in the world. Bad things happen to good people, evil often seems to thrive unchecked, and many children endure unimaginable horrors. But this is not the whole story. Our hope proclaims that love will ultimately win.

Hope is powerful, but it's more than a feeling or an emotion. True hope does not rise or fall depending on our circumstances. In its most powerful form, hope fills us with the knowledge that, no matter what we're facing, we are not alone and our future is secure.

"Hope has a thick skin and will endure many a blow," wrote John Bunyan. "It will endure all things if it be of the right kind."[68]

So what is the "right kind"? Bishop Lesslie Newbigin explained, "The horizon for the Christian is, 'Christ shall come again' and 'we look for the coming of the Lord.' It may be tomorrow, or any time, but that is our horizon. That horizon is fundamental, and that is what makes it possible to be hopeful and to find life meaningful."[69]

Our hope is built on the enduring truths that Christ lived by; the presence, power, and peace that He brings; and the assurance of a hope and home eternal beyond this mortal life. Hope has the power to change everything. So "let us hold unswervingly to the hope we profess, for he who promised is faithful" (Hebrews 10:23).

27 LOVE AIN'T ALWAYS QUAINT

LOVE IS A WORD that we hear about a lot, but to define its meaning is hard. If I look at the great films that always move me, I find that love is almost always at the heart of them.

Often it is the hero sacrificing what he or she has (job security, personal safety, glory, wealth, etc.) in order to save or help or build up someone else. (Maybe it's rescuing a family member, saving the world, or giving the glory of the victory to someone who needs it more.) Hero story lines often look like this, and for good reason. Love inspires and moves us to achieve extraordinary and powerful feats.

This reminds us that love isn't shallow or soppy. Love is the most powerful force on earth. Love gives of itself for others—humbly, quietly, without asking for reward.

I like this description by Paul:

> *Love* is patient, love is kind. It does not envy, it does not boast, it is not proud. It does not dishonor others, it is not self-seeking, it is not easily angered, it keeps no record of wrongs. *Love* does not delight in evil but rejoices with the truth. It always protects, always trusts, always hopes, always perseveres. *Love* never fails. (1 Corinthians 13:4–8, emphasis mine)

Someone once challenged me to replace the word *love* in that scripture with my name and see how I stacked up. (That was a challenging one, for sure!) But if we want to live a rich, full life of love, these words are great compass points to follow: protect, trust, hope, persevere.

RIGHT FROM THE START of Jesus' life, He was in danger from King Herod, dark forces, numerous temple crowds, and religious chief priests. An endless number of people were filled with anger and loathing for anyone who threatened their authority—for anyone who promoted a message of love and mercy.

And so it was that many of the elite always seemed to be conspiring to kill Jesus. Yet He knew it would be like this. The Bible predicted it:

Why do the nations conspire
and the peoples plot in vain? (Psalm 2:1)

But Jesus also knew the solution:

Blessed are all who take refuge in [God]. (v. 12)

When we face the inevitable storms of life, the best thing we can do is to look up. Know that Jesus has faced much worse. He knows what we are going through, and He will always be beside us, helping us.

Trust that goodness will win. These are battles Jesus fought for us long ago and won. Trusting Him with our lives and futures is a powerful sign of faith—and faith, hope, and love will never fail.

"Your Father knows what you need before you ask him." (Matthew 6:8)

29 KEEP GOING

SIR WINSTON CHURCHILL is believed to have said, "Success is the ability to move from one failure to another without loss of enthusiasm."

When we're pursuing a lifelong vision, it can be—and should be—hard work. We need to be diligent, persevere, and not get distracted by the many setbacks and failures we will encounter along the way.

No matter how strong or powerful we think we are, it is nothing compared to when we draw on the strength and power of Christ. This is the task of the Holy Spirit: to keep us close to Christ, to help keep us going, to keep us kind, to keep us courageous—always driven on by love.

Whatever struggle we're facing—whether it's spiritual or physical—God is the ultimate source of victory, and He is on our side.

Since you are my rock and my fortress,
for the sake of your name lead and guide me. (Psalm 31:3)

We gain incredible confidence when we lean on God. We don't have to pretend that we have it all together or that we are successful, strong, and happy all the time. We can be much more honest than that—with ourselves, with others, and with God.

Life is hard sometimes, but whatever we're facing, His hand of love is always there to help us, regardless of our feelings. Trust Him because He is good.

WRITING TOWARD THE END of his life, Paul said, "The time for my departure is near. I have fought the good fight, I have finished the race, I have kept the faith" (2 Timothy 4:6–7). These are the words of a man who had gone through hell and back, who had risked everything. Paul had been tortured, beaten, shipwrecked, abandoned, and starved. He truly suffered greatly and worked tirelessly for the sake of others. He was a man with great vision who had given it his all.

I hope that when my time comes I'll be able to look back and say that I've finished the race and kept the faith. Maybe not as powerfully as Paul but in my own small way. Spreading kindness, goodness, and love to all I meet. That's a good goal.

It's good to remember that this big journey is made up of small steps. As Paul went on to write, "The Lord stood at my side and gave me strength" (v. 17).

So let's never give up. In good times and bad, never give up. When the journey ahead is hard and feels like too much, never give up. Whether we're at the start or the end, with Him beside us, we never give up.

> **WHEN THE JOURNEY AHEAD IS HARD AND FEELS LIKE TOO MUCH, NEVER GIVE UP.**

WISDOM

WHEN YOU'RE ELEVEN YEARS old and a friend dares you to do something cool but dangerous, it's hard to say no, even when your head says it's dumb and you can feel in your bones that it's a bad idea.

That's how I ended up trying to cross the muddy harbor near my home, on foot, at low tide. I'd never seen anybody else do it, and within the first ten steps I knew why. The thick mud and sludge clung to my limbs like cement. The further we went, the worse it got.

We just kept going, of course. But by the time we were about a third of the way out, we were stuck. Really stuck. We were chest deep in black, stinking clay, slime, and mud, and we were exhausted. Each time we tried to move we got dragged down further, and I felt that awful sense of panic you get when you realize that you are into something beyond your control.

Thankfully, two things happened. First, I found out that if I wriggled and extracted one limb at a time, then tried to "swim" on the surface, I could claw my way forward just a little. So we turned around and, inch by inch, made our way back.

The second thing was that someone on the shore spotted us and called the lifeboat. Now I knew we were in trouble—whether we made it out or not. We sped up, and as soon as we made it to the shore—only moments before the lifeboat crew launched—we split and ran home, both looking like monsters from the deep.

Of course my mother found out about it all and sent me around to the coxswain of the lifeboat's house to apologize in person as well as offer myself to do chores for the crew in penance.

It was a good lesson that has served me well in so many survival situations: our decisions have consequences, so don't embark on any adventures without a solid back-up plan, and don't be egged on by others when your instincts tell you something is a bad idea. It's called life wisdom. The smart person learns from it or, even better, learns it from others.

Sadly, it wasn't the last time I messed up big time or had to stumble home covered in dirt. But that's all of our journey in life: we do stuff that is often not so smart, we get beat up by the experience, and then we stumble home, hoping to get mended and promising to be wiser next time around.

When we have unchecked, unbridled power and energy, with no sense of which way to go, it can lead us on paths that bog us down and harm us. It is so tempting to want to write our own rulebook and follow our own appetites in life, but it is actually, and ironically, a surefire way to erode your natural power and influence.

Don't get me wrong, it's good to ask questions of authority, and it's important to take risks, but unless we learn to harness and correctly channel our desire for independence, we can often find ourselves in trouble.

Conversely, when we harness and direct that energy down paths that are right for us and others, we can travel many miles and achieve so much. That's what wisdom is: using our experience, skills, knowledge, and instinct to make smart decisions about what to do and say and follow every day. When we get those decisions right, our lives reflect that, and we produce much harvest.

Thankfully the Bible is full of wisdom, even for strong-willed hotheads. It shows us how to focus and direct our passions and how to take the very best type of risks. And above all, it always points us the way home to Christ and to love.

Isaiah wrote,

> The life-giving Spirit of GOD will hover over him,
>> the Spirit that brings wisdom and understanding,
> The Spirit that gives direction and builds strength,
>> the Spirit that instills knowledge and Fear-of-GOD. (Isaiah 11:2 MSG)

The greatest wisdom we can have starts with fear of the Lord: respect for the Almighty and His truths. Because if we truly fear God (in that biblical sense of holy respect), we need fear nothing and no one else.

Oh, and don't try and cross harbors at low tide when you know it is stupid!

1 TRUST IN ACTION

LIFE IS SHORT—FAR TOO short to worry about things that have little real value in terms of bringing us fulfillment, happiness, and peace. It's all too easy to worry about money, status, or health; whether people like us; or if we are good looking or funny enough. Worries are totally understandable, but we alone give those worries the power to bring us down.

It doesn't have to be that way. Even though there are times when worry threatens to choke us, we have choices. We can choose to see the bigger picture. We can choose to kneel and lift our concerns to the One who knows our lives the best and who will never let us fall.

Amazing things happen when we relinquish our worries and lift them to Christ—to His arms outstretched on that cross for you and me. We no longer have to fear the stuff that we worry about, because He's got it. He's got the situation. He's got you. Have trust and be calm. After all, calmness is simply trust in action.

> Jesus said to his disciples: "Therefore I tell you, do not worry about your life, what you will eat; or about your body, what you will wear." (Luke 12:22)

In the midst of your fears, keep trusting Christ. Keep putting your confidence in Him. Keep listening to Him and following His lead. He will never disappoint you. Whatever you're facing today, there is no need to let the trials of life get you down. We all choose how to react to worries. We can all choose a better, more enlightened way.

Just remember: we are sons and daughters of the Almighty. All will be okay.

2 FINITE UNDERSTANDING

FROM TIME TO TIME people ask me difficult questions about faith: about suffering or justice, heaven and hell, angels and demons, divorce, sexuality, and many more besides. A lot of the time I don't know the answer. But this is what I do know:

- God is more just and merciful than the most loving human being who has ever lived. We can trust Him with our lives.
- This life is not the end. One day everything will be put right.
- Some things our brains are too small to fathom. But often the more that science uncovers, the more I find my faith being affirmed.
- Love and forgiveness trump religion and legalism every time.

And I take comfort that Jesus once said, "You do not realize now what I am doing, but later you will understand" (John 13:7). For some things, that understanding may come in our lifetimes. Other things we will understand only in heaven. Either way, I trust that God is love and that I am His.

Some of the greatest minds ever to have lived have also reached this conclusion, often after a lifetime of questioning, probing, and studying. And if their evidence-based studies have proved sufficient for them, then they are good enough for me.

That's not dodging the issues; it's just saying that I find it hard to wrap my brain around some things, but I trust that God is perfect justice and that He is forgiving and good.

3 MOTION AND STEERING

THERE ARE TWO WAYS to go through life. One is to decide that we are going to be the lords of our own lives, that we can do it all on our own, without God. So we make plans independently of God to please ourselves. It's popular, but it has flaws. The danger, as history all too often proves, is that living for yourself, by yourself, as master of yourself, makes one ineffective, self-centered, and small-minded.

The other way to go through life is to look up, plug in, and receive the blessings of heaven. To live for others, to live with Christ inside us—leading, empowering, and ever challenging and helping us grow and give. We will fall and fail, but time after time His hand will lift us back to our feet. And we keep going on toward the light. This is the way of grace. It takes courage and humility, but it's a path that leads us closer to God.

Humility comes before honor. (Proverbs 18:12)

Choosing to live this way does not mean that we have to stop making plans for our lives. The apostle Paul was a strategic thinker, and he made careful plans for his life. But he also understood that while it's fine to plan, it's vital that our steps are guided by God.

We should make plans—counting on God to direct us. (Proverbs 16:9 TLB)

Cooperate humbly with God. Be willing to give up the ego things that clash with His love-rich purpose for you. And never forget that while the motion comes from us, the power steering is from Him.

4 THE SEARCH

WHILE THE BIBLE IS full of stories about God, the book of Ecclesiastes is very different. Instead, Solomon wrote to reflect on mankind's search for meaning and purpose without God. So how did it work out?

> I said to myself, "Come now, I will test you with pleasure. So enjoy yourself." And behold, it too was futility. (Ecclesiastes 2:1 NASB)

Solomon tried everything:

> I built houses for myself, I planted vineyards for myself; I made gardens and parks for myself. . . . I bought male and female slaves. . . . Also I possessed flocks and herds. . . . I collected for myself silver and gold and the treasure of kings and provinces. I provided for myself male and female singers and the pleasures of men—many concubines.
>
> Then I became great and increased more than all who preceded me in Jerusalem. . . . I did not withhold my heart from any pleasure. (vv. 4–10 NASB)

He gained the whole earth and then reflected on it.

> Thus I considered all my activities which my hands had done and the labor which I had exerted, and behold all was vanity and striving after wind and there was no profit under the sun. (v. 11 NASB)

"Everything's boring, utterly boring—no one can find any meaning in it," Solomon concluded (Ecclesiastes 1:8 MSG).

We're all naturally curious and hungry for meaning. But our appetites can never fully be satisfied with what we can buy or build here. We have to look up for that. There's an ache within us all, and knowledge and power cannot soothe it any more than money and sex can. A life alone, separated from God, leaves us empty. It's a God-shaped hole that only friendship with our Maker can satisfy. We are made like that for a purpose.

The purpose is to bring us all home.

5 BE GOOD NEWS

THE MESSAGE OF MERCY, love, and forgiveness that Jesus brought is the most powerful message in the world. It is good news. It changes lives. It changes cities. It can change the world. So don't waste a single day of the precious life God has given you. Whatever you are called to do, however difficult your circumstances, take pride in your calling and complete your task with joy.

That's how Paul went about his days:

Traveling through the country, passing from one gathering to another, he gave constant encouragement, lifting their spirits and charging them with fresh hope. (Acts 20:2 MSG)

We're here to be like Paul and encourage people wherever we go. This is how we bring the light of Christ to all we encounter. We are all called to show love, kindness, and mercy to others.

6 THE SHOULDERS OF GIANTS

SIR ISAAC NEWTON WAS a great man. He was a mathematician, physicist, astronomer, theologian, and author, and even today he's still considered to be one of the most influential scientists of all time.

But Newton was wise enough to know the truth about his achievements. In a letter to his great rival Robert Hooke, he wrote that his work on the theory of gravity had been possible only because of the scholarship of those who had gone before him. "If I have seen further it is by standing on the shoulders of giants."[70]

I admire him even more for writing that. And I love the way it reminds me of these words of Jesus:

"Do you want to stand out? Then step down. Be a servant. If you puff yourself up, you'll get the wind knocked out of you. But if you're content to simply be yourself, your life will count for plenty." (Matthew 23:12 MSG)

But being humble doesn't mean that we hide away our gifts or fear standing out. Humility is simply part of living wisely.

Humility prepares you for honors. (Proverbs 29:23 MSG)

Ultimately, we are standing on the shoulders of the greatest giant of all: almighty God, who is always wanting to bless us, His children. What a gift!

I promise that I'll bless you with everything I have—bless and bless and bless! (Hebrews 6:14 MSG)

7 THE ANTIDOTE TO ANXIETY

THE ANTIDOTE TO STRESS, anxiety, and fear will never be riches, success, clothes, or diamonds. Even though we try pretty hard to medicate with these things, history shows that it just doesn't work. The harder we chase material possessions, the less they will satisfy.

Conversely, the more we allow ourselves to be shaped by the love of God, the more we experience His peace. Our fears always subside in His presence.

> God is our refuge and strength,
>> an ever-present help in trouble.
> Therefore we will not fear. (Psalm 46:1–2)

To be wise and effective in our lives, we don't need a massive bank balance or a sprawling house any more than we need a degree or a bunch of letters after our name. To grow in character, love, and power, we just need to go to the source of everything beautiful and good, to the Creator of the universe who made us and who cares about our lives so much that He came to be among us and to die for us.

Jesus came so we could be restored to God's presence. When we shed the distractions, the fears, and the self, we clear the way for His light to shine through and out of us. That's the point of empowered living: letting the light and love of Christ lead us out of our fears, stresses, and anxieties and into His blessings.

8 MADE FOR EMOTION

BECOMING WISE DOESN'T MEAN that we drain our lives of all passion. On the contrary, emotion is a key part of all relationships, especially with God. Honesty is good, and expressing raw emotions is natural and healthy. In fact, a little anger from time to time is not a bad thing. Jesus expressed righteous anger, often at hypocrisy and corruption. But let's remember this solid advice from Paul:

> Go ahead and be angry. You do well to be angry—but don't use your anger as fuel for revenge. And don't stay angry. Don't go to bed angry. Don't give the Devil that kind of foothold in your life. (Ephesians 4:26–27 MSG)

It's a great bit of wisdom that can help us as we deal with emotions in our lives. Whenever feelings are running high—whether it's anger or frustration, nerves or sadness—we need to acknowledge rather than bury those feelings. What matters is not being controlled, overwhelmed, or led astray by those emotions.

Develop the wisdom to discern between positive and negative emotions. Lift and relinquish the negative emotions to Christ. Let Him soothe them and bear them. Embrace the positive emotions as God-given fuel to your fire.

He made us emotional beings, so see those emotions as simply part of who you are. Some bits are good, some less so. Discern well. Let emotions enrich your life rather than control it.

9   DAILY FUEL

IF WE DON'T GET the right fuel in our bodies at the start of the day, we regret it later on. It's the same with spending time quietly with God. My days always seem to go better when I start them by quietly connecting with Christ. (Note: Better doesn't always mean easier. Mainly it means I feel calmer, stronger, freer, with more confidence and more clarity. And that always helps the day.)

It's not just about going through the motions, reading a few verses, or repeating some prayers. This isn't about religion or repetition. It's simply about getting in some real fuel for the soul, for the day ahead. Reading a little of the Bible, praying, and listening to our hearts brings us close to the source of all wisdom, Jesus. It doesn't need to take long, but it sets the tone for the day ahead.

Soon the habit becomes ingrained, and then, as we continue with the rest of each day, we will start to notice His presence, even in the busiest of times. We will begin to recognize His voice, His encouragement, His guidance and protection. In other words, the initial "quiet times," where we spend a few moments sensing God's presence, will eventually become our "all the times." This is a great goal for us all.

As Paul wrote,

> My goal is that they may be encouraged in heart and united in love . . . that they may know the mystery of God, namely, Christ, in whom are hidden all the treasures of wisdom and knowledge. (Colossians 2:2–3)

10 DAILY DISCIPLINE

CHARACTER BEATS STRATEGY ANY day. In fact, character is the only thing that counts in the end. It's a message the Bible reinforces again and again. If we want to put down good roots and see strong growth in our life, we need to protect and develop our character.

Jesus set us the supreme example of character, and the hallmarks of His life were humility, service, courage, compassion, integrity, and persistence.

Those who have served well gain an excellent standing and great assurance in their faith in Christ Jesus. (1 Timothy 3:13)

That's why this book exists: to help us together grow in character day by day. Whether you have ever read anything like this before, or this is your first time, it's good to know that you're not alone. It encourages me so much to know we are building a community of people who use *Soul Fuel*, or something else like this book, together every day.

Exercise daily in God—no spiritual flabbiness . . . making you fit both today and forever. (1 Timothy 4:8 MSG)

> CHARACTER BEATS
> STRATEGY ANY DAY.

11 LOVE WINS

WHY IS THERE SO much cruelty and hurt in the world? Why is there so much division around us? Why is there such a battle within even our own lives?

I love this quote, often attributed to Albert Einstein: "I do not fear the explosive power of the atom bomb. What I fear is the explosive power of evil in the human heart."

History shows that it takes very little for humans to turn truly dark in how we treat each other. Evil breeds in the absence of love. Good and evil both start in our hearts. They grow from how we choose to live and what we pursue and value. It's not the first time someone has pointed the finger at human nature.

Where do you think all these appalling wars and quarrels come from? Do you think they just happen? Think again. They come about because you want your own way, and fight for it deep inside yourselves. (James 4:1 MSG)

But the story does not have to end here. We can turn the world and our hearts around by our words, actions, and attitudes. Ultimately, good will always win. Love wins.

Resist the devil, and he will flee from you. Come near to God and he will come near to you. (vv. 7–8)

That's a powerful truth that's worth learning by heart and practicing daily. Walk away from the bad and walk toward the good, keeping your eyes and your heart on Christ. This is the most natural and effective way of living a positive, kind, empowered life.

12 THE HAND OF THE LORD

"This is what the Sovereign LORD says: I myself will take a shoot from the very top of a cedar and plant it . . . on a high and lofty mountain" (Ezekiel 17:22).

"I will give you a new heart and put a new spirit in you." (Ezekiel 36:26)

EZEKIEL'S CALLING WAS CLEAR: he was charged with hearing from God and sharing with others so that they could grow stronger in love and faith. That's the same calling as ours today, and we can learn a lot from Ezekiel. He spent time quietly with God, sensing His presence and guidance, and then he trusted God and obeyed Him. He witnessed some truly horrific times, but he stayed faithful to God.

Ezekiel is a great example of what D. L. Moody said: "The Christian on his knees sees more than the philosopher on tiptoe."[71] Like Ezekiel, we get to experience this incredible intimacy: "The hand of the LORD was on me" (Ezekiel 37:1). Such a promise brings with it great strength.

My young boys often ask me about confidence. I like to tell them that any confidence I have comes from this truth. It's different from self-confidence. It is better. The hand of the Lord brings us confidence; it leads us on and emboldens us in the storms. Our role is to have a faithful heart and willing feet. The guidance and strength come from Him. Ezekiel knew this well, and it was the source of all the effectiveness in his life.

13 WE DON'T KNOW EVERYTHING, BUT WE KNOW ENOUGH

JEHOSHAPHAT HAD EVERY REASON to panic. Three armies had combined to launch an offensive against him, and they were already just a few days' march away. But Jehoshaphat was smart. For years he'd been strengthening the kingdom of Judah, forming alliances in the north and increasing the prosperity of his people. He was a good king with a good brain.

But as the armies marched closer, Jehoshaphat was also not afraid to stand up in the temple and call out to God: "We do not know what to do, but our eyes are on you" (2 Chronicles 20:12).

It takes courage to pray. It takes courage to be vulnerable. It takes courage to bend the knee. But God responded to Jehoshaphat's prayer.

"Do not be afraid; do not be discouraged. Go out to face them tomorrow, and the LORD will be with you." (v. 17)

This same promise applies to us today. God responds to prayer, and He is always with us. So when you're fighting any battle, fix your eyes on the only power you can truly rely on. As Charles Spurgeon said, "Prayer is the slender nerve that moves the muscle of omnipotence."[72]

> IT TAKES COURAGE TO PRAY. IT TAKES COURAGE TO BE VULNERABLE. IT TAKES COURAGE TO BEND THE KNEE.

14 BATTLE AND BLESSING

A FRIEND OF MINE, Nicky, remembers a talk he heard where the speaker began by saying that the Christian life is "battle and blessing, battle and blessing, battle and blessing, battle and blessing, battle and blessing, battle and blessing."

It's such a simple but profound lesson. When life is full of challenges, it's hard to believe the battles will ever come to an end. And when everything is going well, there's a temptation within us to expect it to go on perfectly forever. But life is not like that. Life is indeed a series of battles and blessings.

Wisdom is the art of steering effectively through those battles and blessings and living faithfully in whatever conditions you find yourself.

And here's the good news: if we need more wisdom, all we need to do is ask. Wisdom is one of the things that God never withholds when we ask. Along with forgiveness and His presence, wisdom is a gift that God will always supply us with.

If any of you lacks wisdom, you should ask God, who gives generously to all without finding fault, and it will be given to you. (James 1:5)

So ask, and expect to receive. God loves to bless His children with wisdom and to help steer our lives in a positive direction.

COUNTERCULTURE WISE

THE MORE OF LIFE I do, the more I realize the importance of wisdom. That's why I love these verses from Proverbs:

> Take hold of my words with all your heart;
>> keep my commands, and you will live.
> Get wisdom, get understanding;
>> do not forget my words or turn away from them. (Proverbs 4:4–5)

They remind me that wisdom isn't about making us look clever; its purpose is to bring us into a fuller, deeper, richer experience of life. And the wisdom that God gives is powerful. There's nothing like it:

> The beginning of wisdom is this: Get wisdom.
>> Though it cost all you have, get understanding. (v. 7)

Wisdom isn't about intellect or exam results or perceived accolades. It is about knowing our need for forgiveness, the humility to ask for God's help, and the courage to walk on faithfully, with the love of Christ as our compass.

That's why both the woman who fought her way through the crowds just to touch Jesus' cloak and the thief on the cross next to Jesus had more wisdom than the intellectual Sadducees who condemned Him. God's way has always been countercultural and beautifully back to front. "Wisdom," as the spiritual teacher Joyce Meyer said, "is choosing to do now what you will be happy with later."[73] So let's chase it down in our lives. If we gain this wisdom and understanding, life will be transformed:

> [Wisdom will] make your life glorious.
> She'll garland your life with grace,
>> she'll festoon your days with beauty. (Proverbs 4:8–9 MSG)

16 ANGELS

WISDOM STARTS HERE: WITH the "fear of the LORD," which "is the beginning of knowledge" (Proverbs 1:7).

That word *fear* can be translated as "reverence." It means to respect and honor God. It means building your life, day by day, with Christ at the center. And we don't do it alone. Angels, as well as God's Spirit, guide us. They helped Jesus, and even though we're unaware, they constantly help us too. This verse gives a clue about God's goodness to us and the role of angels:

> Even angels long to look into these things. (1 Peter 1:12)

The Greek word used for "look into" means to stand on tiptoe, as if you are at the back of a crowd trying to watch a parade. It's as if the angels are so eager to see the love of God in action that they stand on tiptoe to marvel at the unfolding plan of salvation in our lives. It's as if they can't believe God's love and mercy to such fallen people.

But that's grace. And the role of angels in the Bible always seems to be to help us look closer at the love of God.

17 HANDLING SUCCESS

BY ALMOST ANY MEASURE, King David was highly successful. He was a great leader and a fearsome warrior, a talented poet and a skilled politician. He ruled for forty years, and on his watch Israel grew to become one of the region's greatest nations. Yes, he also messed up, but he always repented and showed strength and humility in returning to God. David dealt with both success and failure in the best way possible:

I love the house where you live,
the place where your glory dwells. . . .
My feet stand on level ground;
in the great congregation I will praise the LORD. (Psalm 26:8, 12)

David knew where his heart lay, and he did not seek the glory for himself. Instead, he gave all the glory, credit, and thanks to God and encouraged others to do the same. He shone not with his own importance but with gratitude and love for God. He stood among his people, stayed grounded, and lifted his heart and voice to the Almighty.

How important humility and gratitude are in this life. It doesn't matter what our status is. We serve the same God that King David did. Like him, let's always stay among the crowds, shining bright in His love and mercy, sharing goodness, and giving thanks and credit to our Father in heaven.

Handling success well means acknowledging that it is all from Him. Every good thing we have is His—it is a gift to us. So let's always make humility and gratitude our hallmark, never taking success as our own.

18 THE DOOR WITH ONE HANDLE

EVERY DAY I NEED to remind myself of the fact that Christ-centered spirituality is like a door with only one handle. Jesus will never force His way in. We're the ones who have to open the door to let Him into our lives.

Jesus gives us the freedom to choose every day, and our choices matter. They determine our path and what we think and strive toward. What we think about determines our actions; our actions become our habits; our habits become our character; our character becomes our life. The big picture of our life is really just the consequence of a million small decisions. If we want to do life well, we have to remember that it all starts in the heart. That's why we need to get our focus right, just as David did:

But my eyes are fixed on you, Sovereign LORD. (Psalm 141:8)

It is why he was such an effective leader for good.

It is up to each of us whether or not we open the doors of our hearts to the love of God. It's up to us whether we fix our eyes on Christ and whether we want His empowering presence in our lives.

There are no rules or requirements—it is all about our hearts and our will. What do we want to fill our hearts with? Where do we want to draw our strength from?

Whatever our choices, the same truth applies to us all: Christ is waiting for us. He's always ready, and He's got nothing but love, mercy, and goodness to share with us.

19 SIGHS AND GROANS ARE ENOUGH

WHEN LIFE PRESENTS ITS toughest challenges and fears mount inside us, wisdom can be hard to find. We often get blinded by the immediacy of the problems, and panic can cloud our judgment and long-term vision.

It's all too easy to feel trapped. But that's when we need the wisdom to pray more than ever. That's the time to "go to the throne not the phone,"[74] as Joyce Meyer said. Prayer is such a potent weapon. In the sixteenth century, when the Scottish pastor John Knox was imprisoned, it was reported that Mary, Queen of Scots, said, "I fear John Knox's prayers more than an army of ten thousand men."[75]

Prayer has great and genuine power. But sometimes prayer can be tough, and that's okay. It's natural. But in prayer, you're never alone.

Meanwhile, the moment you get tired in the waiting, God's Spirit is right alongside helping us along. If we don't know how or what to pray, it doesn't matter. He does our praying in and for us, making prayer out of our wordless sighs, our aching groans. (Romans 8:26 MSG)

God never scores our prayers for eloquence (Luckily!). He simply loves for us to come to Him in whatever state. And He sends His Spirit to help us pray, even when all we can manage are sighs and groans.

Whatever you're facing, pray. Even if you can't find the words, just let it all out. But above all, get ready for God to respond. He promises never to be far from the brokenhearted.

20 BEND THE KNEE

WHEN WE THINK TOO highly of ourselves, things start to go wrong. In our own lives, in our communities, in our countries, and across the planet, when we believe and act as if we're superior to others, then injustice, suffering, and pain are never far behind.

An abbot once described the opposite of arrogance as this: "Humility is an honest approach to the reality of our own lives and acknowledges that we are not more important than other people."[76] Considering everyone else greater than ourselves is an amazing and freeing way to live.

Remember that "at the name of Jesus every knee shall bow" (Philippians 2:10 TLB; Revelation 19:4, 6). When we voluntarily bend the knee to Christ and give Him all authority in our lives, we become far less worried about the very things that so often burden people, such as self-worth, identity, and purpose. Relationship with Christ answers all those questions.

It takes both humility and confidence to live this way and to hand over authority, and the reins of our lives, to Christ. But when you know that God is truly for you, then it makes total sense. And in this way, we can truly experience freedom.

21 WISE LEADERSHIP

FEW PEOPLE HAVE INFLUENCED the day-to-day management of people and companies more than Ken Blanchard, author of *The One Minute Manager*. His book was so successful in such a short period of time that he had trouble taking credit for its success. So he began to think about God. He started to read the Bible. Blanchard went straight to the gospels because he wanted to know what Jesus did.

He became fascinated with how Jesus transformed twelve ordinary, unimpressive, unlikely people into the first generation of leaders of a movement that continues to affect the course of world history two thousand years later.

The more Blanchard searched, the clearer it became: everything he had ever taught or written about effective leadership, Jesus had already taught to perfection. Any wisdom Blanchard had ever stumbled across, Jesus had taught masterfully.

And so Blanchard discovered the truth about what it really takes to be a great leader of people. He learned that we should lead from who we are more than our position. We should be gentle and unassuming, avoid arrogance and ostentation, and have the courage to confront. We should seek spiritual power, not the worldly sort. And we should always make prayer—time with God—our number one priority.

None of these challenges are easy (wise leadership never is), but they are always worth it.

22 ❚ THE HEART OF THE MATTER

ALEKSANDR SOLZHENITSYN, THE NOBEL Prize winner and most important Russian literary artist of the second half of the twentieth century, was imprisoned and tortured for eight years for criticizing Stalin. He wrote these words: "The line separating good and evil passes, not through states, nor through classes, nor between political parties . . . but right through every human heart—and through all human hearts."[77]

This is such a powerful truth, and it perfectly echoes the wisdom of the Bible. We don't serve a God who is interested in our rituals or our religious displays. We're not involved in some elaborate game where what really matters is some pretense of holiness or righteousness.

A life of faith is simply about knowing and being known by God: finding home and finding peace; being prepared, strengthened, and shielded through the battles; and fighting with love, kindness, and forgiveness.

> Be my safe leader,
>> be my true mountain guide.
> Free me from hidden traps;
>> I want to hide in you.
> I've put my life in your hands.
>> You won't drop me,
>> you'll never let me down. (Psalm 31:3–5 MSG)

Being held by the grace of the Almighty is the greatest gift a man or woman can be given.

23 WHERE WISDOM COMES FROM

KNOWLEDGE, AS MANY PEOPLE have observed, is knowing that a tomato is a fruit. Wisdom is not putting it in a fruit salad! Knowledge is important, and it will help us in life, but knowledge alone does not have the power to save us. We need wisdom as well: the guidance and insight that come from the One who sees the bigger picture.

So how do we get wisdom? C. S. Lewis wrote, "The next best thing to being wise oneself is to live in a circle of those who are."[78] God promises always to provide wisdom whenever we search for it. He reveals it to us through the Bible, through experience, through His Spirit, and through each other. We find wisdom through observing and listening, and we find it in our hearts, through that God-given instinct that helps us know what is smart, right, and true. We also find it through prayer:

> If you don't know what you're doing, pray to the Father. He loves to help. You'll get his help, and won't be condescended to when you ask for it. Ask boldly, believingly, without a second thought. (James 1:5 MSG)

Seek wisdom in all of these places, and it will help keep you rooted in Christ, driven by love, and secure in His grace.

GOD ALLOWS SOME LEVEL of temptation in our lives, although not as much as He did when Jesus spent forty days in the wilderness. Still, our temptation can be very powerful, even to the point of feeling overwhelming and irresistible.

Temptation is a part of all our days and nights, and it is good to be honest about it. It often revolves around sex, power, influence, and desires. But God knows that it is through these tests that our faith is strengthened. Each time we resist, we get stronger, like a muscle being exercised. And when we fail, He will always restore us. It is our hearts He wants, not our failing human attempts at goodness.

God took care of goodness and being restored through Jesus. Being forgiven and being made whole are gifts from Christ, paid for painfully but given freely.

While we are on earth, we live in a fallen world, and temptation is all around. We resist because we want only the things that bring us closer to the love and light of Christ.

And whatever we face, Jesus knows the feeling. The devil first appealed to Jesus' physical appetite when He was both starving and thirsty. He offered to give Jesus instant gratification to His bodily desires.

People do not "live on bread alone," said Jesus (Matthew 4:4). He knew that living only for instant gratification leads to disillusion, emptiness, and despair. But feeding off the presence and truths of God leads to deep joy and purpose.

The devil then tried to appeal to Jesus' selfish ambition. He offered unlimited power and influence if only Jesus would worship him. But Jesus knew the truth: self kills and darkness consumes.

These temptations, like so many others we face, revolve around control of our appetites, our ambitions, and our lives. Ego wants to control your life, but God wants you to know the freedom that comes from being fed and led by the Holy Spirit.

25 ALWAYS A WAY OUT

THERE COMES A MOMENT in every storm when we realize that the worst is over. The skies clear, the winds drop, and we can finally leave our shelter and move on. It's the same with life's storms: a time when we sense we need to stand up, brush ourselves down, and move on.

After the devil tried and failed to tempt Jesus for the third time—trying to intoxicate Jesus with the promise of power—Jesus left. He exited the wilderness and began His life work.

But did Jesus assume that the worst was behind Him? Was there no longer any need for Him to worry about those temptations that the devil threw at Him?

No. Even Jesus, as fully human, would have known the power of temptation every day. After all, Luke says that the devil only "retreated temporarily, lying in wait for another opportunity" (4:13 MSG). This is why the wise person always stays alert. Know that Christ is always beside us in those moments, equipping and encouraging us to make the positive decisions that lead us toward the light and away from the dark.

God is faithful; he will not let you be tempted beyond what you can bear. But when you are tempted, he will also provide a way out so that you can endure it. (1 Corinthians 10:13)

> **THE WISE PERSON ALWAYS STAYS ALERT.**

SUMMITS AND VALLEYS

WHEN WE REACH THE top of a mountain, it is always a special moment. I know that well from experience. We give our all and are often rewarded by incredible summit views.

Life is like that too. We set goals, do our best, and sometimes reach those mountaintops. But we can't stay there forever. We all have to descend the mountain, and then it is back into the struggle and tussle of the valleys.

The disciples learned this lesson for themselves. Having been through the most incredible encounter with Jesus up on a mountain (Matthew 17:1–8; Mark 9:2–8; Luke 9:28–36), they too had to descend to where there were crowds and critics. Then, to top it all, Jesus started talking about His death and the cost of following Him.

There were further tough realities of life awaiting them as well—many failures, lack of understanding, and rivalry. I wonder how often they wished they could have been back up on that mountaintop, alone with Jesus.

While mountaintops inspire us, life's valleys mature us. The experience of the mountain can help us see life down below in a new and different way. The good times can help fuel us through the times when life is tough and we have to dig in and get dirty hands and feet.

I lift up my eyes to the mountains—
   where does my help come from?
My help comes from the LORD,
   the Maker of heaven and earth.
He will not let your foot slip. . . .
The LORD will watch over your coming and going
   both now and forevermore. (Psalm 121:1–3, 8)

God knows what He's doing in our lives. There is a plan. He gives us just what we need at the right time. Whether we're in a valley or on top of a mountain right now, God is with us. And there's nowhere you can go where His love cannot reach you.

27 RETURN ON INVESTMENT

IT IS TEMPTING TO value material possessions or power over wisdom. But God's wisdom is priceless and everlasting, and it will always take us farther and deeper into life and light than mere possessions ever can.

> My benefits are worth more than a big salary, even a *very* big salary;
> the returns on me exceed any imaginable bonus. (Proverbs 8:18–19 MSG)

Wisdom resides within us. It is a God-given instinct for right and wrong, but sometimes it gets hidden under our hurts and fears. Yet it is there, and it will grow within us if we nurture it and feed it.

Because we're made in the image of God, true wisdom can only really be found in Him. If we want to grow in wisdom, we need to go to the source. The more time we spend in God's presence, the more our lives reflect His love and light. To be truly rich, invest your time wisely and feed your heart and mind with His truths. Then your wisdom will grow. It is the wise decisions made day by day that create a life that is both abundant and beautiful.

28 THE POSITIVE PATH TO LIFE

WHEN WE OPERATE OUTSIDE of love, it can drain and destroy so much good in our lives. In my own life, I know that when I am angry, unforgiving, or unkind, ultimately it saps all my energy. Negativity is a heavy weight to carry.

But if we always do our best to act in love and to seek God's truths for our lives, then we grow in character and freedom—we enjoy all the benefits of aligning ourselves with the greatest source of love and goodness in the universe. Operating in this way takes courage, commitment, tenacity, and perseverance. But the worthwhile things in life always do. That's why putting in the positive fuel to our hearts and minds really matters every day.

So let's together be relentless in our determination to stay on the path that leads to life and to be on our guard always against the forces that try to pull us away from relationship and truth.

> Place these words on your hearts. Get them deep inside you. . . . Teach them to your children. Talk about them wherever you are, sitting at home or walking in the street; talk about them from the time you get up in the morning until you fall into bed at night. (Deuteronomy 11:18–19 MSG)

NEGATIVITY IS A HEAVY WEIGHT TO CARRY.

29 STOP. BE STILL. REFUEL.

A FRIEND OF MINE told me about how he once sat next to an eighty-six-year-old woman at a church lunch. She was in a wheelchair, but he soon realized that although her body was failing, her mind was not. She was full of questions and raised some tricky theological issues.

When my friend asked her what she thought the answer to her questions was, she paused. Then, quoting the Bible, she replied, "The secret things belong to the LORD our God, but the things revealed belong to us and to our children forever, that we may follow all the words of this law" (Deuteronomy 29:29). She went on to explain that while there are some things we do know the answer to, there are other mysteries we will never understand in this life.

I like that honesty. The elderly lady knew the fundamental truth that when we are secure in the presence and love of God, it is much easier to trust Him for the mysteries that are hidden from our view.

I love the verse below because it's a way to remain in His presence and to trust Him with all our worries, confusions, and fears:

"Be still, and know that I am God." (Psalm 46:10)

We all need to spend time quietly like this, even if on a bus or in bed at night. His presence is always beside us when we stop. Let's make it a daily thing: Stop. Be still. Refuel. Because when our hearts are humbly His and our feet are following Christ's way, we're heading in a direction that leads to life.

JESUS DID NOT HAVE a degree or any formal training. He never went to theological college, but He knew the Scriptures back to front. And when, in His early thirties, He preached in the temple, the crowds gathered to listen.

> He spent his days in the Temple teaching. . . . All the people were up at the crack of dawn to come to the Temple and listen to him. (Luke 21:37–38 MSG)

He spoke words such as these:

> "I'm telling you, once and for all, that unless you return to square one and start over like children, you're not even going to get a look at the kingdom, let alone get in. Whoever becomes simple and elemental again, like this child, will rank high in God's kingdom. What's more, when you receive the childlike on my account, it's the same as receiving me." (Matthew 18:2–5 MSG)

The words of Jesus remain the most powerful words ever uttered. In fact, whatever your faith, the teaching of Jesus is widely acknowledged to be the greatest teaching of all time. For all our advances in science and technology, no one in the last two thousand years has ever improved on the love-centered teaching of Christ.

Jesus said, "Whoever drinks the water I give them will never thirst. Indeed, the water I give them will become in them a spring of water welling up to eternal life" (John 4:13–14).

These are the kind of words we hope that God would speak: words of life and love. And they're the fuel that empowers me today.

FAITHFULNESS

I'M SO GRATEFUL FOR the fact that the two friends who were my best men at our wedding are still the guys I'd choose for the job today. Our friendship has grown even stronger over the years. It's a constant reminder of the power of faithfulness.

Faithfulness sounds like such an old-fashioned word. But it happens to be one of the most powerful forces on the planet. Like a river gradually smoothing out the rocks beneath it, faithfulness works slowly. But as we make the daily decisions to be loyal and loving to our children, partners, and good friends, our actions cannot fail to make a difference.

When you see faithfulness in action, it's a beautiful thing. Whether it's a man who has been married for seventy years and still holds his wife's hand or a friendship that lasts a lifetime, faithfulness is timeless, and the influence of those bonds will last into eternity.

But it's not always easy. All relationships have their challenges, and faithfulness wouldn't be so powerful if it didn't cost us something. It is most important in our relationship with God. Being faithful to Him can be really hard sometimes. When doubts and fears and failures crowd in and threaten to overwhelm us, it is easy for our hearts to get turned. It is then that faithfulness counts the most.

It is one thing to believe that God loves everybody else, but it can be much harder to believe that God really loves us. But being faithful involves trust in God's promises for our lives. "O good and all-powerful God, who cares for each of us as though each were the only one," wrote Saint Augustine.[79] If you were the only person who had ever lived, Jesus would still have died for you.

God is faithful to us in all circumstances, whether triumph or defeat. Receive that love and show that faithfulness to those around you. It will set you apart and help you shine.

1 GREEN GRASS

FAITHFULNESS DOESN'T JUST APPLY to how we are with God. There's not a single aspect of our lives that can't be improved by loyalty, consistency, and love: work, friendships, generosity, supporting our community—they all benefit when we choose to be faithful.

At some point you'll hear someone try to justify being unfaithful by using the word *love*. Either they've fallen out of love with the old or they've fallen in love with something new and exciting. The trouble is, if the grass looks greener on the other side, it's probably Astroturf! (Or as I also once heard, if the grass looks greener elsewhere, start watering your own!)

If we want anything to thrive long term, it takes consistent effort, loyalty, and commitment. Like the creation of gemstones, it takes time and consistency. Faithfulness is worth all the hard work it requires.

That's why Mother Teresa said, "I am not to be successful but to be faithful."[80] And that is why Jesus placed faithfulness right up there alongside justice and mercy (Matthew 23:23). Faithfulness is a fruit of the Holy Spirit (Galatians 5:22) and is praised in the lives of the Bible greats like Abraham, Joseph, Moses, and Daniel.

> As for you, be strong and do not give up, for your work will be rewarded. (2 Chronicles 15:7)

Be faithful: it is the mark of a strong person.

> **FAITHFULNESS IS WORTH ALL THE HARD WORK IT REQUIRES.**

2 RICH BEYOND MEASURE

IF WE HAVE A home, an education, our health, and a few friends, we're greatly blessed. Add to that a job, food, clothes, access to the words of Christ, and the freedom to meet and speak with others, then we're among those people to whom an extraordinary amount has been given. That comes with a responsibility to honor those gifts and to pass them on.

God is a powerful gift giver, and He loves to give to His children. If we use the gifts, talents, and positions that we've been given wisely, He blesses us by giving more. If we live openly and honestly, following the truth and love of Christ, then life becomes even more full of His goodness. Life will always work in such circular patterns. We reap what we sow.

Faithfulness is hard at times. But knowing how fortunate we really are goes a long way to having a faithful, grateful heart. Developing the determination, strength, and courage to keep going requires practice, and lots of times we will stumble and fall. But we don't travel alone. God is with us, inviting us to get ever closer and go farther with Him.

Wherever you are today, whatever you're facing, God is near. All we have to do is reach out with open arms and open hearts, and say,

Send me your light and your faithful care,
let them lead me. (Psalm 43:3)

> **GOD IS A POWERFUL GIFT GIVER, AND HE LOVES TO GIVE TO HIS CHILDREN.**

3 AN UNBELIEVABLE INHERITANCE!

BEFORE JESUS, ONLY A few elite, chosen people ever got to meet with God. And even then they had to go to special assigned places: Moses went up the mountain, while King David went to the inner holy place in the temple. If regular people wanted to hear from God, they'd have to go listen to one of the prophets. In short, it was all quite hard work because our human mess and failure just do not mix with the presence of the perfect holiness and beauty of God.

That all changed with Jesus. His birth, death, and resurrection—and the giving of the Holy Spirit—remind us that God loves us with an intimacy that surpasses all our dreams. God wants us to have a close, personal relationship with Him: one of togetherness, simplicity, and freedom.

This is an extraordinary honor and privilege. Moses, David, Joseph, Daniel, and others had an intimate relationship with God—but nothing like the quality of intimacy we can enjoy through Jesus. We are offered a constant, never-departing friendship with the Almighty. We no longer need sacrificed lambs to enter an inner sanctuary or some burning bush on a mountain to know His presence.

Jesus bridges all of that for us. He was *the* Lamb. He was *the* Sacrifice. He took our failure and mess. That is His gift to us, and it allows us to enter into the presence of almighty God, which brings great freedom, joy, and power.

> We know who he is, and we know who we are: Father and children. And we know we are going to get what's coming to us—an unbelievable inheritance! (Romans 8:16–17 MSG)

Christ was faithful in His promise to restore us to His presence. In return, let us be faithful to Him: faithful in how we love others, faithful in our determination to walk with Him every day, and faithful in our dependence on His love to sustain us. We were won at a great price.

4 NO CONDEMNATION

EVEN THOUGH I'VE BEEN on this journey of faith and love since I was a young man, every day I need to remind myself of the basics. Especially when it comes to living lightly, living freely, and trusting in the love of God. That's why I love it when Paul stated that "there is now no condemnation for those who are in Christ Jesus" (Romans 8:1). We are not judged and excluded. Just loved, loved, loved. His grace silences our fears, our pride, our pain, our whimpers. We are loved, not condemned.

How different this is to the God who was often presented to me in church when I was growing up. God was often portrayed as scary, aloof, and full of unobtainable rules. Unwinding those lies has been a life journey.

Then Paul ended with the fact that nothing "will be able to separate us from the love of God that is in Christ Jesus our Lord" (Romans 8:39). We are loved, regardless of our failings, and nothing can tear us apart from this overwhelming, unstoppable force. John Stott described the truth of this passage as "a pillow on which to rest our weary heads."[81]

When I remind myself of the truth that God loves and accepts us unconditionally, it changes my heart and my attitude. It refines how I want to live. Faithfulness is so beautiful when you know there's a loving Father cheering you on, calling you ever closer.

Even when the storms hit, we stay faithful because there is always a purpose, and we trust that He is in control.

In all things God works for the good of those who love him, who have been called according to his purpose. (Romans 8:28)

In all the circumstances of our life and the events going on around us, we can trust in the faithfulness of God. He has us.

5 FEELINGS DON'T DEFINE US

BEING FAITHFUL TO GOD is all about trusting that He is faithful and good to us. Will we trust that Jesus is who He showed Himself to be? Will we trust that His love is enough? "Faith," as C. S. Lewis wrote, "is the art of holding on to things your reason has once accepted, in spite of your changing moods." Feelings matter, but they don't define us.[82]

It can be hard to trust God when everything seems to be going wrong. But the Bible is full of stories of people who have faced those sort of challenges, often on a mega scale. Like Job. Despite so much sorrow and suffering, in the face of so many reasons to give up on God, he stood firm and faithful.

> I know that my redeemer lives,
>> and that in the end he will stand on the earth. (Job 19:25)

Sometimes being faithful is simply a matter of being stubborn and refusing to give up on the promises God has spoken over our lives. Don't give up on yourself, because God never will. You are beautifully and wonderfully made and bought at a huge price by Christ on a cross. Hold firm to truth when it is hard. Trust during the storms.

> You gave me life itself, and incredible love.
>> You watched and guarded every breath I took. (Job 10:12 MSG)

I remember this rap that someone wrote at a summer camp I went to after I first found my faith: "Feelings come and feelings go, feelings are deceiving, my warrant is the word of God, nothing else is worth believin'!" I have always remembered that.

It isn't about how we feel, because that changes with the wind. Instead, it's about the strong, humble, quiet determination to let Christ save us anew every day.

6 NO PIT TOO DEEP

ONE OF THE FIRST questions asked in any discussion on faith is this: "If there is a God who loves us, how come there is so much suffering in the world?" It's important and necessary to ask this question, and there are no easy answers. It can be hard to trust God when we think about the way that innocent people suffer, and we cannot pretend it isn't. Yet, in spite of this, God is able to meet us in the midst of suffering and struggles.

Betsie ten Boom, as she lay dying in Ravensbruck concentration camp, turned to her sister Corrie and said, "We must tell them that there is no pit so deep that He is not deeper still. They will listen to us, Corrie, because we have been here."[83]

Extraordinarily, it is often the people who have gone through the greatest suffering who have the strongest faith. They're the ones who describe the way they felt God close by them, strengthening and comforting them in the midst of their pain. That truth helps me so much. If heroes like that can find beauty in horror, then how much more can I hold on through my tiny trials?

One of the most powerful prayers I know is this, and it is so simple. I have often seen it touch those who are going through great suffering and sorrow.

> The LORD bless you
> and keep you;
> the LORD make his face shine on you
> and be gracious to you;
> the LORD turn his face toward you
> and give you peace. (Numbers 6:24–26)

To pray this over those you love is a beautiful and powerful thing.

7 DAY BY DAY

MY GRANDFATHER USED TO start each day the same way: he would kneel beside his bed to pray. He was six foot six, and it was quite a spectacular sight. It was a sign of strength. The act of kneeling is about giving God the authority to come into our lives and shine His love through us.

That's how I also try to start every day. I remind myself of my focus for the day ahead: to love the Lord with all my heart and to love others as myself.

I remind myself to put on the armor of God.

I say sorry and I give thanks.

I ask God for help: to be calm, to be kind, to be generous, to be free, to be His.

And I remember this single, universe-changing truth:

"For the Son of Man came to seek and to save the lost." (Luke 19:10)

I remind myself not to fight but to let Him do His job: to bring us home to His presence. Knowing that we are lost without the love of God around us, and having the humility to acknowledge this need, helps to keep me plugged into the Source.

This is all summed up in the Proclaimers' song "Sunshine on Leith."

My heart was broken . . .
You saw it,
You claimed it
You touched it,
You saved it . . .
While I'm worth my room on this earth
I will be with you
While the Chief, puts Sunshine On Leith

I'll thank him for his work
And your birth and my birth.[84]

That's really the prayer of salvation, life, and gratitude right there.

8   ALL FOR YOU

THERE ARE A FEW things in life I am certain of, but one thing above all is just how often I fail and mess up. Add to that the feeling of just how small we are, and you can understand how humans often feel a little insignificant. Just look up at the night sky.

The Bible says that when compared to God, the people of this world—even its great leaders—are "like grasshoppers" (Isaiah 40:22). He is the Creator of the entire universe, including the billions upon billions of stars (v. 26). Compared to Him "the nations are like a drop in a bucket" (v. 15).

Yet here's the clincher: He made it all for us. The universe and those stars are all for His children, and He loves us more than it all.

The Lord Almighty is beside us: always close, always there to strengthen us when we are in need. He is quick to forgive and quick to save. Or as the Bible says,

The Lord is slow to anger, abounding in love and forgiving sin and rebellion. (Numbers 14:18)

It's all a gift. That's the entire radical, life-changing, life-affirming message of the Bible. God loves little us. So take comfort that despite our feelings and failures, Christ came for you and for me. He is beside us always, and He will not let us go.

Now when you see the stars in the sky, just smile in wonder. It is all for you.

9 FAITH IN ACTION

WHEN ABRAM LEFT HIS homeland, Ur, everything was going well. Life in the city had never been better. But Abram turned his back on all that prosperity for one simple reason: to be faithful to God.

Courage is faith in action. It didn't bother Abram that he did not know where he was going. What mattered to Abram was that he knew who he was going with. Abram discovered that blind trust in God is never truly blind. God sees everything. Our part is to follow. And Abram wasn't the last person to learn this lesson.

> By faith, Noah built a ship in the middle of dry land. He was warned about something he couldn't see, and acted on what he was told. . . . As a result, Noah became intimate with God. (Hebrews 11:7 MSG)

If we want to be faithful to the God of love—experiencing all the blessing and intimacy that go with it—then trust Him. Our first steps in any adventure will most likely be shrouded in darkness and confusion. But walk on.

> Faith is confidence in what we hope for and assurance about what we do not see. (Hebrews 11:1)

We practice being faithful by submitting our hearts to Him and by giving Him the reins of our lives. Have trust and faith, because His promises never fail.

10 LOVE ENDURES

His love endures forever. (Psalm 136)

I LOVE THIS PSALM because it reminds me of one of the beautiful, timeless truths at the heart of the Christian faith: that love wins and endures. Twenty-six times the psalmist repeats the words "His love endures forever." By the end it's almost impossible not to get the message.

God's love will never grow old or wane or fail. We can depend on it to win every battle we face. Love is the answer. Every situation, every relationship, every storm, every fear: love wins and love perseveres. Trust the Source of this love. Christ is for us.

He is a shield to those who take refuge in him. (Proverbs 30:5)

Every day presents you and me with opportunities to share kindness and love with those we encounter. It's small things done constantly. And Christ will supply the love. The fountain will never dry up. That's the role of the Holy Spirit: always beside us, resupplying us, willing us on, challenging us, and leading us toward the light.

So let's together keep giving and keep forgiving. Keep considering others greater than ourselves. Keep serving. It's how Jesus operated, and He still does, because His love endures forever.

11 FIDELITY PROTECTS

I LOVE THE FACT that one of the fundamental founding principles of the Scouting movement is loyalty. It's a powerful expression of faithfulness, and it's a privilege to get to encourage and celebrate it in young people around the world.

Faithfulness melts hard hearts and strengthens relationships. And we all desperately need more of it in our lives. The Bible shows us what happens when we don't value faithfulness and loyalty. There is a pattern that gets repeated over and over again. It started when God blessed His people.

But then they mutinied, rebelled against [Him]. (Nehemiah 9:26 MSG)

It's a pattern that's still familiar today. When we sow disloyalty and infidelity, it hurts us and others. God doesn't ask us to be faithful to Him in order to restrict us. He encourages us to be faithful in order to protect us. God knows that faithfulness leads to prosperity. The more we show it, value it, and protect it, the stronger and more beautiful that faithfulness becomes in our life.

We may fail in this many times, but God never does. He is always faithful. Often I have thanked God that His loyalty to me is so much greater than mine is to Him. And each time He restores me, it makes me a little bit smarter and more determined to show loyalty and faithfulness in return.

Experience has taught me this simple truth: to be rich in life, be faithful.

12 HATTIE MAY WIATT

SIX-YEAR-OLD HATTIE MAY WIATT lived near Grace Baptist Church in Philadelphia, Pennsylvania, in the United States. The Sunday school was always jammed to overflowing, and many children had to be turned away.

The minister told Hattie May that one day they would have buildings big enough to allow everyone to attend. "I hope you will," said Hattie. "It is so crowded I am afraid to go there alone."

He replied, "When we get the money we will construct one large enough to get all the children in."

Two years later, in 1886, Hattie May tragically died. After the heartbreaking funeral, Hattie's mother, weeping, gave the minister a little bag they had found under their daughter's pillow. It contained 57 cents that she had saved up and a little note she had written: "To help build bigger so that more children can go to Sunday school."

The minister acted on this gift and changed all the money into pennies, offering each one for sale. From 57 pennies, he received $250, which was itself changed into pennies and sold by the newly formed Wiatt Mite Society. In this way, her 57 cents kept on multiplying.

Twenty-six years later, in a talk titled "The History of the 57 Cents," the minister explained the results of Hattie's 57-cent donation: a church with a membership of more than 5,600 people; a hospital where tens of thousands of people had been treated; 80,000 young people going through university; 2,000 people going out to preach the gospel—and all this happened "because Hattie May Wiatt invested her 57 cents."[85]

What happened to Hattie's money is nothing new. The theme of multiplication runs throughout the Bible, especially in the stories about the early church.

Give, and it will be given to you. A good measure, pressed down, shaken together and running over, will be poured into your lap. For with the measure you use, it will be measured back to you. (Luke 6:38)

What we give faithfully to the Lord, He multiplies. What we sow, He grows. What we sow, we reap. If we want to have a positive influence in this life, then let's always strive to be generous. Because when we are faithful with the little things, we are blessed with bigger things.

If in doubt, or if supply has seemed to dry up in your life, turn around and look for something to give away. When we give, we receive, and others get blessed, as shown by the beautiful Hattie May Wiatt.

13 SHINE HIS LIGHT

SIX TIMES JESUS TOLD people that if they searched for truth, God would answer them. Why six? Maybe He knows our tendency to doubt. So often we struggle to believe the truth that God really loves us, that He wants good things for our lives, and that He is truly for us. But when we claim these truths and find the courage to ask God for His presence, His forgiveness, His wisdom, and His strength, then He never fails us. And that is when our lives begin to change away from self and out to others.

But what does that actually mean? John Wesley's advice on living a life empowered is so good: "Do all the good you can, by all the means you can, in all the ways you can, in all the places you can, at all the times you can, to all the people you can, as long as ever you can."[86] When we live like that, our doubts and fears begin to lose their grip. It's about looking up for the strength and affirmation of who we are—sons and daughters of God—and looking outward, to shine His light to all those we encounter. That's the way to live.

May all who love you be like the sun
when it rises in its strength. (Judges 5:31)

14 RENEWING OUR STRENGTH

He gives strength to the weary
and increases the power of the weak. . . .
But those who hope in the LORD
will renew their strength. (Isaiah 40:29–31)

How many times have I reminded myself of these words when up against it in the wild, battling up a mountain, and in those moments when I'm simply struggling in life? Life can bring us all to our knees.

But I always remember this great truth: a person is never as tall as when they kneel before God. And the person who kneels before God can stand up to anything. So wait on God faithfully and quietly. Let Him restore you, reenergize you, and empower you to face everything you need to do.

You will fill me with joy in your presence. (Psalm 16:11)

Faith changes everything. It turns a hopeless end into an endless hope.

15 FRONTLINE SOLDIER

BEING FAITHFUL INVOLVES HAVING faith (the clue is in the word!), and faith has an inherent sense of risk about it. Faith should feel edgy and should always take courage. Faith involves stepping into the unknown. But those sort of risks are so good for us.

Then Jesus said, "Did I not tell you that if you believe, you will see the glory of God?" (John 11:40)

That's got to be a good thing!

And Saint Augustine wrote, "Faith is to believe what you do not see; the reward of this faith is to see what you believe."[87] It's empowering to know that the more we choose to trust God, the more exciting life gets. Risk is like that. Yet the irony is that in stepping into the unknown we enter a place of total security and safety.

> Blessed are all who take refuge in him. (Psalm 2:12)

We get to make a difference in the lives of as many people as possible by spreading kindness and forgiveness and being nonjudgmental, affirming, encouraging, and generous. And we never work alone: He is with us always, supplying us with all we need for the day ahead.

16 WALK ON, WALK HUMBLY

THE BIBLE SPEAKS A lot about walking with God, always pointing us toward how better to follow Him faithfully day by day. There are some key traits to such intimacy. First and last is always humility, the courage to bow the head and ask for His presence. He never stays away when we do this. He will always walk beside us when we ask. That part is a gift. Your sins are forgiven, and you are bathed in love and light as His child. Soak it in.

But day to day, what traits can we recognize as hallmarks of walking close to God? We're told to "act justly and to love mercy and to walk humbly with your God" (Micah 6:8). That covers a lot of ground! And we all fall so short.

Both Enoch and Noah "walked faithfully with God" (Genesis 5:24; 6:9). They didn't just wait passively for something to happen. They got up and moved—not just physically but emotionally—allowing God to direct and shape their lives.

C. S. Lewis wrote, "To walk out of his will is to walk into nowhere." [88] But when you walk with God, he will reveal his purpose for your life and you will reach your destination.

When we spend time with God, when we make getting close to Him a priority in our lives, His light reflects off us. Love radiates. Just ask those who have ever met Mother Teresa or the pope. Or the beautiful old lady in church who sits at the back, never saying much but always smiling so radiantly at the little kids.

We will stumble from time to time, even every day. But we are restored almost before we even fall. Christ has our lives and our hearts in His hands. And one day we will walk with Him "dressed in white" (Revelation 3:4).

Walk on.

17 THOUGHTS. WORDS. ACTIONS.

LIVING FAITHFULLY REALLY COMES down to the small steps, the everyday choices we make. And these three areas are key to that:

The Things We Think About

We all get into cycles of thought, but let's make sure they're positive and encouraging. Make that a choice, not a reaction. Choose the positive for long enough, consistently enough, and eventually it becomes us.

> Above all else, guard your heart,
> for everything you do flows from it. (Proverbs 4:23)

The Things We Say

Speak with honesty, respect, and kindness. These are all such good traits to nurture. And less is always more. (Remember: one mouth, two ears. Use in proportion.)

You'll find I'm just what I say I am.

    My words don't run loose. (Psalm 17:3 MSG)

The Places We Go

Keep out of temptation. Be wise about the situations you place yourself in. Don't paddle too close to the waterfalls. In other words, beware of places and situations that play to your weaknesses. Keep your guard up always.

My steps have held to your paths;

    my feet have not stumbled. (Psalm 17:5)

All this advice comes from King David, a man who learned his lessons the hard way. He faced many battles and made a ton of mistakes, but he was blessed by God. And at the end of the day, he was able to say this: "I stood there saved—surprised to be loved!" (Psalm 18:19 MSG).

God's love is the only thing that will restore us—not our wisdom, strength, or skills. But we can use those qualities to keep us from doing things that harm ourselves, others, or our walk with God. That's faithfulness.

18 BREAD OF LIFE

WHEN SOMEONE ASKED JESUS what he needed to do in order to please God, His answer was simple:

"The work of God is this: to believe in the one he has sent." (John 6:29)

We're here on this earth for one simple thing: to allow our Father to bring us home. We're invited to live in a personal, honest, heart-to-heart relationship with Christ. And it is a gift that cannot be earned.

Yet a lot of us live in quiet desperation. We try to fill the ache with fast cars and sparkling homes, but the ache persists. History and experience tell us that the only thing that can truly satisfy our spiritual hunger is a relationship with God.

Jesus said, "I am the bread of life. Whoever comes to me will never go hungry" (John 6:35).

In Christ we find freedom, light, and love. We are called to be courageous and kind, forgiving and humble. Those are universal and beautiful things to shine, and our relationship with Christ is where we find it all. It is the source of life and gratitude.

19 SEEK AND SAVE

BEING LOYAL AND LOVING has positive consequences. Likewise, there are always consequences to our messes and bad decisions. That's just the way of the world. That's why, unless we first can see our own failings, it's hard to comprehend the significance of God dying on an instrument of Roman torture. How can something be mended unless you can see where it is broken?

I just know when I have done wrong. I do it so often that it is a feeling I am all too horribly familiar with. It's a sick sensation deep in my heart. It comes from moments of selfishness and arrogance, from lies, from envy, and from pride.

We see the manifestations of these traits all over the world, and it is painful to witness. Who doesn't feel sick when we see extreme cruelty, gross injustice, bitter hatred, or cold evil? These are all the polar opposite of love.

That is why Jesus knew all along where His life was leading: that He would ultimately take the place and pay the price for all the world's cruelty, for all the damage and hurt we cause.

God Himself, tortured and killed on a cross, as a common criminal. The flawless paying for the flawed. Dying just for you and just for me and dealing with death once and for all. God's rescue at Christ's expense: *grace*. Preordained and perfectly planned since the very beginning of time. When we see life through this lens, what else can we do but kneel in thanks at His love for His children? We thank Him for His forgiveness, for His rescue, and for bringing us home.

"For the Son of Man came to seek and to save the lost." (Luke 19:10)

Now I understand why Jesus said these words with regard to His purpose on earth. His mission wasn't to judge, condemn, or bring religion and a set of rules. His purpose was simpler and more beautiful: to seek and to save you and me.

20 THE HIDDEN TEAM

MOSES OWED HIS LIFE to five brave women. First were Shiphrah and Puah, the Jewish midwives who delivered him, defied Pharaoh, and saved the lives of hundreds of male babies. Next was Moses' sister, Miriam, who was quick thinking and brave when she fetched Moses' own mother to nurse him, and then Moses' mother, who passed on great faith to her three children, Moses, Aaron, and Miriam. Finally, and most surprisingly of all, there was Pharaoh's daughter, who had compassion on Moses. She was ultimately the one who rescued him and raised him as her own child.

Moses had no idea about the work that was going on behind the scenes to save him. But it was happening all the same. God was always at work through the willing hands of those who followed Him.

Our lives are much the same. We might have no idea about what's going on behind the scenes, such as how our words or actions or work fit into God's plan, or what purpose that something currently so painful might actually play in a happier future. But we can know and trust in this promise:

The LORD himself watches over you! (Psalm 121:5 NLT)

He's the One who sees the bigger picture. Our role is to trust Him and to have still hearts that can listen for His voice, whether that comes through our hearts, through His promises, or through others. We can always trust that Christ is working His purpose out through our lives for the better.

Stay faithful and trust that His goodness will shine in your life. Trust Him to do His work behind the scenes.

21 TESTED AND REFINED

THERE ARE TIMES WHEN we all find life hard. The whole notion of having faith in those times can seem impossible. Maybe we feel as if we're facing one test after another, and as the stresses mount up, there seem to be fewer and fewer positives to counter them. God often works most powerfully during those times.

> He trained us first,
>   passed us like silver through refining fires, . . .
>   pushed us to our very limit,
> Road-tested us inside and out,
>   took us to hell and back;
> Finally he brought us
>   to this well-watered place. (Psalm 66:10–12 MSG)

When we're in the middle of one of these periods, it might just be that we're being trained. Like a soldier being put through their paces, we're being stretched and stressed in anticipation of what lies ahead. Struggles always develop strength, and faith is the same. When we learn to hold on tight to the promises of God, especially when it is dark all around us, then our faith becomes real. Faithful in the storms. That's the key to growth.

You can trust God always—not only when things are going well, but also in the difficult times. God, the unchanging, all-loving Father, knows exactly what He's doing. As my friend Nicky Gumbel says, "Regret looks back. Fear looks around. Worry looks in. Faith looks up."

22 SMALL BEGINNINGS

EVERYTHING BIG HAS TO start small, and from God's perspective outside of space and time, who even knows what is small or insignificant anyway? Jesus said that faith as tiny as a mustard seed is enough to move a mountain (Matthew 17:20).

Where we feel weak and fragile, when we see other people doing better than we are, God sees it all so differently. His perspective is not about achievement. It is always about love and edging us onward toward Him and toward home—ever stronger, ever closer.

> Do not despise these small beginnings, for the LORD rejoices to see the work begin. (Zechariah 4:10 NLT)

Nothing you do for God in love goes unnoticed or unrewarded. You may not see the fruits today, tomorrow, or even in this life, but if you're walking close to Christ, listening to Him and loving Him, you are accomplishing God's purpose for your life.

So never give up on the dreams He has given you. They are gifts. Go for them, and don't be discouraged by small beginnings and many failures. Both those impostors are all too often signposts that you are doing something right and that His hand is leading you.

23 LOVE BEFORE RELIGION

MOTHER TERESA SAID, "I believe in person to person; every person is Christ for me, and since there is only one Jesus, that person is only one person in the world for me at that moment."[89] It's beautiful, practical advice. We see it at work all throughout history, especially in the life of Jesus.

Strict laws forbade a rabbi from even greeting a woman in public, let alone having a long conversation with her. But instead of being interested in formal adherence to restrictive laws (especially ones that limited salvation), Jesus chose to stop and help a lone Samaritan woman (see John 4:1–42).

In doing so, He wasn't discounting the old law but rather fulfilling the new law, one of grace and kindness over regulation and religion. Jesus took time to talk with her in public. He listened to her. He challenged her. He treated her with dignity and respect.

The impact was huge. The local community had their eyes opened:

We no longer believe just because of what you said; now we have heard for ourselves, and we know that this man really is the Savior of the world. (John 4:42)

The impact went even further as well. For in that one conversation, Jesus challenged society's prejudiced view of women. As John Stott wrote, "Without any fuss or publicity, Jesus terminated the curse of the fall, reinvested woman with her partially lost nobility and reclaimed for his new kingdom community the original creation blessing of sexual equality."[90]

When the divisions that keep people apart are dismantled, the positive transformation of individual lives is never far behind. Societies change when barriers are broken down. And all of this from one risky, simple, honest, and loving conversation with the person nearest.

That is so very typically Jesus—through and through.

24 MY WAY, YOUR WAY

FRANK SINATRA'S "MY WAY" is the most popular song played at British funeral services. No other song has been covered more times, and if you're in a karaoke bar in the Philippines and you hear it, watch out. "My Way" has even been declared responsible for a number of fatalities, where arguments over performance degenerated into violence![91] What is interesting is that the message of the song is the polar opposite of how Jesus showed us how to live an empowered, blessed life.

There is an amazing contrast between what took place in the garden of Eden and in the Garden of Gethsemane. "I'll do it my way" summed up the response of Adam and Eve to God in the first garden.

Self first.

But in the second garden, on the night Jesus was betrayed, He chose the opposite path:

"Yet not as I will, but as you will." (Matthew 26:39)

Love first.

Doing it God's way led Jesus to suffering and death. But His way also led to the redemption of the world.

If we want to live a faithful life, we also have to accept that God's way may not be easy. But it is the way of great joy and blessing:

The path of the righteous is like the morning sun,
shining ever brighter till the full light of day. (Proverbs 4:18)

The great moments in humanity and history have often involved this principle: short-term pain, long-term gain. Let's also recognize the route to life: a path that denies self and instead commits faithfully to loving others first. It was (and still is) revolutionary, but it is the way of Christ and the way of blessing.

25 POWER AND EFFECT

JESUS TELLS US THAT there are two secrets to living with power and effect. First, there is pruning.

"Every branch that does bear fruit he prunes so that it will be even more fruitful." (John 15:2)

All gardeners know that if they cut back and prune plants well, they will produce even more fruit in time. It's the same with us. Pain, sorrow, sickness and suffering, loss, bereavement, failure, disappointment, and frustrated ambition—they all hurt. Yet these are some of the most powerful ways that God shapes, blesses, and enriches our lives. So don't run from the pruning;

recognize it and acknowledge it. Trust the process, stay faithful in the storm, and see the long game.

The second secret is closeness to Christ.

"When you're joined with me and I with you, the relation intimate and organic, the harvest is sure to be abundant. Separated, you can't produce a thing." (John 15:5 MSG)

You and I cannot take on the giants by ourselves. But with Christ close beside us, we can do all things and endure all things. That's empowered, effective living.

26 HOLDING ON

ALL OF US FACE times when we struggle to keep going. Living faithfully, holding on to the choices we've made, can seem so hard at moments like this. We can feel as though we're under attack, as if the enemies are lining up against us. How long can we hold on?

If that's you right now, you're not alone—and you're not the first person to feel this way. In the storms, trust that God will provide exactly what you need. He will protect you, deliver you, guide you, and strengthen you.

- God is your protector and your deliverer. He guards your life: "Those who love him he keeps safe" (Psalm 97:10 MSG).
- God is your guide. He will show you the right way to go, illuminating the path ahead: "I will instruct you and teach you in the way you should go; I will counsel you with my loving eye on you" (Psalm 32:8).
- God will bring joy and strength to your heart—deep-rooted, quiet,

reassuring joy and enduring, persevering strength: "In the day when I cried out, You answered me, and made me bold with strength in my soul" (Psalm 138:3 NKJV).

You're tired, bruised, and troubled, but you're not alone. Keep going, and never give up, because God's hand is reaching out to you right now.

27 NEVER ALONE

WHEN A NEW MOTORWAY was built, taking passing traffic away from Colonel Sanders's restaurant, his business crumbled. The future looked bleak. About the only thing he had going for him was a mighty fine chicken recipe. Perhaps he could sell the recipe to other restaurateurs and earn a slice of every chicken meal sold. How hard could it be?

The answer: very.

His first day of appointments brought nothing but rejection. So did his second. And his third. In fact, Colonel Sanders knocked on 1,009 doors before someone gave him a yes and the legend and business empire that became Kentucky Fried Chicken was finally born.[92]

Faithfulness isn't always easy. There are times when the setbacks get on top of us and we are tempted to give up. But when it is toughest, look up, don't give up:

"I will give you every place where you set your foot . . . No one will be able to stand against you all the days of your life." (Joshua 1:3, 5)

What a promise this is. In the battles of life it brings quiet assurance to know that we're empowered when we lean on God. Christ Himself and legions of angels cheer us on through the toughest times, always beside us, always bringing comfort and strength when we ask, ever onward toward the goal.

Let us run with perseverance the race marked out for us, fixing our eyes on Jesus, the pioneer and perfecter of faith. (Hebrews 12:1–2)

The journey isn't always easy. Faith and life itself require daily steps of courage and commitment. But faithfulness is always rewarded, and in Christ we are never alone.

28 THE HARDER PATH THAT LEADS TO LIFE

I HAVE MET A lot of people over the years who say they would do whatever it takes to win a race or climb a big mountain. But having the will to win just isn't enough. In fact, those feelings mean nothing if we don't also have the will to train and the determination to do the hard work.

I love the story of Daley Thompson, the British decathlete who won gold at two Olympics. It was reported that his favorite day of the year to train was Christmas Day. He knew it would be the only day his competitors wouldn't be training. That is commitment, and it is part of why he won—he saw it as a chance to get 1/365th quicker than his rivals![93]

Daley chose the harder path that led to success, and it made all the difference.

Being faithful to God is about making the difficult kind of choices that ultimately bring us closer to the source of light, love, and goodness. Choosing to be faithful rather than cheat, choosing to love rather than being jealous, choosing trust rather than fear and kindness instead of selfishness. It isn't always easy to do this, but it is worth it. And the presence of Christ beside us will help us always.

We know that suffering produces perseverance; perseverance, character; and character, hope. (Romans 5:3–4)

BLIND BUT NOW I SEE

I LOVE THE STORY of the blind man Bartimaeus and his encounter with Jesus (Mark 10:46–52). It says so much about our needs and Jesus' supply.

Blind beggars in Roman times were surely in the worst of situations. (There certainly wasn't any welfare state.) All a blind beggar could do was to cry out in desperation, hoping for a little money or food to help him survive the day, because without help he was destined to die.

There Bartimaeus was, blind and begging at the side of the road, when he heard Jesus approach. Yet for some strange reason, at first he didn't ask Jesus for money or food or even for healing. He simply asked for mercy. You can only imagine the poignancy of the scene. Blind Bartimaeus appealed to God Himself for the one thing God has never refused. And soon Bartimaeus was opening his eyes and staring into the very face at Jesus.

I am certain this encounter with blind Bartimaeus had been planned long before in the heavenly realms. And I am certain he is today with Christ.

A lot of us are like Bartimaeus. At many times we're wounded, messed up, and in need of help. But unlike him, we don't always ask for the right thing. We seek possessions, positions, or power, when instead what we really need is to look into the face of Jesus and receive His mercy. By asking for mercy, Bartimaeus showed such a raw, honest, and beautiful desperation for Jesus. He had only one shot, and he took it—and he hit the bull's-eye. Bartimaeus instinctively trusted Jesus, and the result was life changing:

"'Go,' said Jesus, 'your faith has healed you.'" (Mark 10:52)

Blind Bartimaeus got so much more than he ever imagined. He was healed, restored, and freed. That's what always happens when we reach out in honest need for Christ.

30 LAY DOWN THE WORRIES

WE ALL HAVE WORRIES. But how we deal with them determines our lives.

In his book *Affluenza*, the psychologist Oliver James pointed out that "almost a quarter of Britain suffers serious emotional distress, such as depression and anxiety, and another quarter are on the verge thereof."[94]

Society often puts wealth up there as a solution to the likes of depression and emotional distress. Maybe money can help this anxiety? Oliver James continued, "Those earning over £50,000 . . . were recently shown to be more prone to depression and anxiety than those earning less."[95]

So in addition to not being able to buy happiness, money doesn't even seem to bring peace or relief from stress. So where do we turn? How do we live with freedom, joy, and lightness? How do we remove our worries?

David said you should "cast your cares on the LORD and he will sustain you" (Psalm 55:22).

Later on, Paul called you to "cast all your anxiety on him because he cares for you" (1 Peter 5:7).

Cast them not just once, but daily. Each and every day you and I can make a choice: either we try to shoulder the ever-increasing burdens ourselves or we can hand over our fears, worries, and anxieties to Christ. We can freely lay them all before Him. He wants to take the shackles of anxiety and distress off of us. His arms are stretched wide on that cross to bear those loads.

Christ knows all, sees all, will heal all. Your life and your future are secure. He wants us to live light, free, trusting, childlike, in the moment, and worry free. As Jesus once told His disciples on the side of a hill:

> "Look at the birds, free and unfettered, not tied down to a job description, careless in the care of God. And you count far more to him than birds." (Matthew 6:26 MSG)

COURAGE

THE STORM WAS A monster. It was nighttime, and we were four hundred miles off the coast of Greenland, facing subzero, gale-force 8 winds, and waves as big as houses. Five of us were attempting to cross the frozen North Atlantic in a small, open rigid inflatable boat, and we were struggling.

It felt as if it was only a matter of time before one of the walls of roaring white water that were repeatedly smashing over us would soon capsize our little boat, and that would surely spell death so far from rescue in those arctic waters.

All five of us were truly terrified. I will never forget that sickening feeling when you know you have truly screwed it up—and you are going to die. Anticipating a horrible death was a genuine reaction to our situation.

We had been sticking to our order of rotation, taking turns at the wheel, desperately trying to outlast the storm and endure the night. But we were exhausted, tight on fuel, and hundreds of miles from any civilization.

I knew that the times when we changed over the helm were always our most vulnerable moments. It was those dangerous few minutes as the new helmsman started a fresh battle to feel the rhythm of these huge waves in the pitch dark. One slow reaction and we would be over.

Twice we came so close to capsizing at this critical handover point, and instinct told me we might not get so lucky a third time. I made the decision to carry on and helm the boat myself, in a desperate attempt to see the storm through. It was hard to explain, but I just knew that this voice was telling me to keep steering.

Fear can totally break people, but it doesn't have to be the final answer. Courage steels people, but we have to find it from somewhere. Courage isn't the absence of fear. On the contrary, without fear we cannot truly be courageous. To be brave we must first be afraid.

I remember so vividly asking Jesus to be beside me in that storm, to steel me, to sustain, strengthen, and deliver me. And He was there, so much so that one of our crew, Nigel Thompson, who had never known faith in his life before, swore that he saw an angel calmly sitting on the front of our small boat throughout that storm.

Still the winds and waves roared—if anything, they got worse. It was one of the longest, most high-risk nights of my life, but never once did I feel alone. Christ promises never to abandon us. And as dawn broke and the storm subsided, we finally saw the coast of Iceland in the distance. We had been steeled and delivered.

In the moments when we need it most, if we ask, God will supply us with the courage we need. Fear and anxiety might shout louder. But isn't it just like God to answer in the still, small voice of calm? When we ask, Christ will always be beside us, with His angels if necessary. I don't know all the ins and outs of theology, but I know the presence and the courage that God has provided in the tightest of moments.

And that is enough for me.

1 EYES FRONT

HENRY FORD WAS RIGHT: "When everything seems to be going against you, remember that the airplane takes off against the wind, not with it!"[96]

Struggles are a part of life, and we all need renewed courage from time to time. So it's comforting to read words like these from someone as great as King David: "I am in trouble," he wrote. "My eye is clouded *and* weakened by grief, my soul and my body also" (Psalm 31:9 AMP). Nobody can go through life without moments like these. But if we read on we see another essential truth: in the tough times we find out the most about where our trust lies.

> I trust [confidently] in You *and* Your greatness, O LORD; . . . "You are my God." (v. 14 AMP)

When hard times come, it's tempting to look back and long for things to be the way they were. But we are called always to look forward, not back. That's where God is leading us. Look up, not down—ahead, not back. That's where our help comes from, and that's where our courage gets restored and renewed.

2 SHAKEN AND SHAPED

THE PAGES OF YOUR Bible are full of stories of great women and men who faced battles and learned the hard way (is there any other?) that God was on their side. I've lost count of the number of times I've been terrified or brought low—so many of those moments when I mutter in desperation, "Help get me through this one, somehow." But in the storms, let's remind ourselves yet again of Paul's encouragement to us:

We know that in all things God works for the good of those who love him, who have been called according to his purpose. (Romans 8:28)

God uses all things to bring us closer to Him, especially the tough times. Like a refiner's fire, the heat shapes us. If we want to develop courage, we're going to have to face some tough times. Courage means not running from the battle or hiding from the struggles. It means facing them with Christ beside us. It means trusting that what shakes us today will shape us tomorrow and that every storm is a school. Every trial is a test. Every experience is an education. Every difficulty is for our development.

Blessed is the one who perseveres under trial because, having stood the test, that person will receive the crown of life that the Lord has promised to those who love him. (James 1:12)

3 IN THE FACE OF OVERWHELMING ADVERSITY

WE ALL HAVE MUCH to learn about courage from the former-convict-turned-world-leader Nelson Mandela. "I learned that courage was not the absence of fear, but the triumph over it," he wrote. "The brave man is not he who does not feel afraid, but he who conquers that fear."[97]

Jesus was the ultimate example of courage in many ways, even, for example, in how He was continuously scrutinized by the scribes and Pharisees—people who were suspicious and critical of His motives, who watched His every move, waiting to pounce.

How tempting must it have been for Jesus to spend time only with those who loved Him. But that was not Jesus' way. He did not avoid the difficult.

Jesus' courage was like His compassion, and He often demonstrated both at the same time. He'd heal an outcast and then face the people who criticized Him for doing so.

Courage always has a purpose, whether restoring justice or protecting the vulnerable, whether sharing truth or trusting God when we feel up against it.

Ultimately Jesus faced torture, hatred, mocking, injustice, abandonment by friends, isolation from God, and death. And He walked toward it all with love and forgiveness. That's courage.

Unlike Jesus, and because of Jesus, we now never need be isolated from God.

Be strong and courageous. Do not be afraid or terrified because of them, for the LORD your God goes with you; he will never leave you nor forsake you. (Deuteronomy 31:6)

The Bible repeats these instructions over and over and over again: courage, courage, courage.

Be courageous; be strong. Do everything in love. (1 Corinthians 16:13–14)

4 STORMS, BOATS, AND PRAYERS

STORMS AND BOATS AND prayers were made for each other.

Remember the disciples when they were out on the water with Jesus? They were "straining at the oars, because the wind was against them" (Mark 6:48 AMP). They were "shaken *and* terrified" (v. 50 AMP). And then Jesus showed up and spoke to the storm.

Jesus doesn't always respond to our personal storms in the same way. Sometimes Jesus calms them, just as He did for the disciples. Sometimes He lets the wind and the waves continue to rage while He calms us instead. This is one truth that I've learned the hard way. When life starts to present a ton of challenges, we have no idea whether they're going to be over in a flash or whether we're going to need to dig in for the long haul. But either way, the instructions Jesus gave to His disciples hold true:

"Take courage!" He said. "It is I (I Am)! Stop being afraid." (v. 50 AMP)

When we find and show courage, we are obeying Jesus' commands. We are doing life the way it is meant to be done, and He will never let us go under.

5 CHRIST'S PRAYERS

BACK IN THE NINETEENTH century, a minister in the Church of Scotland named Robert Murray M'Cheyne wrote, "If I could hear Christ praying for me in the next room, I would not fear a million enemies. Yet distance makes no difference. He is praying for me."[98]

Jesus is praying for you and me right now, and the implications are massive. Almighty God is continually beside us, always for us, loving us, praying for us. It should give us a courage that is beyond this world.

Those who trust in the LORD are like Mount Zion,
    which cannot be shaken but endures forever. (Psalm 125:1)

The words of this old hymn from a dying clergyman echo through time, as true today as they were then:

Abide with me: fast falls the eventide;
the darkness deepens; Lord, with me abide.
When other helpers fail and comforts flee,
Help of the helpless, O abide with me.
I fear no foe, with you at hand to bless,
though ills have weight, and tears their bitterness.
Where is death's sting? Where, grave, your victory?
I triumph still, if you abide with me.[99]

Beautiful. Honest. Powerful.

6 LIFE WITH JESUS

THIS DAILY INSIGHT IS written by a remarkable young boy, my friend Jonathan Bryan. Jonathan wrote the mind-blowing book *Eye Can Write.*[100] Read about him when you have a few minutes at www.eyecantalk.net. He is the son of my wife's first cousin, Chantal. Jonathan knows Christ really well. And vice versa.

Jonathan wrote,

In choosing to become a man, God in Jesus became the embodiment of vulnerability.

Who, being in very nature God,
did not consider equality with God something to be used to his
own advantage;
rather, he made himself nothing
by taking the very nature of a servant,
being made in human likeness. (Philippians 2:6–7)

Being disabled, I know what it is like to depend on others and a small amount of the sacrifice God's grace paid for us.

Recently I was asked why I thought God gave me cerebral palsy. This question is so flawed. Why would people think God gives out illness?

God is good, and illness was never part of His plan. But illness is not a barrier to God having a plan for you. Through God's grace I am accepted for who I am by a God who loves me as I am. When I invite Jesus to share my life, not because of what I can do but because of who He is, I learn the truth of 2 Corinthians 12:9: "My grace is sufficient for you, for my power is made perfect in weakness."

With Jesus life is richer, life is deeper, life is fulfilled.

Thank you, Jonathan. We love you and admire you so much. BG

7 | NEVER LET US DOWN. NEVER LET US DROWN.

WHENEVER I'M OUT IN the wild, I always keep an eye on the sky. Conditions can shift so dramatically in a few moments that a good situation can quickly turn bad. It works the other way too, of course. Storms can end as fast as they begin. What appears bleak one moment can be transformed the next.

When we feel that situations are out of control and we are powerless to influence them, fear often follows. Look at the fear from the disciples when they were about to drown in a massive storm:

They roused him, saying, "Teacher, is it nothing to you that we're going down?" (Mark 4:38 MSG)

But it doesn't have to be that way, because Christ always gives us a safe place to turn to.

Awake now, he told the wind to pipe down and said to the sea, "Quiet! Settle down!" The wind ran out of breath; the sea became smooth as glass. Jesus reprimanded the disciples: "Why are you such cowards? Don't you have any faith at all?" (vv. 39–40 MSG)

Fear is natural, but where we turn to in those moments is what makes the difference. Life with Christ changes how we respond to tough situations. Turn with faith to the One who will never let us down and never let us drown.

8 WE BECOME WHO WE FOLLOW

WHO WE FOLLOW AND who we admire (whether in books, film, or social media) often reflects the type of character we develop. As humans we grow toward those we love and respect. So who do you want to trust with your character and life? Who do you want to be influenced by?

> Those who trust in the LORD will prosper. . . .
> Those who walk in wisdom are kept safe. (Proverbs 28:25–26)

It takes courage to trust our life and future to Christ, but in Him we have the supreme example of character. When we follow and trust His truths, we prosper and are kept safe. Those are two powerful motives and are sound reasons for walking in His path and light. And when we do this, we provide a great platform for others to follow, whether that be our friends, family, or colleagues. Albert Schweitzer, the French theologian, philosopher, and physician, said, "Example is not the main thing in influencing others—it is the only thing."[101]

Let's always look to Christ for the ultimate example of courage, integrity, and purpose, because that is the key to effective living.

9 THE TASTE OF TERROR

CRUCIFIXION WAS CAREFULLY DEVELOPED to be the most agonizing, brutal way to die: slow, public, desperate, and bloody. It involved having nails driven through one's wrists and ankle joints, suspended by metal on bone and nerves, then a slow death of dehydration and suffocation—all in front of a baying angry crowd, held back by Roman soldiers who would do all they could to add to the mockery and misery of their victims. It was the most modern method of torture and death, chosen by the most advanced nation on earth. And with it, the Romans spread fear and dread among their empire and enemies.

But what is truly extraordinary is how centuries before Jesus, these exact words were written about what was to happen to Him:

> All my bones are out of joint. . . . My tongue sticks to the roof of my mouth; . . . a pack of villains encircles me; they pierce my hands and my feet. All my bones are on display; people stare and gloat over me. They divide my clothes among them and cast lots for my garment. (Psalm 22:14–18)

It's an incredibly accurate prophecy about the suffering of Jesus. But as the writer John Stott explained, here is why it matters: "I could never myself believe in God if it were not for the cross. . . . In the real world of pain, how could one worship a God who was immune to it?"[102]

When we most need courage in our life, Jesus is always beside us. He knows exactly what true terror tastes like, and He will never let us down.

DEATH VALLEY

AT SOME STAGE, ALL of us will see death close up, whether a friend or a family member dies, or we are faced with our own mortality. The hard reality of life is that we will all have to walk "through the valley of the shadow of death" (Psalm 23:4 KJV).

When that day comes, we don't need to let fear overcome us. We can borrow David's words and use them as our own prayer: "You are with me; your rod and your staff, they comfort me" (v. 4). The kind of trust in God that Psalm 23 describes isn't just for the darkest days when our grip on life grows faint. It is as much about how to live life right now to the fullest: close to the Source and enriched by His presence and love.

> Surely your goodness and mercy shall follow me all the days of my life,
> and I will dwell in the house of the LORD for ever. (v. 6 KJV)

A life of faith is about both how to live life as much as it is about how to face death. They go hand in hand. But whichever and whatever we are facing, the truth is still the same:

> He leads me beside quiet waters,
> he refreshes my soul. . . .
> And I will dwell in the house of the LORD
> forever. (vv. 2–3, 6)

Draw on this. I do every day.

11 THE ROPE

AS A YOUNG BOY climbing with my dad, sometimes I would look up at a sheer rock face and feel that to climb it would be impossible. So often I would feel crippled and immobile with fear. But once that rope was connected between us, everything changed. Suddenly the impossible was possible and the fear turned to confidence.

As His children, being close to God has the same effect on us. We all get scared by different things. I'm a bit of an introvert at heart, so stormy seas or lonely mountains cause me less fear than a party full of people clinking glasses. But whatever our fears, the answer is the same: "GOD takes care of all who stay close to him" (Psalm 31:23 MSG).

Even when things are difficult, keep looking up. Ask our Father for help. Listen to His calm voice over us: "Be strong. Don't give up" (v. 24 MSG). Christ is on our side. He protects us (v. 20b) and hears us when we call for help (v. 22b). And the end result is always good: "What a stack of blessing you have piled up for those who worship you" (v. 19 MSG).

12 WE CAN DO THIS

WHEN THEY RETURNED FROM their scouting expedition in Canaan, most of the Israelites were pessimistic. The land was fertile enough, but the cities and soldiers already in place presented significant obstacles. It all just seemed too big a challenge to overcome. In their fear, the scouts spread rumors and wildly exaggerated the risks, telling people that the land was ruled by giants.

Fear does that. It can take a regular-sized problem and turn it into an impassable, insurmountable, unbeatable giant. Joyce Meyer was right when she said that "sadly, we often stare at our giant-sized problems instead of at our God."[103]

Caleb was one of the few who had the right perspective. He knew the land would make a great home for the Israelites, even though it would take courage and discipline to secure it. But above all, he knew he could trust God.

Let's go up and take the land—now. We can do it. (Numbers 13:30 MSG)

Caleb knew that God was greater than the problem the Israelites faced. And God is greater than any problem that threatens to hold our lives back today. Being bold and ambitious is a great thing when done in love and service to others. To prevail, all we need to do is know where to draw our strength and to quiet our hearts to hear the whisper of Christ within us.

"We can do this. We can do this. We can do this."

13 ACTIVELY STILL

FEAR IS NORMAL. IN fact, a lot of the time it's needed. Fear keeps us sharp and is there to heighten our senses for battle. But uncontrolled, it can easily tip over into panic. And when that happens, our courage can evaporate like the morning mist.

Psalm 37 is full of great advice. "Do not fret," wrote David—not just once or twice, but three times (vv. 1, 7, 8). He tells us to turn to the Lord, to bring Him our fears, and to "trust in the LORD" (v. 3).

So the response to fear and worry is to turn and to trust. Instead of letting fear overwhelm us, it can simply become a trigger to turn and to trust. To trust Christ is an active decision. It involves choosing to calm our thoughts, to slow our breathing, and to look to Him. To trust takes courage, but it is the opposite of fear and panic.

"Be still before the LORD," wrote David, "and wait patiently for him" (v. 7).

Being actively still—that's a cool concept. The presence of God brings calm and vanquishes fear. The good drowns out the bad, the light drives away the dark, and quiet confidence replaces panicked fear.

That's the way through fear.

14 GENERATION FEAR

THERE ARE GOOD REASONS why some people call millennials "generation fear." There are many factors. But one of them is the sudden and all-consuming rise of social media. The online world can be vicious, dangerous, and unforgiving, and it can cause huge anxiety.

The Bible is full of people who were scared. It describes so clearly the crippling, life-sapping sensation that robs us of peace. But the Bible also shows a clear answer to fear: trusting in the promises that God speaks over our life. True affirmation, true strength, and true comfort come from being found, being known, and being loved by God.

When we look elsewhere for meaning and purpose, we end up riddled with fear, anxiety, and FOMO (fear of missing out). This is nature's way of saying "wrong place to look." Instead, look up. It's a lesson I have had to keep relearning. But I know this works: in the middle of our fears, the best thing is to put our confidence in the promises of Christ. We are loved. We are forgiven. We are held, strengthened, and given peace through the storms of life. We are safe and are being called home. And love wins all.

When we live like this, we live truly empowered. We are found.

He anointed us, set his seal of ownership on us, and put his Spirit in our hearts. (2 Corinthians 1:21–22)

15 | THE TWO BOOTS

A GOOD FRIEND OF mine once told me that one of the most powerful talks he had ever heard came from a simple, seven-minute sermon by a guy who had joined the army. The speaker wasn't particularly eloquent or erudite; he simply stood there holding his pair of army boots in one hand. Everyone was curious.

"This one's called Trust," he said, dropping the left one on the floor with a bang. "And this," he said as the right boot fell, "is called Obey. Trust and Obey—they're as essential to a life of faith as these boots are to a soldier."

Fear and worry lose so much of their power when we choose to trust and obey God. It is a powerful, timeless truth. We can trust and obey because we are protected and because His nature is good.

> "Yes. I'll stay with you, I'll protect you wherever you go, and I'll bring you back to this very ground. I'll stick with you until I've done everything I promised you." (Genesis 28:15 MSG)

These are strong words for a strong life. Stand on them.

> **FEAR AND WORRY LOSE SO MUCH**
> **OF THEIR POWER WHEN WE CHOOSE**
> **TO TRUST AND OBEY GOD.**

16   BE BRAVE, BE BOUND

"I HAVE ON MY table a violin string," wrote the Indian author Rabindranath Tagore. "It is free to move in any direction I like. If I twist one end it responds; it is free. But it is not free to sing. So I take it and fix it into my violin. I bind it and when it is bound, it is free for the first time to sing."[104]

In the same way that the violin string comes alive when it is bound tight to the violin, so we come alive in Christ. Jesus has always been the great liberator of people. Just look at how He was with every person He encountered on earth. Whether we are like the Samaritan lady, the tax collector, or the fishermen, when we bind tight to Him, He sets us free.

That's why Jesus asked people who they said He was. He wasn't simply curious about whether they recognized Him or not. His question went right to the heart of the matter. Were they willing to bind themselves to Him to find their freedom?

"'Come, follow me,' Jesus said" (Matthew 4:19). He's still inviting us to live like this—twined close to Him.

It takes courage to understand that our sense of worth is not based on what we do, what we look like, or what others think about us. But it is the start of enlightenment.

But as Paul said, choosing to orient our lives around Jesus is a risk worth taking.

> Keep your eyes open, hold tight to your convictions, give it all you've got, be resolute, and love without stopping. (1 Corinthians 16:13–14 MSG)

By Jesus' side is where true freedom has always been found.

17 COURAGE PERSONIFIED

IF I HAD TO choose one moment where both Jesus' divinity and humanity were on full display, it would be this: while His disciples were nearby yet no longer able to stay awake, Jesus prepared Himself to be tortured and crucified. The prospect of what lay in store for Him was so horrendous that He sweated blood.

Beyond the physical agony, He knew the real pain would be that for the first time in His human life, He was to be ripped apart from God the Father. He would experience total darkness and isolation, the scale of which we can never imagine.

Despite the terror of what lay ahead, Jesus made a clear choice: He "knelt down and prayed, 'Father, if you are willing, take this cup from me; yet not my will, but yours be done'" (Luke 22:41–42).

He was humble, faithful, and courageous to the end.

You and I will never face suffering so great as the cross. How could we possibly ever bear the weight of all of humanity's wrong on our shoulders? But there will be times in our lives when we will need to call on God for sure. And when we do, Christ will be there to strengthen us.

18 PROTECTION

AFTER ANY ADVENTURE, REST is often the thing we need the most. It's the same with life: when we're caught up in difficult seasons—the kind where we need a constant supply of resilience and persistence—we can so easily feel worn down and tired out. And when that happens, every challenge intensifies.

Psalm 121 was written for all the weary among us, the stressed, all of those who've been running on fumes for far too long. It's a beautiful psalm that speaks of the Lord's protection over our lives.

> He will not let your foot slip—
>> he who watches over you will not slumber. . . .
> The LORD watches over you . . .
> The LORD will keep you from all harm . . .
> the LORD will watch over your coming and going
>> both now and forevermore. (Psalm 121:3–8)

You know what I love most about it? It starts with the psalmist searching for answers. He was at the end of his rope, scanning the skies, wondering, "Where does my help come from?" (v. 1). It takes courage to admit that we need help, but it's absolutely vital to our survival.

Once he admitted that he was in need of help, the psalmist was able to move on and remind himself of the answer:

> My strength comes from GOD,
>> who made heaven, and earth, and mountains.
> He won't let you stumble,
>> your Guardian God won't fall asleep.
> Not on your life! (vv. 2–4 MSG)

The next time you feel like you're too long in the storm, read this psalm. It's okay to need help, it's good to take time away, and it's strong to look up. Christ will always be with us and will always protect us.

19 GET SET ... GO!

TAKE A LOOK AT elite athletes like Roger Federer and Usain Bolt. Notice how they're able to raise their game those extra few percentage points when it matters most. When the stage is the biggest, when the pressure is at its greatest, when everything is on the line, these are the moments in which champions deliver. But when there's nothing at risk, it can be hard to achieve our best results.

The adventure of faith is undoubtedly the most dynamic, challenging endeavor that we humans can ever pursue. Alone, it is far beyond what we can achieve, but with the Spirit of God on us, anything is possible.

> "The Spirit of the Lord is on me,
> > because he has anointed me
> > to proclaim good news to the poor.
> He has sent me to proclaim freedom for the prisoners
> > and recovery of sight for the blind,
> to set the oppressed free,
> > to proclaim the year of the Lord's favor." (Luke 4:18–19)

It's the ultimate adventure, and we're all included. His Spirit will help us raise our game and fulfill all that potential He has stored in us. We just have to ask for His help. And on this adventure, our weakness isn't a hindrance. It is actually the key to relying on His strength alone, not ours.

So, take your marks ... Get set ... Go!

WHEN WE FIND OURSELVES in the middle of a huge adventure, we can feel more alive than ever. And don't be under any illusion about how much life will be changed, enhanced, and challenged by living with Christ. He promises adventure, hardship, and reward, the likes of which we can't ever imagine.

The church reformer Martin Luther said, "I live as though Jesus Christ had been crucified yesterday, had risen this morning and was coming again tomorrow."[105] Luther lived for the moment, and he knew the truth of these words:

> GOD's your Guardian,
> right at your side to protect you. . . .
> GOD guards you from every evil,
>   he guards your very life.
> He guards you when you leave and when you return,
>   he guards you now, he guards you always. (Psalm 121:5–8 MSG)

On this adventure of faith, we are promised the presence of God inside our hearts, His strength to sustain us, and His peace to surround us—fully equipped, ready to roll.

[CHRIST] PROMISES ADVENTURE, HARDSHIP, AND REWARD, THE LIKES OF WHICH WE CAN'T EVER IMAGINE.

21 FREELY AND LIGHTLY

IN THE WRONG HANDS, religion can be so toxic. It can instill fear, exclude, and suppress, all of which are tragic misrepresentations of the character of Christ. When the life-changing force that is the love of God gets reduced to rules and power plays, it's boring at best and sickening at worst. Thankfully, this is nothing new. Jesus spoke to people who felt exactly the same:

"Are you tired? Worn out? Burned out on religion?" (Matthew 11:28 MSG)

For so many of us, the answer has been yes. But Jesus didn't leave it there. What He said next are some of the most powerful words to live by:

"Get away with me and you'll recover your life. I'll show you how to take a real rest. Walk with me and work with me—watch how I do it. Learn the unforced rhythms of grace. I won't lay anything heavy or ill-fitting on you. Keep company with me and you'll learn to live freely and lightly." (Matthew 11:29–30 MSG)

It can take a lot of courage and a good dose of humility to admit that we need faith to empower our lives. We have to put aside some fears and our religious hurts, and we have to hang up our false aspirations so that we can live life to the full on our own.

Instead, we have to learn to walk to the rhythm of the Almighty rather than marching to our own drum. We'll stumble much of the time. But what matters is that we get up and that we never give up. Because when we walk with the love of God shining inside us, we start to live "freely and lightly"—a life empowered.

22 NO COMPARISON

PAUL SUFFERED SO MUCH in his life. According to his letter to the church in Corinth, the list of trials he faced was long and painful.

Five times he was brutally whipped. Three times he was beaten with rods. He was stoned, shipwrecked three times, and endured nights and days adrift in the open sea. He was on the move constantly and encountered endless dangers in the form of rivers, bandits, hunger, and thirst (2 Corinthians 11:23–27). Yet he said that these sufferings could not come close to comparing to the glory we will see one day:

> I don't think there's any comparison between the present hard times and the coming good times. (Romans 8:18 MSG)

That's courage and vision right there: looking ahead, trusting God, never complaining, and never giving up.

23 ON THE BATTLEFIELD

THE DUKE OF WELLINGTON once remarked about Napoleon, "I used to say of him that his presence on the field made the difference of forty thousand men."[106] When we're fighting alongside a strong, inspirational leader, it has a powerful effect. How much greater is the impact of knowing the incredible power of the presence of God?

What a difference it makes to our lives when we realize what it means to be on the side of total goodness, love, power, and kindness: to be on God's side. For Paul, it changed everything about how he saw the world:

I can do all things through him who strengthens me. (Philippians 4:13 ESV)

The presence of God radically changes our lives and the lives of others. Never take that presence for granted. It is our greatest gift. The Lord is with us now, all the time. Despite our failings and our doubts, we cannot shake off the presence of God in our lives. Live in that truth and be strengthened by it.

24 POWER PERFECT WEAKNESS

"I WAS SCARED TO death," wrote the apostle Paul (1 Corinthians 2:3 MSG).

Trying to tell people the truth about Jesus terrified Paul, and he felt totally inadequate for the task. But he trusted God and "the Message came through anyway. God's Spirit and God's power did it" (v. 4 MSG). That's so often how it works: God uses the weak, broken, fallen things of this world to bring love and light to people. It is in Jesus' DNA.

Just look at the cross on which Jesus died as a state criminal. He was killed on a Roman instrument of death, reserved for the most degraded and despised in Roman society. But eventually the cross (a symbol of weakness, humiliation, and defeat) became the main symbol of Christianity.

It's the topsy-turvy way of grace. It shines throughout the life of Jesus. He chose women (ahead of men) to discover the empty tomb, a Samaritan to show the way to eternal life, a despised tax collector to be one of His best friends.

If you're taking risks and feeling scared, take heart. You're quite possibly exactly where God wants you to be. God uses frailty much more than brilliance. Brilliance doesn't think it needs God. Frailty desperately seeks His help.

My power is made perfect in weakness. (2 Corinthians 12:9)

The same power that raised Jesus from the dead also turns our water into wine and makes the blind see. It is the way Jesus always worked and still does in millions of lives around the world. The weak He strengthens, the broken He heals, the fallen He restores. I know firsthand.

25 WINNING LIFE

WHEN LEARNING TO CLIMB or to skydive, there's a process that we have to follow: we have to push through the difficult, awkward, unfamiliar part if we're going to develop the skills and results for the long haul.

Likewise, if we want to be fit and strong, we have to go through some tough training first. It's a process, like sowing and reaping, cause and effect.

The Bible is full of stories of great leaders whose tough beginnings served them well in the end. For Joseph and Daniel, being taken captive and shipped off to another land taught them hard but vital lessons that nurtured courage and ultimately a strong trust in God. Those traits stayed with them for their whole lives and allowed them to act wisely to the end.

And then look at Jesus. Born and forced to go on the run to escape genocide, He grew up within the brutality and corruption of Roman rule, but He grew up trusting God.

"Stand firm, and you will win life." (Luke 21:19)

It's hard sometimes to see beyond this present struggle, but we're not alone. Stand firm, trust, look up, and have faith. Draw courage and remember the pattern from those heroes before. The dawn will come, and we will be found strong. With Christ within us, we will hold on and be faithful in the storms.

26 ▌I AM WITH YOU

I WONDER WHETHER IT'S a coincidence that as faith and respect for God decreases in our society, so our fears have increased. Genuine, quiet faith is rarely seen or celebrated, faith communities become more fractured, and those who kneel before their Maker in strength and humility are rarely heard among the shouts of those seeking headlines and attention.

Yet our world is more riddled with anxiety and loneliness than at any point in the history of humanity. Even with faith, life is hard. Without it, I see people weighed under with anxiety and doubt. We aren't good at living alone without knowing our purpose and our destination.

It's an old problem.

Do not be afraid, for I am with you; I will bless you. (Genesis 26:24)

The expression "do not be afraid" is one of the most frequent commands in the Bible. When we aim to follow God's way, we begin to understand the truth of being protected, loved, and guided through challenges. It changes and empowers our lives.

God is in control and He loves you deeply—so deeply that "even the very hairs of your head are all numbered" (Matthew 10:30).

When we decide to commit our day to Christ and summon the courage to step out in faith and trust His promises for our life, we don't need to fear anything or anyone.

27 SEALED FOR LIFE

IN THE ANCIENT WORLD, whenever a package was dispatched, it was stamped with a wax seal to indicate where it had come from and to whom it belonged. That's why Paul chose his words carefully when he wrote, "When you believed, you were marked in him with a seal, the promised Holy Spirit" (Ephesians 1:13). Paul wanted us to know how significant it is that the Holy Spirit has come to live within us. It's an unbreakable bond. We have been sealed with the Holy Spirit, and we belong to God.

Those are massive statements to make—so big that they cover every aspect of our life, from the beginning to the end.

> You watched me grow from conception to birth;
>> all the stages of my life were spread out before you,
> The days of my life all prepared
>> before I'd even lived one day. (Psalm 139:16 MSG)

You are precious in God's eyes. He has a perfect plan for your days on earth—not always an easy plan, but your plan, and full of purpose. We are called to know Him and to be known by Him. Breathe in that truth and let it direct your day.

> **WE HAVE BEEN SEALED WITH THE HOLY SPIRIT, AND WE BELONG TO GOD.**

WE OFTEN THINK OF Moses as this great leader, strong and bold. But the reality was so different. Moses was terrified. He was the most reluctant of leaders. He was flawed and riddled with inadequacy, and he even killed a man out of anger. But he was also a friend of God.

Moses had an extraordinary relationship with God. "The LORD would speak to Moses . . . as one speaks to a friend" (Exodus 33:11). Moses is like us all. We've all done so many things to disqualify us from being close to God, yet despite that, God still invites us to be with Him. The same promises that God made to Moses—"My Presence will go with you, and I will give you rest" (v. 14)—are given to us today. And Jesus spreads the invitation to all people.

"I no longer call you servants, because a servant does not know his master's business. Instead, I have called you friends." (John 15:15)

Jesus doesn't want us to see ourselves as followers. He wants us to be His closest friends, like brothers and sisters. Through Him we can call God "Abba Father," the most intimate, childlike phrase—more like Papa or Daddy.

This resurrection life you received from God is not a timid, grave-tending life. It's adventurously expectant, greeting God with a childlike "What's next, Papa?" God's Spirit touches our spirits and confirms who we really are. (Romans 8:15 MSG)

Christ gives us an unbreakable bond that is dependent not on our deeds but only on who we are. We are all His.

29 NOBODIES OVER SOMEBODIES

CHURCHES ARE NOT MEANT to be full of perfect people. No. Church should be a gathering of imperfect people: old, young, all walks of life and race, with scars and limps, struggles and failings.

There weren't a lot of people in the early church who were influential or who came from high-society families. They were just a ragtag bunch of everyday nobodies, ordinary folk with ordinary problems. "I don't see many of 'the brightest and the best' among you," wrote Paul in his first letter to the church in Corinth (1 Corinthians 1:26–31 MSG). (I love that verse: it means hope for us all.) But Paul knew exactly why God chooses the "nobodies" over the "somebodies":

God chose the foolish things of the world to shame the wise; God chose the weak things of the world to shame the strong. (v. 27)

If you ever feel like the message about what it means to follow God is simple, don't be afraid, because it is. There's a lot about this journey of faith that seems foolish to other people. Forgiveness, for example, can seem crazy—until you know how much you are forgiven.

We don't need to dress up Christ's message of love, and we certainly don't ever have to pretend to be someone good or religious. (The first doesn't exist and the second is bereft of life.) Instead, let's follow Paul's lead:

I deliberately kept it plain and simple; first Jesus and who he is; then Jesus and what he did. (1 Corinthians 2:2 MSG)

When we live and share Christ, we are living and sharing love, freedom, humility, redemption, and kindness.

KISS. Keep it simple, stupid.

THE INVISIBLE HAND

EVERYTHING WAS LOOKING BLEAK for the country of Judah. Their king had been dethroned and the people exiled to Babylon. Yet again they were slaves, living far from home. But they regathered, fought to survive, and started to rebuild what had been destroyed. Just as before, God found someone to help shepherd His people to safety. And Ezra knew exactly how important it was to trust God completely:

> Because the hand of the LORD my God was on me, I took courage. (Ezra 7:28)

God's invisible and intangible hand is also on you. You might not have to lead a nation back to freedom, but you have a job to do that involves leading, guiding, encouraging, protecting, strengthening, and sharing love and light with others.

When Jesus came to earth, He didn't just lead a nation out of slavery, but all people for all time—out of bondage and into life—including you and me. And He's with us in power today, with His invisible hand on our lives. First, let His presence encourage, restore, and refresh you; then pass it on to others. In Christ, you have a well of resources that can never run dry.

> **GOD'S INVISIBLE AND INTANGIBLE HAND IS ALSO ON YOU.**

FORGIVENESS

IF I THINK ABOUT it, there have definitely been a small handful of people over the years who have wronged me and my family in various ways. We've all known people who have either ripped us off, bad-mouthed us, hurt or betrayed us—it's simply part of life.

In fact, the bigger the platform we get, the more criticism we will often attract. If we're going to get out there and try to live differently, making a positive impact on the world around us, criticism is almost inevitable. After all, not many people like change (except a baby with a wet diaper!).

But being wronged goes two ways, and when I think about the people I've intentionally or unintentionally wronged, it makes me wince. Sometimes it's things I've said or done. Other times I've damaged those I love without knowing it. But I've hurt people, there's no doubt about it.

It can be tempting to try to bury both shame and hurt deep within us—to pretend it never happened. But the unavoidable truth is that we all need forgiveness, and we all need to forgive. One of the strongest reasons for forgiving someone (as well as for asking for forgiveness) is the bitter alternative. When we refuse to forgive or refuse to let go of our own guilt in return, it really hurts us. We're the ones who get burned up inside. We're the ones who suffer.

However hard it might be to give and to receive forgiveness (and I don't underestimate the power and hold that many hurts can have over us), we have to find a way. That way is to ask for God's help. Be still, breathe it in, ask for His presence to melt the hurts, and keep asking, repeatedly, for His help. It will come. And always remember how much we have been forgiven first. The one helps to release the other.

If I've learned one thing about people who forgive easily and ask for forgiveness quickly, it is this: they live lightly. They're free. They know they've made mistakes and that mistakes have been made against them, but they let them go. And they are better and richer for it.

Unforgiveness is like a river. If we try to dam it up, hold it back, or stop it flowing, it goes stagnant. The water starts to stink, as do we when we refuse to let go. Hurt, shame, anger, bitterness, and revenge will always ultimately fail.

Forgiveness is the opposite: it frees, releases, liberates. That's why Jesus placed it front and center when it comes to our own needs on how to live a life empowered. Un-dam the river. Live un-dammed.

It all starts in our hearts. And without giving and receiving forgiveness, we can never travel far.

1 AGE-OLD ISSUES

I LIKE THE STORY of Hezekiah (see 2 Kings 18–20). He was such a good guy. As a king he was faithful, humble, and brave, and he trusted God. Yet, like all of us, he messed up. But Hezekiah did not wait long before he said he was sorry. He did not let his pride get in the way. Even when he felt that God was absent, he stayed faithful.

It is interesting how times change but our challenges stay the same. Life still involves struggles, relationships, tests, temptations, difficulties, and battles. How we respond determines so much. Again, we see that the way to live an effective, empowered life remains constant: Be "gracious and compassionate, slow to anger and rich in love" (Psalm 145:8). And always remember that "With us is the LORD our God to help us and to fight our battles" (2 Chronicles 32:8).

Hold on to that powerful truth when all around is dark—and above all, never give up.

2 THE TRUTH ABOUT FORGIVENESS

FAMILY BREAKDOWNS, CONFLICTS BETWEEN communities, and so many relationship troubles often share the same root cause: unforgiveness. It destroys the bonds that hold us together and leads us down many a destructive path.

Forgiveness is hard, and C. S. Lewis was right when he wrote, "Everyone thinks forgiveness is a lovely idea until they have something to forgive."[107]

But forgiving someone does not mean approving of what they've done. It doesn't mean that we excuse it, deny it, or pretend that we're not hurt either. Forgiving means being aware of the wounds the other person has inflicted on us, yet still choosing to let go. It means laying aside all malice, revenge, and retribution and offering heartfelt forgiveness instead.

I'm so grateful that God does not put a limit on how often He forgives me. Yet when I have been hurt in some way by someone, it is all too easy to think, *I can forgive once, or maybe twice, but much more than that and I'm out!* Then I remember Jesus on the cross: the ultimate picture of what true forgiveness looks like. It cost Him everything. But it also opened the way for us to return to God, and it dealt fully with all our mess and hurt and pride—not just as a one-off, but forevermore.

> Get rid of all bitterness, rage and anger, brawling and slander, along with every form of malice. Be kind and compassionate to one another, forgiving each other, just as in Christ God forgave you. (Ephesians 4:31–32)

Let's cultivate in our hearts the same attitude toward others that God has toward us: grace and mercy, love and forgiveness. Without it we can never truly be free.

3 WASH ME ALL

I LOVE THIS SAYING: "Man is never as tall as when he kneels before God; and the man who kneels before God can stand up to anything." It's a paradox. Not only does it go against so much of the so-called wisdom of today, it's also a powerful reflection of where true strength and humility lie. Strength comes from knowing our true place before God, knowing our need for forgiveness, and trusting His promises for our life. Humility comes from knowing our need to be restored in our friendship with God.

I love the way Peter interacted with Jesus at the Last Supper: "Lord, are you going to wash my feet?" (John 13:6). Hotheaded Peter was appalled that Jesus would take on the role of a servant. Peter wanted to be the one who would do the washing. But that wasn't God's purpose. The purpose was for Jesus to show that all of mankind would need to be washed by Him, inside and out: you, me, everybody.

When Peter finally got it—that he had to let Jesus wash his dirty feet—he went all in, asking for not just a foot bath but a whole body wash (v. 9)! I love it. I would be the same. When we understand that God wants to restore and refresh us, to bring us home and to keep us close to Him forevermore, it changes our impetuous, numbskull hearts.

I think that's why Jesus loved Peter so much. And I think that's why He loves you and me.

4 THE PRODIGAL SON: PART 1

JESUS SHOCKED THE RELIGIOUS leaders of the day. The way He spoke, and the things He did, were so offensive to them that they couldn't stop grumbling and plotting against Him. How could this guy take in sinners and eat meals with them, treating them like old friends, when He knew their past?

Jesus' answer to this was incredible. In what is probably the greatest short story ever told, Jesus presented an amazing revelation of what God is really like: an astonishing father, full of love and compassion and mercy, who will give beyond your imagination.

The parable of the prodigal son* starts with something that the audience would definitely have found offensive. If a younger son ever dared to request his inheritance while the father was still alive and in good health, people would have been shocked. In traditional Middle Eastern culture, this is as good as saying, "Father, I want you to die." Any traditional father would have thrown the son out of the house.

But, in an extraordinary gesture of generosity, the father radically broke from tradition. He gave his son the full freedom to sell all his portion of the estate—an act that would also bring shame on the whole family. Many would say the father was totally foolish, recklessly extravagant, to give his son such freedom and such riches. We might think he was bound to abuse it. With his pockets full of cash, the son left town as quickly as possible.

The son's request was shocking indeed. But the father's gift was even more so: total self-sacrifice at the father's expense. Jesus knew exactly what He was saying when He told the first part of this story. And Jesus knew exactly the parallel to what lay ahead in His own life.

> But God put his love on the line for us by offering his Son in sacrificial death while we were of no use whatever to him. (Romans 5:8 MSG)

Growing up, I inherently seemed to believe God would be judging, tight, ungracious, and demanding, like some bad-tempered old man. But this story is shaping up very differently, and without doubt, it throws up in the air everything I assumed God the Father to be like.

---

* Jesus never called this the "story of the prodigal son"—I think it could more accurately be called the running father. We will see why.

5 THE PRODIGAL SON: PART 2

MANY PEOPLE TODAY, MYSELF included, have experienced a little of what the prodigal son found while he was away from his father—"freedom" to live as he wished: first perceived freedom, followed by disillusionment, followed by despair.

After squandering all of his inheritance on false highs, the son realized he was wasting his life. He was trapped and felt empty inside. He was alone, and all his plans had failed. In desperation, the son knew that he was in dire trouble. His only option was to head back home. After all, even his father's servants lived better than he did right now. He was reduced to working with the pigs and wasn't even allowed to share their swill.

He prepared his confession, though he doubted it would work. He certainly didn't anticipate being welcomed back; he rather hoped simply to be able to work for his father's estate—just to survive.

At the time of Jesus, a Jewish boy who lost the family inheritance to Gentiles would be punished by the entire village in their support of the wronged father, and then the community would have nothing to do with the wayward son. Those listening would have known that. Yet the father's reaction is truly extraordinary.

"When he was still a long way off, his father saw him. His heart pounding, he ran out, embraced him, and kissed him." (Luke 15:20 MSG)

This is the beating heart of the story: "when he was still a long way off," implying the father had been waiting and hoping and looking for his son, from the outer reaches of his estate, every day. Jesus is showing us the true nature of God the Father: hoping, searching, breathlessly waiting.

Then the father saw his son, and with "his heart pounding" and seemingly uncontainable joy, he "ran out, embraced him, and kissed him." To hear that the wronged father was now running toward the son would have been in itself shocking to the crowd listening to this story. And then the whole notion of embracing and kissing the wayward son would have been wildly extravagant and recklessly forgiving, beyond all reason.

But this is why Jesus told the story. He showed us a glimpse of the reality of how our Father in heaven sees us, despite our mess and all our selfishness. His joy, when we look up and seek home, is uncontainable.

6 THE PRODIGAL SON: PART 3

THE PRODIGAL SON TRIED to begin the speech that he had prepared. But he was exhausted and broken and desperate. The father stopped him before he could even start.

It is almost as if the son's prepared speech got drowned out by the overwhelming love and tears of the father holding his precious son in his arms, as if the father's embrace was muffling the sobs of his son.

The father was not even listening—he was too excited and full of joy! He quickly shouted to his servants to bring clean clothes and gifts, and he told the others to start preparing a massive party. After having placed the family ring on his son's finger and sandals on his feet (this alone was an act of unbelievable grace, which to the audience would symbolize total restoration to the family), the father spoke to the rest of his family at the banquet:

> "This brother of yours was dead, and he's alive! He was lost, and he's found!" (Luke 15:31–32 MSG)

This is the story of so many powerful lives through history, from John Newton, the slave trader turned slave abolitionist; to Martin Luther, the great reformer; and many millions of others. They were dead and afraid but now are alive and secure. Or, as the words of "Amazing Grace" so beautifully say, "Amazing grace! how sweet the sound, that saved a wretch like me; I once was lost but now am found, was blind but now I see."

It is our story too. Jesus is in the business of finding lost people and bringing them home. Our job is simply to receive, to let Christ reinstate us all as children of God. It is the ultimate gift that can never be earned.

Isaiah's prophetic words express this truth so powerfully:

> *That's* how much you mean to me!
> *That's* how much I love you!
> I'd sell off the whole world to get you back,
> trade the creation just for you. (Isaiah 43:4 MSG)

7 DO YOUR BEST. DYB. DYB. DYB.

WHEN I MESS UP (which I do often), I can't help but feel distant from God. It's not that God withdraws but rather that my mess clouds His presence for me—as if goodness and badness don't mix. That's why God warns us to keep away from the things that hurt us. He gives us guidelines to follow: Love each other. Forgive each other. Go the extra mile for each other. Love justice and mercy. Be kind. We're given these guidelines for the simple reasons that they protect us and He wants us to stay close to Him.

Living like this brings blessings. We see it time and time again in the Bible, when men and women live with—and then without—the presence of God.

> If you fully obey the LORD your God and carefully follow all his commands I give you today, the LORD your God will set you high above all the nations on earth. (Deuteronomy 28:1)

I want to make obedience to the way of love my default because I know that throughout time, God showers blessings on those who make faithfulness to Him their life. We will fail often, but God loves it when we do our best. That's why I love this verse:

In God we'll do our very best. (Psalm 60:11 MSG)

It's perfectly echoed by the promise that all Scouts make: to do your best. (DYB. DYB. DYB.) Maybe this verse is where Lord Baden-Powell, the Scouting founder, took this motto from. It's smart, and it is good.

I am often struck by how many great organizations are, at heart, mere reflections of the path of God and the way of love. I like that. Today, let's choose that path of life and be faithful to Christ's words of love.

8 THE SACRIFICE

A LITTLE GIRL WAS suffering from a rare and serious disease. Her five-year-old brother had miraculously survived the same disease and developed the antibodies she now needed. The little girl's only chance of survival was a transfusion.

The doctors explained the situation and asked the little boy if he would be willing to give his blood to his sister. He hesitated for a moment before taking a deep breath and saying, "Yes, I'll do it if it will save her."

As the transfusion progressed, the brother and sister lay next to each other in their beds. When the color started to return to his sister's cheeks, the little boy smiled at first. But soon he frowned. Looking up at the doctor, his voice trembling, he asked, "Will I start to die right away?"

The little boy had misunderstood the doctor. He had thought that he was going to have to give his sister all of his blood in order to save her. He loved his sister so much that he was willing to die if it meant saving her. He was willing to be her substitute.

God loves us: that's the radical and life-changing message of the Bible. Jesus Christ came to earth to die in our place.

> "For even the Son of Man did not come to be served, but to serve, and to give his life as a ransom for many." (Mark 10:45)

Understanding and living within this truth is a life journey, but when we begin to get it, it changes everything. And the promise is that He will lead us on this journey if we simply let Him.

9 FIRST THINGS FIRST

KING DAVID IS A hero of the Bible. He's described—not once, but twice—as a "man after [God's] own heart" (1 Samuel 13:14; Acts 13:22). He's one of the really good guys, right? Yet he was also a liar, a cheat, and a murderer. He fell and failed big-time. It's a healthy reminder that however heroic and good people seem to be, they aren't! None of us are. We all, like David, need one thing above everything else: forgiveness.

We might be tempted to consider physical healings, miracles, or raising Lazarus from the dead to be the most impressive part of the amazing things Jesus did. Cool as they were (I still wish I could walk on water like Peter!), Jesus always showed that forgiveness trumped them all.

That's why, when He met the paralyzed man whose friends had lowered him down from the roof, Jesus first of all said, "Son, your sins are forgiven" (Mark 2:5). Forgiveness was the priority. Once that was dealt with, the healing followed.

It was the same in the Old Testament. Joshua encouraged people to repent and "throw away the foreign gods" (Joshua 24:23). He wanted them to clear out the bad stuff first to make room for God.

Whoever we are, whatever we have done, however bad, we all have the chance to put things right with our Creator. That's what He wants for us, and that's why Jesus came. It is priority number one. Because of this we can say we're sorry for our mess and failings, and trust that they've been dealt with. Then, like so many great men and women through history, we can walk on, into the light.

10 WILD AT HEART

IF ANYONE WAS WILD at heart, it was Samson. He had extraordinary strength and ability. And he made some extraordinary mistakes. But when we read about Samson in the New Testament, he's described as one of the heroes of faith (Hebrews 11:32). He's the perfect illustration of the fact that God uses all types of people. And He uses us in spite of our failings and weaknesses.

Samson's great physical strength was a gift from God, and he used it ferociously. But Samson's failings came when the pressures of life got too much and he eventually relented to the charms of Delilah.

Who can't sympathize with this sort of thing? None of us are immune to the charms and attention of those we are attracted to, and Delilah was, I am sure, quite a looker!

When we fail to draw on God's strength and we give up or relent, the consequences almost invariably damage us. But our failings are never our endings. They are simply part of being human and of our journey back to Christ— back home.

Samson ended up bound, blinded, and in chains. But the story didn't end there. Samson's strength and success were always greatest when "the Spirit of the LORD came powerfully upon him" (Judges 14:6, 19; 15:14). On the ultimate occasion when the Spirit of the Lord fell on Samson, "the ropes on his arms became like charred flax, and the bindings dropped from his hands" (Judges 15:14).

This is what happens when we submit and seek the presence of Christ in our lives. God helps release us from our weaknesses, bad habits, obsessions, and addictions. And we all have them.

Samson's story reminds us that what God did in the Old Testament in a physical way, He also did in the New Testament in a spiritual way. The arms of Christ are always open, willing us on, and strengthening us against the arrows of life that seek to damage us. He tenderly removes the bindings from our hands.

"Seek first his kingdom and his righteousness, and all these things will be given to you as well." (Matthew 6:33)

11 WHAT FORGIVENESS IS

WHEN JESUS WASHED HIS disciples' feet, He didn't just demonstrate what love is; He also gave a clear picture of forgiveness. As Jesus moved to wash Peter's feet, Peter resisted. But Jesus' response was emphatic. "Unless I wash you," said Jesus, "you have no part with me" (John 13:8).

Such strong words to Peter. But in true style, Peter quickly changed his mind and asked Jesus for a top-to-toe bath instead! Peter was always impulsive and led by his heart. But his response was understandable: Forgive me everything. Cleanse me inside and out. I need it all.

Jesus' intent is clear: our primary need in life is forgiveness. And when we put our faith in Him, we are made totally clean. Let Him wash our feet. Jesus knows what we really need.

> If we confess our sins, he is faithful and just and will forgive us our sins and purify us from all unrighteousness. (1 John 1:9)

So let's keep coming back to Christ every day for this forgiveness. Don't allow the dirt to build up on our feet for too long. As soon as we mess up, let's ask God to forgive us, to cleanse us, and to restore us. It is why Jesus came to earth.

12 WHAT LOVE IS

SOCIETY MAKES IT EASY to be seduced into believing certain falsehoods about love: first, that love has something to do with being really well known (I am famous, therefore I am loved); second, that love is about sex (I fancy them, therefore it's love); third, that love is addiction (I can't do without this, so it must be love). None of these are ultimately true. To truly know love, we need to see it in action.

In the final hours before He was arrested, Jesus was eating with His friends. At one point He stood up, removed His outer garment, and, like a slave, started washing people's feet. The roads of Palestine were unsurfaced and uncleaned, and in a wealthy household the second-lowest slave of the household would untie visitors' sandals. The lowest slave would wash their feet. Jesus was taking the place of a person at the bottom of society, the lowest place. It was (and still is) a total reversal of many flawed models of leadership.

When Jesus had finished, He asked the disciples something profound: "Do you understand what I have done for you?" (John 13:12). It is a powerful question.

Can we understand that love is not about what we can get but what we can give? Can we understand that love is about treating people better than any of us deserve? Love is about the extra mile, kindness, humility, and an open heart.

We'll never fully master it. And when looked at like this, I realize I am so far away. But faith and love are journeys. And Jesus' hand is beside us, always leading us on in gentleness and love. We're never alone.

13 AMAZING GRACE

AS A YOUNG MAN, John Newton was not a fan of church, or of God. He was a militant atheist, a bully, and a blasphemer. When he was eighteen he was press-ganged into the navy, where he broke the rules so recklessly that he was publicly flogged for desertion.

He then became a slave trader of the worst kind. He was hated and feared by his crewmates. John Newton delivered and dealt in cruelty and death. He was altogether a wild and angry young man.

And then, at the age of twenty-three, Newton's ship almost sank when it encountered a severe storm off the coast of Ireland. As the ship filled with water, Newton became increasingly desperate. Eventually, he called out to God, begging for help. God answered his prayer and saved him, and Newton knew it deep down.

John Newton began a totally new life. Eventually, he joined William Wilberforce in the campaign to abolish the slave trade, becoming a leading light in the campaign. His life had been transformed and healed.

Today, Newton is best known as the author of the hymn "Amazing Grace": "Through many dangers, toils and snares, I have already come; 'tis grace has brought me safe thus far, and grace will lead me home." To be rescued is to be brought home, set free, delivered from danger, and protected from harm.

David said, "He brought me out into a spacious place; he rescued me because he delighted in me" (2 Samuel 22:20).

This is the story of our faith. Jesus has always been in the rescue business. It's what He does.

14 LAVISH WITH FORGIVENESS

EVEN THOUGH WE CAN never hope to fully understand God, Jesus leaves no mystery about how we reach Him. If we want to grow in strength and spirituality, we need to turn away from the things that separate us from the light. "I am the light of the world," said Jesus. "Whoever follows me will never walk in darkness, but will have the light of life" (John 8:12).

But turning away from darkness is only part of the story. We also need to turn up toward the light.

> Let them turn to the LORD, and he will have mercy on them,
>   and to our God, for he will freely pardon. (Isaiah 55:7)

No matter how far we've wandered, no matter how many times we've stumbled, God will forgive us. It's in His nature. He is "lavish with forgiveness" (Isaiah 55:7 MSG).

I know only too well how many mistakes I make, but I also know how much God loves me. That's grace. And whenever I doubt if that love is really possible, I read Paul's words:

> For we are God's masterpiece. He has created us anew in Christ Jesus,
> so we can do the good things he planned for us long ago. (Ephesians
> 2:10 NLT)

Our life has a purpose, our story is important, our dreams count, and our voice matters. We were born to make an impact. We can trust God to help us walk our path. He has planned it carefully. Trust that it is good and walk on with His courage and confidence.

15 TAKE A KNEE

I ONCE HEARD ARROGANCE defined as being unaware of our need for forgiveness. It's true. There is no man or woman living, present or past, who has never done anything wrong, said an unkind word, or had an impure thought. We are all flawed. Being aware of this is the first step of enlightenment. That's why I love the raw honesty in this verse: "Christ Jesus came into the world to save sinners—of whom I am the worst" (1 Timothy 1:15).

Jesus has always been the life transformer. He changes everything, turning our guilt and shame into freedom and love. We see it over and over in the life of Jesus, especially when He dealt with Peter. Peter's continual mistakes never separated him from Jesus. Every time Peter admitted his errors and asked forgiveness, he was embraced and trusted with more. That's the way it works.

Long before Jesus' birth, Isaiah wrote this beautiful and powerful description of the way our lives would be transformed by Jesus:

You will go out in joy
     and be led forth in peace;
the mountains and hills
     will burst into song before you,
and all the trees of the field
     will clap their hands.

Instead of the thornbush will grow the juniper,
and instead of briers the myrtle will grow. (Isaiah 55:12–13)

The power of Jesus' love is the greatest force on earth. Thorns become pines. Death becomes life. Failure becomes triumph. But it all starts with the humility to acknowledge our need for His presence, forgiveness, and help.

Together let's take a knee.

16 THORNS IN OUR SIDE

WE ALL HAVE THINGS we struggle with—thorns in our sides. I have so many it isn't even funny. Paul had real battles too. Listen to this from the great apostle:

What I don't understand about myself is that I decide one way, but then I act another, doing things I absolutely despise. (Romans 7:15 MSG)

And it was an ongoing fight for him:

It happens so regularly that it's predictable. The moment I decide to do good, sin is there to trip me up. I truly delight in God's commands, but it's pretty obvious that not all of me joins in that delight. Parts of me covertly rebel, and just when I least expect it, they take charge. (vv. 21–23 MSG)

I find it so reassuring that Paul had these struggles too. The Bible shows that ever since the garden of Eden people have turned away from goodness and light. It's human nature, and we are all fallen.

"Did God really say?" asked the snake in Genesis 3:1. Doubt and untruths. "You will not surely die," he told Eve, putting another seed of doubt and untruth in her mind. We're just like Adam and Eve. Before we swallow forbidden fruit, we always swallow a lie about God. Then, as we lose our peace, we begin to doubt even further. That only makes the lie all the more tempting.

But there's always a way back. We can all find that peace again by coming home to the presence of Christ and then staying there, close, clinging on. Focus on the light. That's the journey of faith.

17 THE LOWEST POINT

IF JESUS WAS WITHOUT sin, why did He allow John the Baptist to baptize Him?

John asked the same question: "I'm the one who needs to be baptized, not *you!*" he stated (Matthew 3:13–14 MSG). John knew that Jesus had no sins to wash away. Yet Jesus insisted.

The location matters. The River Jordan flows into the Dead Sea. At more than 1,300 feet below sea level, it's officially the lowest surface point on earth. So when Jesus was submerged beneath the surface, He was below the lowest point on earth—below anyone else on the planet. This was all so beautifully planned. Salvation would involve Jesus going to the lowest point—taking on the worst of humanity, the bottom of the pile, as the servant king. His baptism here was such a symbolic moment. The Bible says that heaven opened and a voice spoke:

This is my Son, whom I love; with him I am well pleased. (v. 17)

A dove descended. Jesus rose out of the water. His ministry, His mission, now began, and it all started in the exact place that God intended.

HIS AMBASSADOR

PAUL WROTE THAT WE are "Christ's ambassadors" (2 Corinthians 5:20). Being an ambassador is a great privilege. Ambassadors represent their sovereign or country in a foreign land. But they never operate alone. They gain their authority and power from their governments. They act as spokespeople for their countries' wishes.

Likewise, as an ambassador for Christ, we can't do it solo. We have to stay connected to the Source every day afresh. In order to be effective and to have the strength to do our duty, we have to stay close to Christ.

> Look to the LORD and his strength,
>> seek his face always. (Psalm 105:4)

Jesus gave us His full authority over demons and dominions (Luke 9:1). This is what Jesus says. Whatever we ask for in His name, He will provide (John 14:13)—mountains moved, lives healed, relationships mended. Love and forgiveness can change everything, and nothing is impossible for those who are found in Christ.

> I can do all this through him who gives me strength. (Philippians 4:13)

As Christ's ambassadors, let's walk humbly, draw our daily resource from above, and be His representatives on earth—sharing goodness, kindness, and love.

THE BASIS FOR A CHARGE

ACCORDING TO THE MAN with the power to release Him, Jesus was completely innocent. "I find no basis for a charge against this man," declared Pilate—not once, but twice (Luke 23:4, 14). But the crowd wanted the murderer Barabbas to be freed and Jesus to be killed. There was no persuading the religious elite otherwise. And so Jesus, the innocent one, was condemned to crucifixion, while Barabbas, the fallen man, went free.

The symbolism of Jesus' trial and crucifixion is clear. Jesus, the innocent one, died so that we, the fallen, who have messed up so many times that we can't even remember, may go free. The only charges against Him were all our own charges—all our sins.

As Jesus was nailed to that wooden cross, having been beaten, whipped, and bloodied, He cried out:

"Father, forgive them, for they do not know what they are doing." (Luke 23:34)

He was speaking on behalf of you and me. And if Jesus is who He claimed to be, Savior of the world, then these are surely some of the most powerful, beautiful words ever spoken.

20 MERCY, NOT RELIGION

IN JESUS' TIME (AND far too often still today), religious people thought they should stay away from really messed-up sinners. No wonder the religious elite despised Jesus. He spent all His life breaking down barriers, reaching all sections of society across the barriers of class, lifestyle, and social position. But overall, Jesus spent the vast majority of His time with the outcasts, the socially stigmatized, and the downtrodden. These were the very people the religious leaders always tried to turn away.

That's why, when He met the woman who had been sleeping around, He knew she didn't need a lecture; she needed love, mercy, and kindness, just like us all. And that's exactly what He gave her.

"Whoever drinks the water I give them will never thirst." (John 4:14)

We've all messed up and done things we're ashamed of. But we all are offered the same relationship, acceptance, and forgiveness that Jesus offered the Samaritan woman that day in the scorching heat by the well. Jesus didn't come to condemn any of us. He came to revive us. It was a message that the religious elite could not accept. He said, "I'm after mercy, not religion" (Matthew 9:13 MSG).

21 WILLING, HUMBLE, AND BRAVE

JOSHUA AND RAHAB COULDN'T have been more different. One was leading the nation of Israel; the other was a prostitute. But God doesn't see us according to our titles, successes, or failures. God sees our hearts and uses those who are willing and humble.

When an angel appeared to Joshua, he took off his sandals and fell facedown on the ground (Joshua 5:13–15). And when Rahab met two spies who had been sent by Joshua to scope out the city she was living in, she offered them kindness and protection (Joshua 2).

There are times in life when we need to bow down in awe of God. And there are times when we need to take a risk and stand up for what is right. Centuries after Joshua and Rahab's time, the writer of the book of Hebrews singled them out:

> By faith the walls of Jericho fell. . . . By faith the prostitute Rahab . . . was not killed with those who were disobedient. (11:30–31)

It wasn't Joshua's military skill that won him the day, and Rahab's background certainly didn't dissuade God from using her. What mattered were their willing, humble hearts and the fact that they were prepared to take a risk. They both had the courage to trust God and to say yes to whatever He called them to do. That's a strong model for us all in our journey of faith.

22 IT'S ALL ABOUT PERSPECTIVE

I READ A STORY about an art critic standing in a gallery, staring at a painting of Mary holding the infant Jesus on her lap. In his book *The Vision and the Vow*, Pete Greig described the way the critic admired the painter's skill but somehow found the proportions all wrong.

The critic wasn't the first to criticize the painting, but as he stared, he had a revelation. What if the painting had never been intended to hang in a gallery but in a place of prayer? The critic dropped to his knees and suddenly saw what generations of art critics had missed. The picture finally made sense, everything in perfect proportion.

It was not the perspective of the painting that had been wrong all these years; it was the perspective of the people looking at it. It was only when the critic got to his knees that he saw the power and the beauty of what the painter intended.[108]

We can try to go through life as critics—standing and staring, looking for flaws and faults in the world around us. But we weren't created for that. We were made for more, and we find it when we kneel down before God, trusting Him with our lives.

"The Father will honor and reward anyone who serves me." (John 12:26 MSG)

And who doesn't want the blessing of almighty God on our lives?

23 TERROR TO TRIUMPH

I SOMETIMES THINK ABOUT the similarities between Peter and Judas. They were both part of Jesus' inner circle. They both walked with Him as He entered Jerusalem in His final week. And in those final days, both of them failed Jesus. But it's the differences between them that really stand out, especially when we look at how they reacted to failure.

Judas fled the scene and tragically hanged himself. But Peter stayed close, even though he was scared. Although he had publicly disowned Jesus to save his own life (not once but three times), Peter ultimately didn't hide. When Jesus rose from the dead, Peter was there. He was repentant, forgiven, and restored. This gives us all hope. Like Peter, our mess of yesterday can become our message today. Our test can become our testimony. And like Peter, we no longer have anything to fear.

> He destroyed the Devil's hold on death and freed all who cower through life, scared to death of death. (Hebrews 2:14–15 MSG)

So many people cower through life. And people's fear of death is sometimes monumental. But it needn't be this way. The hold over all of our terror has been broken. And like Peter, we can stand up and walk on, hand in hand with Christ, empowered.

24 RICH IN LIFE

WHEN WE REACH OUT for God in our hearts and ask for His presence, something happens. The changes that follow are often slow, but like the roots of a tree that search out the life-giving water beneath the surface, we are gradually being transformed for the better. The roots go down for water, and the branches grow up toward the light. That's us. The water is the promises of Christ for our future, and the light is His Spirit and presence in our lives. It's a great natural state of positive existence.

When we choose to live with Christ, we don't need to search so hard for love and affirmation in other places. We discover that our status is not determined by our success or wealth, nor by our possessions, trophies, or influence. We have found true meaning and relationship when we inherit the enriching presence of God Himself. That's what Jesus meant when He said these words:

"I have come that they may have life, and have it to the full." (John 10:10)

The presence of God is all we ever truly need in life.

25 WATER INTO WINE

AS A KID HAVING to attend church on the occasional day throughout the year, it was easy to assume that a life of faith would mean becoming very somber, sober, and sullen. It was so surprising, when I eventually found a quiet faith in my life, to discover that the way of Christ would involve such a radical, life-affirming adventure that turned dirty water into extravagant wine.

I should have guessed, though, looking at the life of Jesus. He transformed lives for the better wherever He went. And it is our calling to draw on His resources and spread love, light, and laughter.

Jesus' first miracle in His ministry was saving a wedding party that was at risk of being a failure and transforming it into possibly the greatest party of all time! Jesus didn't just save the bridegroom from the embarrassment of running out of wine; He made sure the guests had never tasted anything quite as good. And the wine just kept flowing.

> Everyone brings out the choice wine first and then the cheaper wine after the guests have had too much to drink; but you have saved the best till now. (John 2:10)

Isn't that just like Jesus? He constantly surprises us and challenges our historical, preconceived ideas about how God works. And isn't it like Him to make a wedding—and no doubt the marriage it launched—so much better?

Jesus turns the water of life without Him into the wine of life with Him. He transforms fear and failure into valor and victory. And how totally cool that Jesus' first miracle wasn't somber but was extravagant and outrageous and fun. I can almost imagine Jesus winking at His mother across the dance floor as the tempo, laughter, and joy of the party suddenly increased!

26 PLAN LIGHTLY

WHEN LIFE IS BUSY and our workload is full, we naturally have to make a lot of plans. But when we make plans for our lives, it matters that we try to do so with humility.

You know the old expression: if you want to make God laugh, tell Him your plans. Wisdom says to focus on our hearts before we focus on our plans. We need to care about the relationship with our Father more than we care about the outcome of our plans. Some plans work out, and some get thwarted. It's okay. Let's just hold them lightly. They don't matter as much as our walk with our Father.

I have had a huge personal journey in this respect. I used to care far too much about my plans and let my feelings be determined by the outcomes. Nowadays I worry much less about the outcomes. I make plans, yes, but I don't worry about them so much. I know Christ is a better driver of the ship than I am.

It's like the writer of Proverbs said, "In their hearts humans plan their course, but the LORD establishes their steps" (16:9).

Ultimately this is all about calm, courage, and trust.

27 PEACE WITHIN

HOW DO WE FORGIVE people who really hurt us or those we love? It's not easy. But it's not impossible either. The answer is written all throughout the Bible as well as in countless other books and songs: forgiveness leads to peace. Conversely, a lack of forgiveness eats us up.

This hymn lyric written by a bishop living more than a century ago is powerful: "Peace, perfect peace, in this dark world of sin? The blood of Jesus whispers peace within."[109] This peace melts our hard hearts. I have known this myself.

The word that the Bible uses for peace means far more than just an absence of hostility. It means wholeness, soundness, well-being, oneness with God, and every kind of blessing and good. It is a peace that "transcends all understanding" (Philippians 4:7).

True peace surpasses both our ability to cope with and our anxiety about what is to come. And it holds the key to our letting go of the hurt, anger, and resentment we might hold against those who have wounded us.

We forgive because we have been forgiven. And we forgive because the alternative is a lack of peace. It's not always easy, especially when the hurt runs deep, but the soft voice of Christ is always edging us toward grace and mercy— the same grace and mercy He shows to us.

Let the peace of Christ rule in your hearts. (Colossians 3:15)

There is no hierarchy of hurts, just as there is no limit to the love of God, the depths it can reach, or the times we can be forgiven.

28 DID YOU OR DID YOU NOT?

A BRILLIANT PROFESSOR OF philosophy at London University, C. E. M. Joad, was not a man of faith, but when he was asked on a radio program which one historical figure he would most like to meet and ask just one question, he didn't hesitate.

"I would meet Jesus Christ and ask him the most important question in the world—'Did you or did you not rise from the dead?'"[110]

You see, if Jesus Christ really is risen from the dead, it changes everything. It means that every word, every claim, every statement He ever made is true: That He came to bring life, to save the lost, to bring us all home. That He came to set us free from religion and rules. That He wants us to live lightly. That we can move mountains and heal the sick. That we are all His children. And that ultimately He won't let harm come to us.

But it all hinges on His resurrection. If He didn't rise again, then His claims about Himself were not true.

In the words of C. S. Lewis,

A man who was merely a man and said the sort of things Jesus said would not be a great moral teacher. He would either be a lunatic—on the level with the man who says he is a poached egg—or else he would be the Devil of Hell. You must make your choice. Either this man was, and is, the Son of God, or else a madman or something worse.[111]

But if He did rise again, then how?

The compelling evidence for the resurrection is hard to argue against. I have tried. Many of the greatest minds of our time have tried. The evidence is so stacked toward it being the truth that many scholars have found faith *after* setting out to discredit it.

So if He did rise again, it means this also is true:

"I am with you always." (Matthew 28:20)

And if He is right here, right now—beside us, for us, and within us—then our day really should be full of joy and assurance!

Jesus with us. Truth. Soak it in.

29 BUILD ON THE ROCK

MANY PEOPLE TURN AWAY from their perception of who God is based on the injustices they see around them. I can so understand that. The ills of this world are horrible to see: illness, poverty, false imprisonments. The list goes on, and it ever grows. But one thing I feel certain of is that when we face God's judgment, there will be no doubt about the just nature of His decisions.

Everyone will say, "That is absolutely right." If God is love and God is perfect, then how could His decisions ever be imperfect or unjust?

On that day God will put everything right. That's His promise to us. No matter what challenges we have faced in life, no matter how many mistakes we have made, no matter how many times we have been let down or hurt, God will put all things right. All our misunderstandings and disappointments; our unfulfilled longings, doubts, and setbacks; our tears born of pain and of our own shame will all be put right. So let's be wise right now. Let's do as Jesus says:

> "Therefore everyone who hears these words of mine and puts them into practice is like a wise man who built his house on the rock." (Matthew 7:24)

There's no greater source of love, power, and strength than the words of Jesus. Hold them close, live by them, and build on the rock.

30 RIGHT FROM THE START

THE BIBLE IS ONE long invitation to come to God. It starts with God's call to Adam, full of love and anguish: "Where are you?" (Genesis 3:9). And it ends with the invitation from the Spirit and the Bride who say, "Come!" (Revelation 22:17).

Jesus often invited people: "Come to me" (Matthew 11:28); "Come to the wedding banquet" (Matthew 22:4); "Come to me and drink" (John 7:37). And everything is a gift—given freely—that is impossible to earn by good deeds.

> Hey there! All who are thirsty,
> come to the water!
> Are you penniless?

Come anyway—buy and eat!

Come, buy your drinks, buy wine and milk.

Buy without money—everything's free! (Isaiah 55:1 MSG)

As we come to the end of this journey around forgiveness within *Soul Fuel*, let's go back to the beginning of the Bible and the promise that God made to Jacob:

I am with you and will watch over you wherever you go. (Genesis 28:15)

Those words echo loud across all time. They are true for all people, in all places, in all times. This is history—His story. He is with us. He has never left us, and He never will.

FREEDOM

ACCORDING TO THE SAILOR Sir Robin Knox-Johnston, "There is no such thing as an atheist in the Southern Ocean."[112]

In the times I have been truly afraid and alone, my Christian faith has given me such hope and courage. When I have been at my weakest, faith has helped me find true strength. And when I have felt trapped, the presence of Christ has helped me learn to live lightly and freely. But what about the everyday? Can faith help us then?

Faith in Christ can be difficult to articulate. It's like describing ice cream or swimming: words will get us only so far. Some things are best experienced. But what I can say is that my faith tells me that I am known, that I am loved, and that I am forgiven—regardless of how many times I fall and fail.

I've tried to do without it. And I've survived—for a while—but alone we can never be fully empowered. Time and many adventures have taught me that to be complete and fully alive I need the life-giving presence that faith provides.

It is almost as if, over the years, I have found the courage to admit that my longing for this life of love and faith is stronger than the pride that says we must do it all alone. It's a point of awareness. It takes some humility to relinquish control. But it is the starting point of true adventure.

Some might call faith a crutch. But what does a crutch do? It helps us stand and gives us a weapon to fight with. (I like that analogy.) And as time goes on, there's no doubt I need that strength more and more, every day, to tackle the battles of life and to climb the mountains we all face.

Faith is different from religion, though. I meet a ton of people who don't want religion. I get it. I have always felt the same. So did Jesus, ironically. He was the least religious, the most free, and probably the wildest character I know of. He loved a party and hung out with the rejected, the un-tamed, and the outsiders. Karl Barth is believed to have said, "Jesus Christ came to destroy human religion." I love that. The only people Jesus ever seemed to get angry with were the overly religious hypocrites.

Faith, though, is a journey. To walk in it in our everyday lives takes courage. All too often it's the tougher path. But life and the wild have taught me that the tougher path almost always ends up being the most fulfilling one.

When it comes to quietly bowing the knee and asking for His presence to bring you peace, strengthen your spirit, and lead you into light—well, we have nothing to lose and everything to gain. That's grace. That's true freedom.

1 GIVE!

SO OFTEN I HAVE been hard-hearted and tightfisted when I have seen poverty and need. So often I have put my head down and passed the person by. So often I have been so wrong.

Jesus always encouraged people to be openhanded, always to give generously and not be judgmental or cynical. We aren't called to judge, only to give.

Jesus said, "When you give a banquet, invite the poor, the crippled, the lame, the blind, and you will be blessed" (Luke 14:13–14).

Jean Vanier, who founded the L'Arche community for people with disabilities, has done this every day for more than fifty years. His life has been a rich blessing machine, overflowing with grace and mercy.

When we see money for the great tool that it can be—rather than a reward in itself—we're freed from so many of the worries that plague people.

> Give to them as the LORD your God has blessed you. (Deuteronomy 15:14)

Let's never fall into the common trap of loving money and using people; instead, let's always try to use money and love people. That's the way it is truly intended.

2 GUIDELINES TO EMPOWER

FREEDOM ISN'T ABOUT RULES. But without rules there can be no freedom.

Just as the rules of football do not stop the passion and fun of the game, God's guidelines enable the game of life to be lived and experienced to the full. Imagine a game of your favorite sport with no rules. That would not be fun. It would be chaos and carnage and would end in violence and anger, no doubt. So when it comes to this life of love and faith, how can we talk about freedom without talking about smart guidelines to protect and empower us?

God's guidelines are simply there to help steer us toward Him, toward life, and toward happiness. Obeying some guidelines can never be the cause of our redemption. Being rescued by Christ has nothing to do with our feeble deeds or abiding by any set of rules, period. Being made a son or daughter of Christ is a gift, one that cannot be earned.

His boundaries are a guide for life, given out of His love for us. And those boundaries are not designed to restrict our freedom. Instead, they exist to give us freedom to live with passion, love, strength, courage, and kindness.

With Christ, we are no longer bound by customs or convention. We are set free to be who God intended: brilliant and beautiful. That's why this advice is so important for us:

> Keep my words
>> and store up my commands within you.
> Keep my commands and you will live;
>> guard my teachings as the apple of your eye.
> Bind them on your fingers;
>> write them on the tablet of your heart. (Proverbs 7:1–3)

Like the guide who knows the only way out of the caves, God guides us through life. He's the One who knows the pitfalls and dangers, and He's the One whose voice we can trust and listen to.

3 LIKE THE CHILDREN

BEING THE CHIEF AMBASSADOR to World Scouting is the best job I've ever had. I have one role: inspiring and encouraging young people to go for it in their lives and to know the power of friendships, adventure, and positive life values. Everyone involved in Scouting knows the power of kids having fun. It is unquantifiable and beautiful.

Not a lot of people saw the world that way two thousand years ago. Jesus was born into a society that did not think much of children. This made the way He treated them even more remarkable.

"The kingdom of God belongs to such as these," He said, hugging them (Mark 10:14).

In fact, Jesus tells us that whoever we are, however old we are, we all need to learn from children when it comes to living in the kingdom of God:

"I tell you, anyone who will not receive the kingdom of God like a little child will never enter it." (v. 15)

Jesus is not suggesting that we become like children in every aspect. We're not supposed to give into every childish whim or assume no responsibility for our actions. But, like children, we are meant to be open and receptive and honest about our feelings.

Children are often such strong examples to us. They are free to express their love and emotions, free to have fun, free to be honest and vulnerable, and free in how they see the world around them with wonder and gratitude. That's surely what Jesus meant for us.

4 STRONG TO THE END

WE LIVE IN EXTRAORDINARY times. There is so much good in the world but so much bad as well. If ever there was a need for men and women of faith to shine the light of hope, love, and truth on the world around them, it is now.

Jesus knew the days would get dark, far into the future. After He had been brutally whipped to within an inch of His life, Jesus was marched to the place of crucifixion. As He stumbled under the weight of the cross He was carrying, some women started weeping for Him. Jesus turned and gently told them not to cry (Luke 23:28). He wasn't being overly dramatic. He simply knew what was coming. He knew that truly tough times lay ahead for the world.

The challenge for us—whether we're involved in the good things or witness to the bad that's happening in the world—is the same: Will we keep our eyes on the promises of God for our lives? Will we stay true and remember the ways of Christ, right through to the very end? It's not going to be easy, but we're never alone. Jesus promised us His presence always:

"The Advocate, the Holy Spirit, whom the Father will send in my name, will teach you all things and will remind you of everything I have said to you." (John 14:26)

The great truth for how to live is quite simple: know that you are not alone, know that you are loved beyond all reason, and live with Christ's generosity overflowing through you.

5 NO PEER PRESSURE

I LOVE THE STORY I read recently about a 104-year-old lady who was asked what the best thing about being her age was.

"No peer pressure," she replied.

When people feel scared in life, the fallout manifests itself in various ways. Sometimes it is an overwhelming pressure to fit in or conform, or having to keep up with our peers, or projecting an image of perfection. Fear leads to pressure to compete, to make ourselves better than people, to put others down, to hide or overpromote ourselves. We become anxious of missing out and of not doing well enough. All of these emotions weigh us down and rob us of our freedom. And it all starts from the fear of being alone, abandoned, and not good enough.

Matthew's gospel starts by stating that Jesus is "God with us" (1:23). And in the very last verse of the gospel, Jesus reminds everyone who chooses to follow Him that nothing has changed. He said, "I am with you always" (28:20).

If we want to live a life that is full of freedom and power, we don't have to wait until we're the last one standing to be free, like the 104-year-old lady. Instead, we can plug into the ultimate source of freedom and power: Christ Himself.

Never alone, always empowered; no peer pressure, just love and freedom—that's the life Christ brings.

> **FEAR LEADS TO PRESSURE TO COMPETE, TO MAKE OURSELVES BETTER THAN PEOPLE, TO PUT OTHERS DOWN, TO HIDE OR OVERPROMOTE OURSELVES.**

6 DON'T FEAR WEAKNESS

I OFTEN FEEL INADEQUATE because of my many weaknesses. But sometimes God works through our weaknesses better than through our perceived strengths.

We see it in Gideon. Chosen by God to lead an army, he didn't feel that he was up to the job. "'Pardon me, my lord,' Gideon replied, 'but how can I save Israel? My clan is the weakest in Manasseh, and I am the least in my family'" (Judges 6:15).

Often our doubts and fears only really surface when we're about to be tested. But our sense of weakness is no barrier to God. "I will be with you," said God to Gideon. And He says it to us too.

I often draw strength from the words of the apostle Paul:

Therefore I will boast all the more gladly about my weaknesses, so that Christ's power may rest on me. . . . For when I am weak, then I am strong. (2 Corinthians 12:9–10)

Don't run or hide from your weaknesses. Accept and embrace them, and lay them before the Almighty. He longs to enter, transform, and empower our lives. It is what He does—but only when asked, and only when there is room for Him to work.

A false sense of self-confidence often gets in the way of our progress in life. There's a power to weakness, strange as it sounds. But when we admit that we're unable to fight the big battles alone, that is when we learn to effectively rely on a stronger power. God-confidence is always going to win over self-confidence. Gideon knew that, as have so many of the most empowered men and women throughout history.

THE CURTAIN BETWEEN MAN AND GOD

IT IS ARGUABLY THE most poignant moment in human history: Pilate turned and looked at Jesus. Covered in blood, a crown of thorns biting into His scalp, soldiers on either side, Jesus didn't look like much of a threat to the Roman ruler. I imagine Pilot half sneering, half despairing as he spoke: "Don't you realize I have power either to free you or to crucify you?" (John 19:10).

But Jesus' reply was so calm and clear: "You haven't a shred of authority over me except what has been given you from heaven" (v. 11 MSG).

It must have looked to many as though it was game over, as though Jesus' life had been a failure—that hatred, jealousy, and ego had conquered over mercy, forgiveness, and love. But in reality, the greatest victory in the history of the world was about to be won. The conquered one, the man who looked as if He'd failed, was about to reveal a source of new life, a new vision for humankind, a new road to peace and unity.

> At that moment, the Temple curtain was ripped in two, top to bottom. There was an earthquake, and rocks were split in pieces. (Matthew 27:51 MSG)

Whenever we're struggling with the circumstances of our lives, let's see beyond what other people see as failure and look instead to what God's doing behind the scenes in our lives. Let's choose to remember that the greatest triumphs sometimes occur when the circumstances seem to be hardest.

> He went through it all—was put to death and then made alive—to bring us to God. (1 Peter 3:18 MSG)

When we think life is dark, Christ knows better. Look up. The light is coming.

8 BUYING FREEDOM

THERE'S A LOT OF pressure to buy our way to happiness. If we're feeling anxious, we think maybe a little retail therapy will give us the boost we need. But it rarely does. Likewise with drugs, riches, and accolades. A lot of the time, the more we chase, accumulate, and stuff these things inside ourselves, the more we actually hunger and thirst and ache.

> Whoever loves money never has enough;
>> whoever loves wealth is never satisfied with their income.
> (Ecclesiastes 5:10)

Instead of freeing us from our worries, things can create whole new ones. If we want to be truly refreshed, God's the source to turn to. Spending time with Christ is the way to fuel up on all the things we most need: strength, happiness, peace, love, forgiveness, and guidance.

It can be hard to go against the grain of society, but this verse reminds me who the real heroes are in this world, and it helps to keep my aspirations in check:

> It's better to live humbly among the poor
>> than to live it up among the rich and famous. (Proverbs 16:19 MSG)

Money, glory, and drugs will never deliver freedom to the soul. But the light and presence of Christ bring a freedom that is both rare and powerful.

9 PERFECT FREEDOM

SAINT AUGUSTINE WROTE THAT God was the master "whom to serve is perfect freedom."[113] It's the beautiful paradox.

I used to fear that if I believed in God and tried to follow His ways, then I'd lose my freedom—that His rules would tie me down. What I discovered is that the opposite is true. Living for ourselves is, in fact, a tragic form of slavery. It's a hard one to explain. But His ways set people free and set human hearts ablaze. Maybe this verse does it best:

> Those who enter into Christ's being-here-for-us no longer have to live under a continuous, low-lying black cloud. A new power is in operation. (Romans 8:1–2 MSG)

Living this way changes everything. We learn to see ourselves as a child of God, someone who is deeply loved, accepted, and empowered by God's unconditional love. We get to live free from guilt, fear, loneliness, and society's false promises as to where freedom is found—the sort of "promises" that tie people up in knots and say we have to be rich, good looking, or important to be worth anything.

Knowing God "in the new way of the Spirit" (Romans 7:6) is the way to perfect freedom. And Christ is at the very heart of that freedom.

> **HIS WAYS SET PEOPLE FREE AND SET HUMAN HEARTS ABLAZE.**

10 CRACKED VESSELS

THERE'S A BEAUTIFUL ART form in Japan called kintsugi. Instead of throwing away broken pottery, the pieces are carefully glued together using a lacquer mixed with gold. The cracks are not covered over—they're revealed, celebrated.

It is our many cracks that make us human. We are all flawed, every single one of us. We mess up, we carry damage, and we fall down and get broken. Cracks are simply part of that story, part of life. There is no need to hide them.

And yet hiding is exactly what a lot of us do.

When we put on a pretense of perfection, it is living a lie. And it denies Christ His purpose to redeem and rescue us, to set us free. Indeed, the light needs our cracks to shine through. Our failings remind us of our great need for Christ. The cracks are actually made beautiful by the light.

That's why God never completely removed whatever it was that Paul called his "thorn in my flesh" (2 Corinthians 12:7). It kept Paul humble and leaning every day on the grace of God.

> These limitations that cut me down to size—abuse, accidents, opposition, bad breaks. I just let Christ take over! And so the weaker I get, the stronger I become. (v. 10 MSG)

The point of true strength starts with humility and knowing our great need for Christ within us. This was the source of all of Paul's power and effectiveness.

11 MONEY MANURE

ARE THERE ANY OF us who have never been ensnared by money worries in some way? Sometimes we think money is the answer to all our problems. At other times we see it as the root of all the world's problems. Either way, we can all so easily find ourselves tied up by it.

The book of Proverbs can help us get free of that. It reminds us that having money—as well as not having it—is neither wholly good nor wholly bad. Money in itself is inanimate. It is how we use it, how we view it, and how much focus we place on it that matters.

The writer encourages us to use whatever we have wisely and to know that while there is nothing wrong with wealth in itself, there are so many more important things in life. It's all a question of priorities. Either money controls us or we control it. When we learn to use money wisely and generously, and to hold it lightly, we are often then entrusted with more of it.

And right here is the key to handling money well:

> Whoever is kind to the poor lends to the LORD,
>> and he will reward them for what they have done. (Proverbs 19:17)

So be generous and give boldly. Let's use what we have to make life a little better for everyone. As Francis Bacon said, money is like manure: it only works when it is spread around![114]

12 EVER TOWARD THE LIGHT

A LIFE OF LOVE and faith doesn't just bring freedom to some areas of our lives. It has the power to transform everything. You can be free from guilt and shame. Free from condemnation. Free from the fear that you're not good enough and can never hope to match up. Free from selfishness. From pride. Free from legalism and free from the fear of rejection. Free from peer pressure. Free from the need to compare yourself to other people. Free from past pains and future worries. Free from the fear of death.

This is not some far-off hope. You have been set free already. Right now you are free to use your life and energy to help, love, and strengthen others. You are free to be the unique person that God made and that He delights in— free to be you.

That old, constricting legislation is recognized as obsolete. We're free of it! All of us! Nothing between us and God, our faces shining with the brightness of his face. And so we are transfigured much like the Messiah, our lives gradually becoming brighter and more beautiful as God enters our lives and we become like him. (2 Corinthians 3:17– 18 MSG)

It's a beautiful vision, and some of these freedoms may take a while to come. All of us are on a journey that lasts a lifetime, but as we focus on Jesus, the change happens, little by little. We move ever toward the light.

13 WHO WE ARE

SOME OF THE GREATEST battles humans face are with our sense of self and self-worth. The repercussions of a false image of ourselves (whether over- or underinflated) have led to some of the greatest tragedies of all time. Likewise, in our own lives the effects of how we view ourselves have great consequences: if we think we are too great, we fall flat; if we think we are too insignificant, we never even get up.

God's view of us is both surprising and empowering.

For we are God's handiwork, created in Christ Jesus to do good works, which God prepared in advance for us to do. (Ephesians 2:10)

That's quite a promise, but what does this mean for how we live? It means we are loved, and it means we are valued and have purpose. And it means we have power.

With Christ beside us, this promise comes true:

No weapon turned against you will succeed. (Isaiah 54:17 NLT)

Our true identity and worth are rooted in the fact that we are His. We are precious in His eyes. We are trusted with the universe, and we have the power to succeed. And if that isn't enough, God has given you "endless energy, boundless strength!" (Ephesians 1:19 MSG).

So claim this, walk humbly with this strength, and know the source is always the love of God inside you. Take heart and have confidence in the truth of who you are. We are His children, children of light. That's our confidence and our identity.

14 THE GREAT CALLING

I LOVE THE STORY of Daniel. He showed such resilience and courage in the face of so much fear and oppression. He survived the lions' den and evil plotters, and he knew where the true source of power was. He did not deviate from the course set for him. As a result of his integrity, and through a gift of God, he rose higher up the ranks than anyone else.

> Daniel was preferred above the presidents and officials because an excellent spirit was in him. (Daniel 6:3 MEV)

But having this great power was not his calling—it was just his job, no more important than anyone else's. All of our jobs are different, but our calling is always the same: to love the Lord our God with all our heart and to love others as ourselves. This is what really matters, and it is something we all have in common. And just like Daniel, God offers us constant encouragement as we keep our eyes on Him:

> And you? Go about your business without fretting or worrying. Relax. When it's all over, you will be on your feet to receive your reward. (Daniel 12:13 MSG)

Jobs come and go, and successes and failures will visit us all. Treat them lightly. But our calling from Christ will never change. It is beautiful and simple, and it is rooted in humility, service, and kindness.

15 YOUR TRUE ID

WE ALL STRUGGLE WITH self-image from time to time. And many factors come into play. The ever-widening gap between the public life people share online and the private life people struggle through alone means that our self-image is constantly under attack. We find ourselves often pigeonholed into a role and a title that becomes hard to shake off. You are the accountant, the football player, or the doctor. You're the fat guy or the tall girl; you're the wild cat or the stay-at-home dad. You name it, society puts labels on us and says in a loud voice: that's who you are.

But Jesus always sees beyond the labels, right into our hearts.

You are a chosen people . . . God's special possession . . . called . . . out of darkness into his wonderful light. (1 Peter 2:9)

One of my favorite bits of the Bible is a little-known phrase that the disciple John used to describe himself time and time again. Instead of using his own name, John always referred to himself simply as the one Jesus loved.

It's genius because when we see ourselves as simply a child of God, deeply loved and truly free, it changes everything. We are no longer our label; we are His, and that's all we ever need to know. That's the important part of our identity.

The answer to self-image comes flowing through these simple words:

It's in Christ that we find out who we are and what we are living for. (Ephesians 1:11 MSG)

That's a beautiful and empowered way to live.

16 I WILL UPHOLD YOU

THE WHOLE BIBLE TELLS the same story about God's desire and purpose to free His people. Like a father, God longs for His children to know what it means to live without fear, loneliness, and worry.

Faith is a journey, and for every step forward we will slip and fall and stumble many times. But grace picks us up, restores us, refreshes us, and tends to our wounds. The whole story of our freedom is rooted in God's love for us. It is this love that sets us free.

When we hurt others or ourselves, it ties us in knots. Guilt hurts inside. How do we feel when we have done wrong? Deep inside it aches. But the forgiveness that Christ brings is complete. He holds nothing back when it comes to our restoration. That gives us courage, confidence, and strength. We can live in that freedom, full of gratitude and full to overflowing for others.

> So do not fear, for I am with you;
>> do not be dismayed, for I am your God.
> I will strengthen you and help you;
>> I will uphold you with my righteous right hand. (Isaiah 41:10)

Many times I have held on to this verse, and many times it has helped me.

> ## THE WHOLE STORY OF OUR FREEDOM IS ROOTED IN GOD'S LOVE FOR US.

17   THE TORN CURTAIN

WE MIGHT HAVE BEEN trying to live God's way for years, or maybe we've only just started. Wherever we are on the journey, the same truth applies: the way of love and Christ leads us to total freedom.

The whole Bible tells the same story about God's desire and purpose to free His people. But freedom takes many forms. Sometimes it's freedom to be able to do things. Other times it's freedom from having to do things. We're free to take a stand, to embrace courage and risk our lives for the sake of saying yes to God. And we're free to turn our backs on the things that lead us away from Him. We're free to be different, free to stand out for all the right reasons.

One of the clearest images of freedom in the Bible comes at the moment of Jesus' death. At sixty feet high and at least one inch thick,[115] the huge and heavy curtain that hung in the temple had always been the physical barrier and symbol that separated people from the presence of God.

> Jesus, with a loud cry, gave his last breath. At that moment the Temple curtain ripped right down the middle. When the Roman captain standing guard in front of him saw that he had quit breathing, he said, "This has to be the Son of God!" (Mark 15:37–39 MSG)

Imagine that moment, when this huge, heavy curtain of solemnity that had hung forever in the holy temple, the house of God, the place that represented the presence of the Almighty on earth—was torn in two with a crack! Those Jewish worshipers inside must have almost died with shock!

But the death of Jesus marked the point at which we were all given access to God. The curtain has been torn, our sins forgiven, our freedom secured. Life would never be the same again. The whole of humanity's history came together in this one moment, across time and across the universe for us.

18 THE WORST OF SINNERS, THE STRONGEST OF MEN

THE APOSTLE PAUL STARTED out by describing himself as "the least of the apostles" (1 Corinthians 15:9). Later on he called himself "less than the least of all the Lord's people" (Ephesians 3:8). Finally, he described himself as "the worst of sinners" (1 Timothy 1:16)!

Was Paul's behavior getting worse? No. He was simply becoming increasingly aware of the beauty and overwhelming love that is found in the presence of God.

It seems that the deeper Paul went with Christ, the more aware he became of his need for forgiveness. But from that point of ultimate awareness, Paul also inherited a strength—a streak of steel that ran through him.

David commented on it many years before Paul: "It is God who arms me with strength" (Psalm 18:32).

The same God who empowered David also empowered Paul. And He's the same God who holds His arms out to you.

In the presence of God, we inherit life and light like no other. It is enriching, empowering, humbling, tender, kind, and strong. We begin to live.

In His presence is unearthly strength, refreshing humility, and perfect freedom.

19 FIRST AND LAST

SOCIETY PEDDLES THE UNTRUTH that the rich, the powerful, and the famous are the ones to look up to—that they've made it, that they're a success. The poor, however, are often simply overlooked and ignored. In the kingdom of heaven, the reverse is true. The message is that Christ is all about rescuing the poor in resources and the poor in spirit.

One day, when Jesus was trying to explain this to the disciples, they asked a logical question. If someone who's rich and influential doesn't earn access to heaven, they reasoned, "Who then can be saved?" (Matthew 19:25).

Jesus looked hard at them and said, "No chance at all if you think you can pull it off yourself. Every chance in the world if you trust God to do it" (v. 26 MSG).

This is the powerful truth about God's upside-down kingdom. God isn't impressed by our futile displays of strength, wealth, and power. But He cares desperately about those that society overlooks and marginalizes. If you want to know the heart of God, look at how He sees the poor and afflicted.

It's just like Jesus said: "Many who are first will be last, and many who are last will be first" (v. 30).

Freedom comes from living counter to our culture. It comes from honoring the poor and serving the vulnerable. This is the way of freedom because it is the way of Christ.

20 GIVE AND IT WILL BE GIVEN

MOTHER TERESA ONCE DESCRIBED meeting a beggar who was desperate to give her the few pennies he had. "I said to myself, if I take it, he may have to go to bed without eating; if I don't take it, I will hurt him, so I took. And I've never seen the joy on anybody's face who has given his money or food or thing as I saw on that man's face; that he, too, could give something for somebody. This is the joy of loving, and I will pray for you that you will experience that joy of loving and that you share that joy of loving first in your own family and with all you meet."[116]

Her words echoed those of Jesus:

"Give, and it will be given to you. A good measure, pressed down, shaken together and running over, will be poured into your lap. For with the measure you use, it will be measured to you." (Luke 6:38)

If we want true financial freedom, then we are wise to give away ever more of what we have. When we give to the poor, we always receive in return, and we remind ourselves of the heart of what it means to belong to Christ.

"He defended the cause of the poor and needy,
    and so all went well.
Is that not what it means to know me?"
    declares the LORD. (Jeremiah 22:16)

21 FREEDOM BREEDS COURAGE

WHEN WE KNOW WHO we are, who we follow, and who we can trust, it breeds an incredible freedom, especially from fear.

In AD 250, the church was growing so rapidly that it was said that "all of Rome were finding a faith in Jesus Christ." As a result, Emperor Valerian increased his persecution of Christians.

In an effort to stop him from stealing their money, the church leaders decided to distribute the believers' cash and treasures among the city's poor. Valerian was enraged. He ordered all the church leaders to be arrested and executed, but he offered the treasurer, a man called Lawrence, a pardon if he handed over the wealth.

Lawrence asked for three days to get everything ready.

When the time came and Valerian arrived to see the church's treasures laid bare, Lawrence flung open the doors. What he revealed was a room full of the blind, the poor, the disabled, the sick, the elderly, widows, and orphans. "These are the treasures of the church," he cried.

Valerian was livid. He decided that beheading was not cruel enough for Lawrence, choosing instead to have him roasted alive. As his body was tortured by the flames, Lawrence apparently even joked with his executioners, "This side is done, turn and eat."[117]

What courage, what freedom he knew. Lawrence had such a profound understanding of the message of Jesus, echoed in the words of Paul:

Give thanks in all circumstances; for this is God's will for you in Christ Jesus. (1 Thessalonians 5:18)

Lawrence understood that the poor are the true treasures of the church and that death—no matter how cruel or painful—is not the end of the story. How do we honor Christ? We love, protect, and are generous to the poor.

22 A KIND OF GIVING

SOME PEOPLE IN LIFE are givers. Some are takers. According to King David, this is a key difference between the righteous and the wicked:

The wicked borrow and do not repay,
　　but the righteous give generously;
those the LORD blesses will inherit the land,
　　but those he curses will be destroyed. (Psalm 37:21–22)

Being generous isn't something we choose to do just to make us nicer people to be around. It's not about having perfect manners or even showing that we have a great character. It's not just something we do occasionally or on Sundays. No. It is deeper and more fundamental than any of that. It's a way of life. Generosity is right at the very heart of all that the Christian faith is about, and we're called to give as God did: freely, with joy and without reservation.

C. S. Lewis defined the whole of Christianity itself as "a kind of giving."[118] He's right. God has poured out His generosity to you and me through the life, death, and resurrection of His Son, Jesus. And you and I are invited to respond by embracing generosity ourselves.

A generous person will prosper;
whoever refreshes others will be refreshed. (Proverbs 11:25)

We can give in so many ways: our care, our time, our encouragement. We can give resources like money and gifts; we can give love and hope and kindness. They all lead to Christ, and the more closely we follow this path of generosity, the richer our lives become.

23 FREEDOM TO FAIL

WHEN I WAS A kid, my dad and I would sometimes hire a couple of horses and go riding on the beach near our home. They are some of my best childhood memories, even though there were many times I fell off onto the hard, wet sand.

I remember one time when I took yet another tumble and tears began filling my eyes. I felt annoyed and embarrassed to have fallen yet again. But just at that moment, my dad, with a big smile on his face, started to clap.

Applaud the fall? But why?

Dad wanted me to understand that I could become a good horseman only if I had fallen off a great number of times—that the only way to proficiency is through many failures.

In Christ we have something so special. We are set free from the fear of failure. Our identity isn't in trying to show a facade of perfection; our identity is found in being close to God—restored, empowered, set free.

That means we are free to fail and therefore to grow. It is the great irony: once we lose the fear of failure, we grow stronger and more competent in all we do.

In Christ we are empowered beyond the norm. We might fall, but we are always safe.

> We are hard pressed on every side, but not crushed; perplexed, but not in despair; persecuted, but not abandoned; struck down, but not destroyed. (2 Corinthians 4:8–9)

Always remember this: "Whoever trusts in the LORD is kept safe" (Proverbs 29:25).

24 MAKING THE UNIVERSE SKIP A BEAT

DID YOU KNOW THAT every time we express love and thanks to God—even if it's just a silent cry from deep within us—the whole universe quivers with delight? There are many references in the Bible to the stars and universe praising God:

> The heavens declare the glory of God;
>   the skies proclaim the work of his hands. (Psalm 19:1)

Even Jesus told us that if we ever stopped praising, the rocks themselves would cry out!

The whole crowd of disciples began joyfully to praise God in loud voices for all the miracles they had seen:

"Blessed is the king who comes in the name of the Lord!" . . .
    Some of the Pharisees in the crowd said to Jesus, "Teacher, rebuke your disciples!"
    "I tell you," he replied, "if they keep quiet, the stones will cry out."
(Luke 19:37–40)

There have been times in my life when I've sensed this phenomenon for myself. I've sat watching the stars on a still night, high on a mountain or silently paddling down a remote jungle river at dawn. It is like I can feel the rhythm of the universe and its delight in its Creator.

When our hearts sing like this with wonder, we join with billions of faith-filled men and women—those alive now as well as those in heaven. We add our heart songs to this epic crowd, a mighty family united in joy that Christ is alive and with us. It's the biggest picture, the greatest adventure, the wildest ride of our lives.

I like what C. S. Lewis wrote on the subject: "How little people know who think that holiness is dull. When one meets the real thing . . . it is irresistible."[119] A life of faith is about life in full color.

As Jesus said,

"The Spirit gives life; the flesh counts for nothing. The words I have spoken to you—they are full of the Spirit and life." (John 6:63)

The Holy Spirit right now is ministering to you. And He brings authority greater than any president, comfort deeper than any counselor, and healing more wonderful than any doctor.

That's a lot of positive universe power!

25 FREEDOM MEANS . . .

AS CHILDREN OF GOD, our life is primarily about being set free.

"If the Son sets you free, you will be free indeed." (John 8:36)

A life with Christ is a life unshackled—no longer weighed down under the burden of anxiety, addiction, peer pressure, or loneliness. We are free to laugh and cry, dance and leap, mourn and weep, and to give and ask for no return. People will always naturally gravitate toward you when you live like this.

Great freedom brings great strength. Great freedom is rare, but with it comes power. You become a vessel for the light of Christ. Use it well to bless others.

God never forces His way into our lives, but when we kneel and open the door to our hearts, He answers. Christ is longing to help us live with this freedom, to enrich us, and to use us.

Be ready for that, and take on this challenge today:

Christ has set us free to live a free life. So take your stand! Never again let anyone put a harness of slavery on you. (Galatians 5:1 MSG)

26 THE MEANING OF LIFE

ACCORDING TO THE MAN whose signature appeared on almost every British banknote created during the 1990s, money isn't the answer. "I am clear that the meaning of life can only be properly understood in the context of our relationship with God," said Chief Cashier of the Bank of England, Graham Kentfield.[120] His financial wisdom and authority gives these words such insight. The Chief Cashier knew that wealth alone does not have the power to satisfy us, let alone bring freedom to our lives. However much money you may acquire, it doesn't guarantee success in life.

As Jesus said, "What good will it be for someone to gain the whole world, yet forfeit their soul?" (Matthew 16:26).

The way of true riches is to commit our way to God. Sometimes this brings material wealth, sometimes not. But what is guaranteed is that following Christ always delivers spiritual riches. His plans for us are "good, pleasing and perfect" (Romans 12:2).

Putting love and faith first in our life is fundamental to prosperity and happiness.

God's love has been poured out into our hearts through the Holy Spirit. (Romans 5:5)

That's true wealth.

27 FOUR WAYPOINTS TO LIFE

IT'S ANOTHER OF THOSE topsy-turvy truths that I have experienced: the narrow path in life leads to the widest expanse of freedom and joy.

And here are four waypoints on the map to help you find that path:

1. "Love the Lord your God with all your heart and with all your soul and with all your mind." (Matthew 22:37)
2. "Trust in the LORD with all your heart and lean not on your own understanding." (Proverbs 3:5)
3. "Give thanks to GOD with everything [you've] got." (Psalm 111:1 MSG)
4. "Whatever you do, work at it with all your heart, as working for the Lord, not for human masters." (Colossians 3:23)

And the result?

"If you practice what I'm telling you, you'll never have to look death in the face." (John 8:51 MSG)

Waypoints to life, indeed.

28 SLATE WIPED CLEAN

IF WE WANT TO really appreciate how great it is to be dry, warm, and fed, we need to know what it is to be wet, cold, and hungry. Likewise, finding our way home is even sweeter when we've first been lost.

It's the same with freedom. If we really want to know what true freedom means, we have to understand what it feels like to be chained. Addictions, anxieties, and the pressures of peers and society can shackle us all. We lose our zest, our peace, our sense of perspective, our love of life and fun.

In Christ we can refind our lives and shake off these shackles. It is what Jesus always did best with all He encountered. He set people free. As the Scottish theologian P. T. Forsyth pointed out, if we want to truly appreciate the "breathless wonder of forgiveness," we first have to know the "despair of guilt."[121]

I love David's description of what it felt like when he was forgiven:

Count yourself lucky, how happy you must be—
    you get a fresh start,
    your slate's wiped clean. (Psalm 32:1–2 MSG)

God wants to give us all a fresh start—that freedom of spirit that we all need. He wants to wipe the slate clean and, as C. S. Lewis said, to surprise us with joy.[122]

29 THE GOOD NEWS

THE BIBLE TELLS THE story of God opening His arms to His people.

Jesus was no different. He was continually inviting people to eat with Him, to follow Him, to become His friend and discover the greatest possible purpose of their lives. It's no coincidence that when He died on the cross, His arms were outstretched, inviting everyone to approach. His death, like His life, was a beautiful and powerful illustration of the words that the prophet Isaiah wrote centuries earlier:

> Come, all you who are thirsty,
> > come to the waters;
> and you who have no money,
> > come, buy and eat!
> Come, buy wine and milk
> > without money and without cost. (Isaiah 55:1)

I have the same hope in this book, *Soul Fuel*. It's a flawed, determined effort to share the love, light, and goodness of Christ with you. It is about an invitation that is universal and without restriction.

> "Come to me and I will give you rest—all of you who work so hard beneath a heavy yoke. Wear my yoke—for it fits perfectly—and let me teach you; for I am gentle and humble, and you shall find rest for your souls; for I give you only light burdens." (Matthew 11:28–29 TLB)

That's why the story of Christ is called the good news.

30 NEVER GIVE UP

AT THE END OF this mini *Soul Fuel* journey through freedom, let's get back to the most life-enhancing, life-empowering, life-transforming message of all. When Jesus was facing His most agonizing challenge—just hours away from brutal torture and eventual death—He cried out these words:

> "Right now I am storm-tossed. And what am I going to say? 'Father, get me out of this'? No, this is why I came in the first place. I'll say, 'Father, put your glory on display.'" (John 12:27 MSG)

Jesus chose to keep going, not turn away. He chose to trust His Father above, not give in to fear and doubt. When facing a death He did not deserve, He decided to never give up.

That's what it means to live this life of love and faith. The clothes of authentic faith are not the purple robes of an emperor. They're the crown of thorns of a Savior. We're called to carry the cross, not the throne, no matter how much it costs us.

Never give up. These are the words that turned the world around when Jesus died, and they continue to turn the world around today. When people of faith make up their minds to keep going, to keep sharing the love of Christ, the world around us is transformed. Relationships are transformed. Hearts are transformed. The love of Jesus wins all.

So together, let's start each day just as we did the last: knees down, eyes up. Get the good news in.

RISK

THE SECOND TIME I saw the summit of Everest, I was alone. Instead of climbing the mountain, my friend Gilo and I were each flying a powered paraglider, which is basically just a parachute with a propeller engine strapped to your back. We were higher than anyone had ever flown a powered paraglider before. It was minus 65 degrees, oxygen levels were dangerously low, and we were still some five thousand feet below the summit.

Then, all of a sudden, Gilo's engine developed a fault and stopped. He had no choice but to glide down and turn back. I suddenly felt vulnerable and alone, without my wingman. But I knew this was our chance. The weather and wind conditions were as good as we would ever get up here. For us both, I pressed on.

It was both humbling and terrifying to look down on these giant Himalayan peaks below me; they all looked tiny. The fear inside kept trying to rise up within my throat, but I knew I could do this. I just had to keep going, keep looking up, and have faith that I could make it. There was so much that could go wrong. There always is in life. But sometimes we have to push the fears and doubts aside, look up, and press on.

That expedition was worth the risk. We achieved a world first, we fulfilled the dream, and we came back alive and as friends. Mission successful.

Life is so inherently full of risk that if we never train to deal with it we become woefully ill-prepared to deal with life. There is risk in relationships, business, hobbies, and in all our aspirations and hopes. There is risk in living a life of faith. We might face ridicule, persecution, and worse. But risk always has a converse positive side: it is called reward. And the game of life is to balance the two and seek the rewards.

But first will always come the risk.

Risk is like a muscle. The more we use it, the stronger our ability becomes to deal with the fear, judge the dangers, and trust our instinct. The more risks we take, the bigger risks we can manage. We know what we can and can't do.

If we never want to have an impact on anything or anyone, then we should stay at home, be "safe," and accept the fact that there will be no ripples emanating from our lives. But if we want to live the fullest version of life possible, we need to become a ninja at dealing with risk. Sometimes we might push it a little far, and life will often sharply remind us of our limitations. Again, we must listen and learn from the universe. Stay alive, stay smart, and learn from the lessons.

Weirdly, as I look back on that Everest mission, the most dangerous part of that whole adventure wasn't when we were up in Everest's death zone. It was beforehand, at home in England, getting ready to leave. A helicopter was filming one of our early test flights, and as we reached five thousand feet, I got hit by the rotor wash when the chopper flew too close in front of us. I got violently spun upside down, over and over, lines all wrapped and tangled. I was falling fast and knew I was about to die. To make matters worse, I had been foolishly flying with no reserve chute in an effort to save weight.

By the grace of God, a small part of the main canopy was inflated just enough to stop my fall, and I crashed into the ground at high speed. But I survived. I knew I should have died that day. The chances of the prop not having cut the lines or the chute not being a little more wrapped as I fell were slim. The consequences would have been terminal.

It was the second time I had nearly died falling from the sky, the first time being my skydiving accident in Africa while I was serving in the British Special Forces. This latest incident somehow felt like an even closer call. Even though I learned vital lessons about paragliding near helicopters and about always carrying a spare chute, it didn't put me off the actual Everest adventure itself.

Whatever doesn't kill us makes us all smarter, and our experience is really just the sum of all our near misses. I am not advocating that we should take these levels of risk all the time, but life should also be an adventure.

And in terms of faith, the rewards will always far outstrip the risks. Faith is a battle that has already been won for us. Christ Himself bore all the real risk and prevailed. Our journey is to surf a little bit of the wake of His risk and to claim the great reward of His salvation. It's a gift He longs to share.

We shouldn't try to avoid the scars that inevitably accompany risk and a life well lived. I'm covered with marks and scars, and they each tell a story. I like that. I've learned that life doesn't require us to be perfect and free of blemishes. What a waste that would be, bereft of history and endeavor. Life simply requires that we keep on giving of ourselves and that we keep getting back on our feet.

Life says not to fear the risk but to use it. Life reminds us that risk is the key to all growth and progress in life, love, faith, and adventure.

1 DEEP ROOTS, GREEN

THE TEACHING OF JESUS is widely acknowledged to be the greatest of all time. We have advanced so much in science and technology, yet in the last two thousand years no one has ever improved on the moral teaching of Jesus. His are the greatest words ever spoken.

Whatever we're facing, however great the risks, and no matter how many fears and doubts are pressing in on us, we can hold on to this truth:

> Blessed is the one who trusts in the LORD,
>   whose confidence is in him.
> They will be like a tree planted by the water
>   that sends out its roots by the stream.
> It does not fear when heat comes;
>   its leaves are always green.
> It has no worries in a year of drought
>   and never fails to bear fruit. (Jeremiah 17:7–8)

Those same words that were written thousands of years ago are just as true today. When we take a risk to trust God, we begin the greatest adventure of our lives. We do not fear the heat, we have no need to worry in the drought, and our lives will bear much fruit. That's life in Christ.

2 THE LIVING ARK OF THE COVENANT

AS A KID I was determined that I would be the one to find the ark of the covenant. Indiana Jones 2.0. I wanted to be an explorer and a warrior, and to find the source of eternal life! (Hey, you got to dream big, eh?)

The irony is that the ark itself doesn't contain jewels or bones, nor some magic potion for eternal youth. The ark contains the old stone tablets of the Ten Commandments. It is a marker. It points the way. The ark of the covenant is the precursor to the living covenant that is fulfilled in Christ Himself. Christ is the living ark that leads us all home to God.

The irony is that I got to become all the things my heart hoped for as a kid. And I found the ark! Because we are all explorers and warriors of faith, and in Christ, we have found the very keys to eternal life.

Nowadays, when I kneel down and read these beautiful words, I know the reason I was born: that through grace, I can now walk hand in hand with the Lord.

> The LORD your God is with you,
>   the Mighty Warrior who saves.
> He will take great delight in you. (Zephaniah 3:17)

3 BUT AS FOR ME AND MY HOUSEHOLD

A lawyer named Charles Finney regularly preached in New York churches in the 1830s. A lot of fellow lawyers came to hear him speak, including, one night, the chief justice of New York.

As the chief justice listened silently from way up in the gallery, he concluded that everything Finney said about Christ, based on the evidence presented, held true. The chief justice felt a stirring in his heart to take positive action rather than passively doing nothing. He left his seat and went to the back of the stage.

While Finney was still preaching, the chief justice tapped on his shoulder and whispered to Finney. When he finished, Finney turned back and looked at the faces staring at him. "The Chief Justice says that if I call people forward, he will come too. I ask you to come forward now if you would like to receive Christ into your heart."

The chief justice went forward, and so did almost every lawyer in Rochester, New York. It is said that one hundred thousand people discovered faith in the next twelve months in that area.[123]

Life is full of choices. They really matter, and sometimes, like with the chief justice, they have life-affirming consequences for other people as well.

At age sixteen I made a quiet choice to ask Christ to come into my life and help me through my days. It felt like an edgy, scary choice to make at the time. The best decisions are always a little like that at first. But that decision has influenced every part of me from that moment forward—for the stronger, for the better. I know now where I stand.

But as for me and my household, we will serve the LORD. (Joshua 24:15)

4 THE POWER OF AUTHENTICITY

IT'S TEMPTING TO POST just our best pictures, to present the world with the edited highlights of our life, to hide the truth and polish the veneer. But there is great power in authenticity. As the saying goes, "be yourself; everyone else is already taken!"

You and I are at our most effective when we are true to ourselves. As Saint Catherine of Siena put it, "Be who God meant you to be and you will set the world on fire."[124]

I love the classic Bible story where David takes on Goliath. After he'd struggled to move wearing the armor that King Saul insisted he wear, David realized the best course of action wasn't to protect himself with leather and metal but was simply to walk forward and to fight as he knew best.

And that was his power. He approached the battle uncluttered, not weighed down by anyone else's expectations. He was authentic, walking with only the protection of God and a small slingshot.

Taking the armor off was the risk David had to take. It was the moment he decided simply to be himself. And it worked out well.

> So David triumphed over the Philistine with a sling and a stone; without a sword in his hand he struck down the Philistine and killed him. (1 Samuel 17:50)

> Blessed are those who trust in the LORD
>> and have made the LORD their hope and confidence. (Jeremiah 17:7 NLT)

Living like this has power. Being true to yourself, and at times being vulnerable, can feel a little scary, but it is magnetic and beautiful as well. Authenticity has power because it is living as the original version of who God created you to be, and that will always be impossible to improve on.

5 THE GREAT GUIDE

SURVIVING IN THE MOUNTAINS is all about managing risk and trusting the right people. As a young mountaineer, learning my trade, I encountered some great guides and a few less good ones. I learned so much about the mountains and survival through these experiences.

If we head off with an inexperienced guide, we will fast find ourselves in unnecessary danger and will make little progress. It is risk for the sake of risk rather than for any purpose. And ultimately we are more likely than not to end up in a ditch somewhere and probably injured.

Conversely, when we find a great guide, when we are ready to work hard and commit to trust that person's decisions (even when they feel frightening), then we will travel far. Yes, there will be risk and danger, but we will be in safe hands and heading in a positive direction. And eventually we will reach that mountaintop, together, uninjured, and the place will take our breath away.

That's the key with life and with faith. Choose your guide wisely. Christ is the ultimate Guide, and with Him all the risks are worthwhile and surmountable. Wisdom and trust conquer dangers and risk.

This verse below has followed me on many adventures. It was written on a small scrap of paper, tucked away in the top of my pack, when I eventually stood on the summit of Everest at age twenty-three.

> Be my safe leader,
>   be my true mountain guide. . . .
> I've put my life in your hands.
>   You won't drop me,
>   you'll never let me down. (Psalm 31:3–5 MSG)

6 THE GREATEST RISK

IT IS TEMPTING TO want to avoid risk, especially when life feels a little fragile. When all we can see are obstacles around us, it can be tempting to want to reduce risk at every turn and sit tight, immobile. But there will always be danger, often even more so when we do nothing. The greatest danger in life is to risk nothing.

If we are too cautious, we will never achieve anything. "Whoever watches the wind will not plant; whoever looks at the clouds will not reap" (Ecclesiastes 11:4). We must try our best not to be daunted by obstacles. They are often opportunities in disguise. We must not be put off by wind and clouds.

Adventurers understand this. They know "nothing ventured, nothing gained." And it's true when it comes to how we use the resources that God has given us as well:

> Be generous: Invest in acts of charity.
> Charity yields high returns.
> Don't hoard your goods; spread them around.
> Be a blessing to others. This could be your last night. (Ecclesiastes 11:1–2 MSG)

If we're unsure about taking risks with and for God, just study the Bible. The more we give, the more we get. The more we give, the greater our wisdom grows. We have to keep giving because even if it doesn't seem to come back to us, it does. It will. It is impossible to sow in the kingdom of God and not to reap a greater harvest.

This is one of the fundamental laws of the universe: you can't out-give God, and everything we have was always His.

7 INCLUDE, NOT EXCLUDE

OF ALL THE RISKS we can take, loving others can sometimes feel the most dangerous. The temptation is to surround ourselves only with people who are like us. But love can be so much bigger and bolder than that. Jesus hit the mark with this:

> "If you love those who love you, what reward will you get? Are not even the tax collectors doing that? And if you greet only your own people, what are you doing more than others?" (Matthew 5:46–47)

Instead, we're invited to take a risk and welcome and love all people, whether they're a different age, background, status, or faith or if they have a different outlook on life. We are called to include, not exclude.

I love this quote from Trent Sheppard: "Jesus showed us that holiness is about how we treat others, especially those who are suffering and those who are different, those who may well be outsiders to your way of living, your way of voting, and, yes, your way of believing."[125] It's a great echo of the Bible:

> "For I was hungry and you gave me something to eat, I was thirsty and you gave me something to drink, I was a stranger and you invited me in, I needed clothes and you clothed me, I was sick and you looked after me, I was in prison and you came to visit me." (Matthew 25:35–36)

True love reaches everywhere.

8 MANAGING CRISIS

I HAVE ALWAYS LOVED the observation that John F. Kennedy made: when written in Chinese, the word *crisis* is composed of two characters. One represents danger, and the other represents opportunity.

Was JFK correct? I don't know. But I do know that when we find ourselves facing difficulty, it's right to be alert to the danger but also vital to think positively about the opportunities it presents. The Bible adds a key third element to this equation that it often repeats:

Do not fret or have any anxiety about anything. (Philippians 4:6 AMPC)

That's a strong command that allows us to walk amid both crisis and opportunity with courage and confidence. But how?

In every circumstance *and* in everything, by prayer and petition . . . with thanksgiving, continue to make your wants known to God. (v. 6 AMPC)

And when we do that, here's the result:

And God's peace . . . which transcends all understanding shall garrison *and* mount guard over your hearts and minds in Christ Jesus. (v. 7 AMPC)

Crisis is both danger and opportunity, but the key to managing them is laying them both before God, leaving worry behind, and then walking on in the peace and presence of Christ. It's a smart formula for life.

9 TWO SIDES OF THE SAME COIN

THERE'S NO DOUBTING THE truth that 2 + 2 = 4. There's no faith necessary to believe it either.

But if someone says that they love you, that's a different matter. Do they really? What do they mean by *love*? Can we trust them? To believe that someone's "I love you" is true requires a little faith. But that doesn't mean love doesn't exist.

Putting our faith in God has a lot more in common with believing that someone loves us than understanding a simple math sum. We're never totally free from doubt, because faith and doubt are two sides of the same coin. Without doubt, faith would not be faith.

It's not wrong to question God, and the Bible is full of examples of people getting mad, frustrated, and angry with God.

Habakkuk looked around him and didn't like what he saw. He was surrounded by violence, injustice, and conflict, and it made him confused and fearful. Worst of all was the fact that—as far as Habakkuk could see—God wasn't doing anything about it.

> How long, LORD, must I call for help,
> but you do not listen? (Habakkuk 1:2)

How often have we felt the same way? But that's never the end of the story. Yes, he expressed his doubts, but Habakkuk took the long-term view and committed himself to faith:

> Though the fig tree does not bud
> and there are no grapes on the vines . . .
> I will rejoice in the LORD. (Habakkuk 3:17–18)

Having faith doesn't mean denying our doubts, frustrations, and fears. And expressing them does not mean denying our faith. The key is always our response, and to trust among the doubts takes courage and a risk-taker's spirit. That is why faithfulness is so beautiful on our journey.

Love is indeed a risk—as is faith—but the Bible continually shows that both are always richly rewarded.

10 THE GREATEST IRONY

AS MANY AS SIXTY million people were horrifically killed in Russia during the twentieth century. When Aleksandr Solzhenitsyn, the great novelist, asked why his homeland had suffered so greatly, he came up with a simple answer: "Men have forgotten God; that's why all this has happened."[126]

The promises and truth of Christ are rooted in service, kindness, mercy, and humility. All of this is summed up by love. When we come close to God, we find love; and when we love others, we shine that same service, kindness, mercy, and humility.

Under the name of religion, legalism, and extremism, millions have tragically lost their lives. Yet under the truth and promises of Christ, people find their lives. It's the greatest and most tragic of ironies. How close the two at first appear, yet how far apart religion and Christ are in truth.

> "Love each other as I have loved you. . . . I no longer call you servants, because a servant does not know his master's business. Instead, I have called you friends. . . . I chose you and appointed you so that you might go and bear fruit—fruit that will last. . . . This is my command: Love each other." (John 15:12–17)

Jesus stated it so clearly: it starts and ends with love. Let's make sure our lives reflect this love and goodness at every turn: never judging, never religious, always kind.

11 THE STILL VOICE

RISKY DECISIONS COME IN many shapes and sizes—emotional, physical, social—but one thing they all have in common is this: they involve us having to step into the unknown. I love this verse from Isaiah:

> Whether you turn to the right or to the left, your ears will hear a voice behind you, saying, "This is the way; walk in it." (30:21)

It is telling that the voice is "behind you." It's not ahead of us or to the side. It's back out of sight, leaving us in front to take the leap of faith. That feels risky and takes courage, but right there is faith in a nutshell.

When we take the kind of risks that God invites us into, a life of adventure with Him, we have to accept that we won't always know exactly where we are going. The ultimate destination is clear, but the waypoints are the adventure.

Even though we step out into the unknown, we are not alone. There's always that voice behind us, whispering guidance and encouragement. We experience that guidance and encouragement through the promises of the Bible, the sensation of the Holy Spirit, through the wisdom of others, and sometimes even through direct divine intervention. So let's always be spiritually alert to that still voice and bold in our response.

12 THE LAND IS MINE

HISTORY IS FULL OF stories of those with worldly power who have gone to extraordinary lengths to gain ever more property and possessions. Little has changed today. Yet, if we read the Bible, we see that over the long term, people never really own anything:

> "The land is mine and you reside in my land as foreigners and strangers." (Leviticus 25:23)

God was teaching His people that there is no such thing as permanent worldly wealth. We are only ever stewards. This is how we should regard property and possessions. They belong to God and are on loan to us. We have what we have, but only for a season.

When we learn to view possessions and wealth like this, then generosity isn't so risky. After all, if God owns it all, then how much fun is it to give away stuff that isn't ours in the first place?

The irony is that when we relinquish this determined pursuit of money and stuff for ourselves, God often blesses us with much greater stewardship of those very things in return.

> "I'm giving you every square inch of the land you set your foot on— just as I promised Moses. From the wilderness and this Lebanon east to the Great River, the Euphrates River—all the Hittite country—and then west to the Great Sea. It's all yours. All your life, no one will be able to hold out against you. In the same way I was with Moses, I'll be with you. I won't give up on you; I won't leave you." (Joshua 1:3–4 MSG)

So hold things lightly and know their season. It is all His, so use it accordingly.

13 WHAT COULD POSSIBLY MATTER MORE THAN MONEY?

ACCORDING TO THE POPULAR Jim Carrey quote, more money just means more problems: "I think everyone should get rich and famous and do everything they dreamed of so they can see that it is not the answer."

Deep down, most of us know money alone can't buy happiness, not to mention life after death. However, for a lot of people it still feels like a massive risk not to dedicate their every living effort to the pursuit of money, possessions, and status. What else could possibly matter more?

Paul was the greatest cynic ever to have lived, a violent hater and persecutor of those who professed to believe in this Jesus, the carpenter from Nazareth. Yet Paul's life was transformed from living for himself to living for Christ. Paul discovered something worthy of his every living effort.

> He set off. When he got to the outskirts of Damascus, he was suddenly dazed by a blinding flash of light. As he fell to the ground, he heard a voice: "Saul, Saul, why are you out to get me?"
>
> He said, "Who are you, Master?"
>
> "I am Jesus, the One you're hunting down." (Acts 9:3–6 MSG)

That encounter on the road to Damascus that Paul experienced seems to be one of the few times in history, and in the Bible, that God didn't give man much choice in deciding if God exists or not! Paul was struck down blind, and Jesus Himself spoke to him. (That would be a hard one to argue against. I guess God figured He wanted mankind to hear more about His Son through Paul.)

The great persecutor and hater would become the great proclaimer of truth and love. And through it all, Paul went on to discover the ultimate empowered way of living. He became one of the most humble, powerful advocates of love ever to preach the good news. Paul knew what life was truly about:

So, my very dear friends, don't get thrown off course. Every desirable and beneficial gift comes out of heaven. The gifts are rivers of light cascading down from the Father of Light. (James 1:16–17 MSG)

God invites us into this life of true abundance. It isn't found in status, money and possessions, or anything so restricting and insignificant as that. Life is found in the abundance of Christ's love, and it is the greatest treasure on earth.

14 GIVING AWAY AND GAINING THE NEW

JESUS ONCE SAID, "GIVE away your life; you'll find life given back" (Luke 6:37–38 MSG). What does this mean, though? If we want the best life possible, one filled with power and purpose and the kind of adventures that are worth dropping everything for, this seems to be the key: giving our old, self-serving life away and taking up a new life—a better, stronger, freer life.

It's about relinquishing the desire just to get wealthy or powerful, well known or influential. It's about choosing a braver, more empowered route. Because if we are to find the deepest satisfaction possible, we must take our hands off the wheel and hand it over to Jesus.

"Hands off the wheel." It sounds risky, but it isn't when the driver is this good.

"Give away your life; you'll find life given back, but not merely given back—given back with bonus and blessing. Giving, not getting, is the way. Generosity begets generosity." (Luke 6:38 MSG)

Let Christ lead, and trust Him when He says that giving, not getting, is the way to bonus and blessing.

15 PRODUCTIVITY OFF THE SCALE

JESUS TOLD MANY PARABLES about crops multiplying and investments growing. He wants us to live a highly productive life. But the productivity He spoke about wasn't simply aimed at becoming a wealthy entrepreneur. After all, Jesus died financially poor.

Jesus' entire life was continually blessing, healing, restoring, and saving people. His truths are about everlasting abundance and productivity, and the more we line up our lives with His purposes, the more fruit our lives produce. It all builds and builds if we stay faithful to the way of love.

Investing in anything is all about taking a risk on the future. And for that we need an ambitious spirit.

"With God all things are possible." (Matthew 19:26)

This verse is about so much more than the power of positive thinking. It is the power of God that makes what seems impossible, possible. We hear the same words again and again.

Nothing will be impossible with God. (Luke 1:37 ESV)

So if we're wanting the fullest life possible, with the maximum productivity, committing to the truths that Christ spoke to our lives is smart. His truths revolve around trusting Him, spending time with Him, drawing on His resources, and then giving to others.

16 GREAT LEADERS ARE GREAT SERVANTS

EVERYTHING RISES AND FALLS on leadership. If a business is well led, it tends to do well. If a community is well led, it usually flourishes. And if a nation has good leaders running it, a lot of the time it will prosper. So what is the secret to being a good leader?

Leadership isn't just about being in charge; it's about taking care of those in our charge. As the saying goes, no one cares how much you know until they know how much you care.

Good leaders don't see themselves as the biggest person on the block. They see themselves more like shepherds caring for their flock. They understand how vital it is to build good relationships. Good leaders care; great leaders serve.

For some, service seems like quite a risk. Will people still trust a leader if they stop "fearing" that leader? Can a leader really show vulnerabilities and weaknesses and still command respect? The Bible answers those questions clearly:

> Love and truth form a good leader;
> > sound leadership is founded on loving integrity. (Proverbs
> > 20:28 MSG)

That means love and integrity are key. These will always trump power and fear.

There's no greater model for leadership than Jesus—the King who chose to be born into poverty, who washed His disciples' feet, and who gave His life for us all.

> "You know that the rulers of the Gentiles lord it over them. . . . Not so with you. Instead, whoever wants to become great among you must be your servant . . . just as the Son of Man did not come to be served, but to serve." (Matthew 20:25–28)

Whether you're a leader with many people reporting to you, or a kid with younger siblings who look up to you, Jesus' words are the most inspired model of leadership known to humankind. That is why billions of souls, and so many of the world's most positive leaders, profess to the quiet truth that Christ is their King. Great leaders are first great servants.

17 THE TWO THIEVES

ON EITHER SIDE OF Jesus hung the two thieves—beaten, battered, bleeding, holding on to life by the thinnest of threads. Little did they realize that they would become two of the most famous thieves in history.

One thief mocked the bleeding Jesus: "Some Messiah you are! Save yourself! Save us!" (Luke 23:39 MSG).

The other thief knew true goodness when he saw it: "We deserve this, but not him—he did nothing to deserve this" (v. 40 MSG).

In so many ways the two thieves reflect each of us. We have all messed up. Some, like the first thief, will mock, belittle, or ignore the way of love that Jesus showed us. Others, like the second thief, will humbly and honestly open their hearts to Jesus and ask for His help.

> Then he said, "Jesus, remember me when you come into your kingdom."
>
> Jesus answered him, "Truly I tell you, today you will be with me in paradise." (vv. 42–43)

It is probably the most extraordinary encounter in history. And it was the last encounter Jesus had as a human on earth. Yet again it was rooted in mercy, forgiveness, and love. I know which thief I would choose to be.

18 WHATEVER THEY DO PROSPERS

THE NINETEENTH-CENTURY EVANGELIST GEORGE Müller took the kind of risks that turned society on its head. Driven by his faith, he showed such care and love for the poor that he was accused of making impoverished children rise above their natural stations in life.

His devotion was equally strong at home, and throughout his life he read the Bible four hundred times. He kept track of what he asked of God and how God responded, and he once claimed that during his lifetime he'd seen fifty thousand prayers answered.

Living this way shaped his character and taught him plenty about what it means to be with Christ. The more he prayed, the more convinced he became of the fact that prayer is absolutely essential for the person of faith.

Life taught him a vital lesson: God is better at meeting our needs than we are. As he once said, "Four hours of work after an hour of prayer will accomplish more than five hours of work without prayer."[127]

And my God will meet all your needs according to the riches of his glory in Christ Jesus. (Philippians 4:19)

Going all in with God might look risky from the outside, but those like Müller, who put their faith, trust, and hope in Christ, inherit riches beyond their wildest expectations.

Blessed is the one . . .
whose delight is in the law of the LORD,
    and who meditates on his law day and night.
That person is like a tree planted by streams of water,
    which yields its fruit in season
and whose leaf does not wither—
    whatever they do prospers. (Psalm 1:1–3)

19 USE IT OR LOSE IT

JESUS TOLD THE STORY of three men who were each given money to invest. The first two doubled theirs, but the third was too afraid of what might happen if he lost it, so he buried his in the ground. It didn't work out well for him, and Jesus called him the "wicked, lazy servant" (Matthew 25:26)! The servant had given up on the dreams and gave in to fear.

You and I need to be wise and not give in to fear of failure. We have to take hold of what God has given us—use it or lose it. Maybe we think we're too old. Wrong. There's no magical age at which excellence emerges or success suddenly comes knocking. With God we're never too young or too old to be blessed or in turn to bless others. Thomas Jefferson was thirty-three when he drafted the Declaration of Independence. Michelangelo was doing some of his finest work at eighty-seven.

Seize the day. Live for the "now" moments of your life; they are a gift— that's why we call it the present. The time you're waiting for may never arrive, so live in the moment and—undeterred by fear or failure—keep moving forward:

> Let us throw off everything that hinders and the sin that so easily entangles. And let us run with perseverance the race marked out for us. (Hebrews 12:1)

It's our race to run. God has laid it all out before us, but we have to grab it, live it, and embrace it—even the failures, those hidden stepping-stones that lead us toward success and the light.

> Jesus looked at them and said to them, "With men this is impossible, but with God all things are possible." (Matthew 19:26)

MAKE YOUR TENTS LARGE

WE ALL WANT TO make some sort of a positive impact with our life, right? Whether it's on a handful of people or a whole nation, we all hope to leave the world a little better than when we entered it. But while it can be easy enough to daydream about the destination we'd like to end up at, taking those first steps can often be tricky. So just begin. Step out in faith. Make a plan and then take positive action to carry it out. If we don't take a few risks, we will never find out the true potential of the opportunities that we've been given.

When God gives us big goals, it often begins as a small idea. So protect and respect those dreams; they are often God-given. And remember: a mighty oak tree is just a little nut that held his ground. God likes it when we think BIG.

> Make your tents large. Spread out! Think big!
> Use plenty of rope,
>   drive the tent pegs deep.
> You're going to need lots of elbow room
>   for your growing family.
> You're going to take over whole nations. (Isaiah 54:2–3 MSG)

Like everything in this journey of faith and love, it comes back to the simple question: Are we prepared to put our trust in God and to step out with courage?

> Trust in the LORD with all your heart
>   and lean not on your own understanding;
> in all your ways submit to him,
>   and he will make your paths straight. (Proverbs 3:5–6)

Know who to lean on and who to draw strength and resources from. And keep going through the storms. Never give up, because you are beautifully and powerfully made.

21 THE TOUCH AND WORDS OF LIFE

ALL OF LIFE IS one long risk. We can't avoid risk and danger, but we can become wise and well trained in how we deal with it and approach it. When the storms approach on a mountain, the waiting and anticipation can often be the hardest part. Life is like that too—waiting for a hospital operation or watching loved ones growing old and struggling, being beside your kids when they are hurting or dreading that impending job review.

But I have learned that it isn't weak to turn to God in the big moments. It is strong. It shows humility and courage. We want to deal with the battle fully equipped. No soldier wants to take on the enemy without every positive resource for victory. Likewise with the journey of faith.

One of my favorite stories from the Bible is the old woman who had been hemorrhaging blood for so many years. When she saw Jesus, in her need and in faith and desperation, she instinctively knew she just had to touch Him. Call it what you will: need, courage, faith, desperation, it doesn't matter. What counts is the result and where these things lead us. For her, it meant taking a risk and reaching out and touching Jesus' coat as He walked through the crowds. "Jesus turned—caught her at it. Then he reassured her: 'Courage, daughter. You took a risk of faith, and now you're well'" (Matthew 9:22 MSG).

That interaction with Jesus healed her. His touch and His words brought life to that lady, and they bring life to us.

IT'S NOT EASY WHEN we've got a big decision weighing heavily on our shoulders and we don't know the best way to approach it. When Jesus was preparing to select twelve of His disciples to be His closest confidants and friends for His journey ahead, He followed a clear plan.

> At about that same time he climbed a mountain to pray. He was there all night in prayer before God. The next day he summoned his disciples; from them he selected twelve he designated as apostles. (Luke 6:12–13 MSG)

Jesus often took Himself off to a quiet place to pray. It was all part of His process to make sure He made the right choices. But there's more to it than this. Jesus didn't stay up all night to double- and triple-check His decisions or to repetitively bang out prayers. He didn't do it because it took Him that long to get through to God. He stayed up because He loved being with His Father. It was His safe, cozy, empowered place.

Staying up all night talking and planning is the kind of thing we do when we're about to embark on the adventure of a lifetime with someone we love. And when we hear the words of God over us, we become empowered and equipped—ready for that risky adventure ahead.

> So do not fear, for I am with you;
>> do not be dismayed, for I am your God.
> I will strengthen you and help you;
>> I will uphold you with my righteous right hand. (Isaiah 41:10)

We all want less fear in our life and more strength. Whatever we're facing, there's no preparation like time alone with God. Just be, with no formal prayers. Soak in His presence. It changes us from the inside out.

23 THE ENEMIES LINED UP

IF YOU FIND YOURSELF facing some opposition and getting criticized for standing up for the right stuff, don't worry. You're in good company. Gustave Flaubert once wrote, "You can calculate the worth of a man by the number of his enemies, and the importance of a work of art by the harm that is spoken of it."[128]

According to Flaubert's sums, the apostle Paul was about as valuable as they come. Everyone was out to get him. His life was full of trials and troubles, opposition and setbacks. Years of faithful service to God and others brought him a ton of trouble and a martyr's death. On his fifth and final visit to Jerusalem, God appeared to Paul and said,

> "It's going to be all right. Everything is going to turn out for the best. You've been a good witness for me here in Jerusalem. Now you're going to be my witness in Rome!" (Acts 23:11 MSG).

I love that. Sometimes we are battling in Jerusalem and then we get called to Rome. That's okay. We aren't the general; we are the soldiers. Our role is to put our hand in the hand of the Almighty, then to trust and to walk. Whatever difficulties we are facing in our life, whatever the opposition, God can turn them all into opportunity. Just keep trusting and keep walking.

IF YOU FIND YOURSELF FACING SOME OPPOSITION AND GETTING CRITICIZED FOR STANDING UP FOR THE RIGHT STUFF, DON'T WORRY. YOU'RE IN GOOD COMPANY.

24 FROM DARK TO LIGHT

HAVING WITNESSED SUCH HORROR and brutality, Lt. Gen. Roméo Dallaire, who was in charge of the UN mission to Rwanda following the genocide there, was asked how he could still believe in God. "I know there is a God because in Rwanda I shook hands with the devil. I have seen him, I have smelled him and I have touched him. I know the devil exists, and therefore I know that there is a God."[129]

Terrorism, human trafficking, torture, institutional abuse, and modern-day slavery—there is just so much darkness in the world today. But the heart of the Christian faith is that ultimately light will win over darkness.

Wherever Jesus went He led people out of this darkness and into the light, away from hate and into love. It was what He came to do.

"I am the light of the world. Whoever follows me will never walk in darkness, but will have the light of life." (John 8:12)

We really can make a difference to the world around us. It will be risky, but remember: Christ is within us. You will never out-dream God. He will give you resources according to your aspirations. He will lead, protect, bless, and encourage you.

Maybe it starts today.

25 THE TREE OF LIFE

KNOWLEDGE MATTERS, ESPECIALLY THE knowledge of who God is. But knowledge alone is never going to be enough. It is not enough for salvation, nor for true happiness. You and I must also have love. But love is risky. Knowledge is safe. It's binary—something is either right or wrong. But knowledge alone can so often lead to pride and arrogance. (By the way, that's why people say that knowledge is like underwear: it is useful to have, but it's not necessary to show it off.)

Love is always going to be more important than knowledge. When God measures a person, He puts the tape around the heart, not the head. That's why it is no good just knowing or hearing or reading about God. The real journey of life begins when we give Him our hearts, not just our knowledge. As Lord Byron wrote, "The tree of knowledge is not that of life."[130] Life begins when we let Christ fill us with love for Him and for others. In other words, it's not what we know, it's who we know.

> Sometimes our humble hearts can help us more than our proud minds.
> (1 Corinthians 8:2 MSG)

How often do people fail in this respect? They seek great knowledge and yet miss the real treasure in front of them. It is our humble hearts that lead us to the foot of the cross. And they lead us on in joy and freedom into life.

SIR WINSTON CHURCHILL ONCE said, "When I look back on all these worries, I remember the story of the old man who said on his deathbed that he had had a lot of trouble in his life, most of which had never happened!"[131]

All of us experience moments where we worry unnecessarily. A lot of the time, the things we worry about never actually emerge. But sometimes they do. Sometimes our worries are real, and we carry them with us for years. Either way, the words of Jesus are poignant for us all:

> "Come to me, all you who are weary and burdened, and I will give you rest. Take my yoke upon you . . . and you will find rest for your souls. For my yoke is easy and my burden is light." (Matthew 11:28–30)

Jesus would have made a few yokes when He worked as a carpenter. They're the wooden frames that are used to join two oxen together at the neck so that they can share the hard work of hauling a heavy cart or plow. Yokes make our burdens lighter and give us a partner to work alongside.

It doesn't always feel comfortable to ask for help. We fear we might look weak and vulnerable. But trusting the promises that Jesus made for us, and looking to Him for help, is one of the bravest, wisest decisions we can make each day. No matter how big or small the burden, let Christ help you with it. He knows a little about shouldering burdens. It is His great strength and promise to us all: He takes the worries as His own.

27 LOOK TO THE STAR

TODAY THERE ARE SO many people who worship the stars. Some look to celebrities, others to lifestyle gurus. Some put their faith in astrology. They are hoping to find guidance, insight, and hope to empower their lives. But looking down dead-end alleys is often not only futile, as well as energy and time consuming, it is also at times dangerous. It's a good rule of thumb not to mess with things we don't truly understand. The occult and idolatry take many forms. It is good to be smart about these matters and be wary of dark stuff posing as light stuff.

As far as our future is concerned, Christ has shown Himself as the ultimate source of goodness, mercy, and power. He's the only Guide we will ever need, the only One whose true nature is forgiveness and love.

The following statement by Paul is a rock-solid foundation on which to base our lives:

> I am convinced that neither death nor life, neither angels nor demons, neither the present nor the future, nor any powers, neither height nor depth, nor anything else in all creation, will be able to separate us from the love of God that is in Christ Jesus our Lord. (Romans 8:38–39)

There's no need to worship the stars when we can hold the hand of the One who made them.

SUCCESS DOES STRANGE THINGS to people. It can so easily go to the head and lead people to think that they're special, set apart, and somehow elevated above others. People can start to get self-centered, and if it goes unchecked, it makes them unhappy and isolated.

I have seen it a lot. And I'm always reminded of this powerful truth: if you are lucky enough to experience worldly success, you must fight hard to stay twice as humble. It's the only way to counter the over-importance that the world falsely places on what they see as success.

But success, in whatever form we experience it, doesn't have to be a negative thing. All success—like money, fame, and power—really does is amplify the character traits we already have, positive or negative.

In other words, if we strive to be kind, then riches, fame, and power can help you do this really well. It all comes down to the choices we make, like choosing to become a person of integrity. That doesn't mean being perfect. It means being honest, down to earth, and authentic.

This verse is a good guide:

Therefore, as God's chosen people, holy and dearly loved, clothe yourselves with compassion, kindness, humility, gentleness and patience. (Colossians 3:12)

It's about talking less and listening more, being ever more generous with what we've got, and making it our mission to try to affect people's lives for the better.

29 LOVE IS THE ANSWER

IT'S RIGHT TO ASK questions and look for answers, especially when it comes to God. There's no reason why we should ever hold back from expressing ourselves to Him.

A lot of questions get answered in the Bible, but sometimes it is hard to see the trees for the forest, especially when we are hurting and asking questions of God such as why there is so much suffering.

"The whole Bible," observed Saint Augustine, "does nothing but tell of God's love."[132]

The love of God is the answer to all the "whys" we could ever ask. Why free will? Why creation? Why the birth of Jesus? Why the cross? As Father Raniero Cantalamessa wrote, "This is the message that supports and explains all the other messages."[133]

If the Bible could be changed into a spoken word and become one single voice, this voice, more powerful than the roaring of the sea, would cry out, "the Father himself loves you" (John 16:27)!

Whatever we're asking of God, whether it's why certain things are happening or why other things are not, trust in His love. Have faith that this love will win in the long term. We may lose many skirmishes here on earth, and many people will continue to suffer greatly, but love will eventually win through.

Jesus saw to this on the cross. Love wins. Love heals. Love is the answer.

GOD IS PREPARING YOU and giving you an increasing authority for what He is calling you to do. This isn't a guess or some pithy saying. This is the truth. God never sends people out on a mission without the right tools, and the deeper we go in this life of love and faith, the more power He gives us.

> "I have given you authority to trample on snakes and scorpions and to overcome all the power of the enemy; nothing will harm you." (Luke 10:19)

As we reach the end of this *Soul Fuel* journey, I hope that, at the very least, you've learned this: we can rely on God alone to give us the power we need each day. Just keep going back to the Source. Keep asking God to empower you. Keep reminding yourself that God watches over you with love, pride, and pleasure.

> The LORD your God . . . will rejoice over you with singing. (Zephaniah 3:17)

Putting time and energy into our relationship with the Almighty is the smartest, most effective, most powerful thing we can do for our lives and our families. Let His truth and His presence steady you, let them settle you, provide you with a firm foundation, and calm and empower you for every day.

It's all a gift. Your gift. Soak it in.

CONCLUSION

REMEMBER THIS:

You have a light within you, the Holy Spirit, and wherever you go you will bring a light greater than the darkness around you.

> The Life-Light blazed out of the darkness;
> > the darkness couldn't put it out. (John 1:5 MSG)

NOTES

1. James Bell Jr. and Stan Campbell, *The Complete Idiot's Guide to the Bible*, 3rd ed. (London: DK Publishing, 2005).
2. Scott Cohen, "Madonna: The 1985 'Like a Virgin' Cover Story," *Spin*, May 1985.
3. Clayton Kraby, "Napoleon Bonaparte's View of Jesus," *Reasonable Theology*, https://reasonabletheology.org/napoleon-bonapartes-view-of-jesus/.
4. Thomas A. Harris, *I'm OK—You're OK* (New York: Quill, 2004).
5. The poem "Footprints," is © 1964 by Margaret Fishback Powers. All rights reserved. Published by arrangement with HarperCollins Publishers Ltd., Toronto, Canada.
6. C. S. Lewis, *Mere Christianity* (New York: HarperOne, 2001). *Mere Christianity*: copyright © C. S. Lewis Pte. Ltd. 1942, 1943, 1944, 1952. Extracts reprinted by permission.
7. C. S. Lewis, *The Weight of Glory* (New York: HarperOne, 2001). *Weight of Glory*: copyright © C. S. Lewis Pte. Ltd. 1949. Extracts reprinted by permission.
8. Quoted in R. C. Sproul, "Ancient Promises," https://www.ligonier.org/learn/articles/ancient-promises/.
9. *The Writings of Mother Teresa of Calcutta*, © by the Mother Teresa Center, exclusive licensee throughout the world of the Missionaries of Charity for the works of Mother Teresa. Used with permission.
10. DC Talk, "Honor Your Mother," in *Jesus Freaks: Martyrs: Stories of Those Who Stood for Jesus* (Bloomington, MN: Bethany House, 2012).
11. "The Alternative Jesus: Psychedelic Christ," *Time*, 21 June 1971, https://schooloftherock.com/3rd_party_articles/times_jesus_movement_article.htm.

12. Kaylena Radcliff, "A War Story: "There Is No Pit So Deep God's Love Is Not Deeper Still," *Christian History* no. 121, "Faith in the Foxholes" (2017).

13. *Share*, no. 29 (2015).

14. Elizabeth Hanly, "Listening to Koko: A Gorilla Who Speaks Her Mind," *Commonweal*, June 21, 2018, https://www.commonwealmagazine.org /listening-koko-0. © 2004 Commonweal Foundation, reprinted with permission. For more information, visit www.commonwealmagazine.org.

15. Peramangalam Job, *Why God, Why?* ((India: Sabine Printing, 2003).

16. Michael Reeves, "Suffering Taught Him to Look to Christ: Charles Spurgeon (1834–1892)," Desiring God, October 19, 2018, https://www .desiringgod.org/articles/suffering-taught-him-to-look-to-christ.

17. Used by permission of Joyce Meyer. https://www.joycemeyer.org/.

18. "The Hand of God," Bible in One Year, https://www.bibleinoneyear.org /bioy/commentary/362.

19. *The Writings of Mother Teresa of Calcutta*, © by the Mother Teresa Center, exclusive licensee throughout the world of the Missionaries of Charity for the works of Mother Teresa. Used with permission.

20. *International Standard Bible Encyclopedia*, ed. Geoffrey W. Bromiley et al. (Grand Rapids: Eerdmans, 1979).

21. Isaac Watts, "When I Survey the Wondrous Cross," Timeless Truths, https:// library.timelesstruths.org/music/When_I_Survey_the_Wondrous_Cross/.

22. Bill Hybels, *Holy Discontent: Fueling the Fire That Ignites Personal Vision*, (Grand Rapids, MI: Zondervan 2007).

23. Raniero Cantalamessa, *Life in Christ: A Spiritual Commentary on the Letter to the Romans* (Collegeville, MN: Liturgical Press, 1990). Copyright 1990 by Order of Saint Benedict. Published by Liturgical Press, Collegeville, Minnesota. Used with permission.

24. Erwin McManus, *Soul Cravings* (Nashville: Thomas Nelson, 2006).

25. Paul J. Achtemeier, Joel B. Green, and Marianne Meye Thompson, *Introducing the New Testament: Its Literature and Theology* (Grand Rapids: Eerdmans, 2001).

26. John Pritchard, "Bible Sunday," Bible Society, https://www.biblesociety .org.uk/content/get_involved/bible_sunday/2016_resources/Bible-Sunday -Sermon-notes.pdf.

27. Kathleen L. Wensel, *Freedom Is...A Book/Journal with a Twist* (Bloomington, IN: Trafford Publishing, 2008), 240.

28. John Lennon, "Beautiful Boy (Darling Boy)," *Double Fantasy*, 1980.

29. Gary Inrig, *Forgiveness: Discover the Power and Reality of Authentic Christian Forgiveness* (Grand Rapids: Discovery House, 2005).

30. "The Cracked Pot," https://www.comp.nus.edu.sg/~tankl/pot.txt.

31. Joyce Meyer, *The Everyday Life Bible: The Power of God's Word for Everyday Living* (New York: Hachette, 2018). Reprinted by permission of Faith Words, an imprint of Hachette Book Group, Inc.

32. James Rampton, "James Cameron: My Titanic Obsession," *The Independent*, August 9, 2005, https://www.independent.co.uk/arts-entertainment /films/features/james-cameron-my-titanic-obsession-304772.html.

33. Raniero Cantalamessa, *Come, Creator Spirit: Meditations on the Veni Creator* (Collegeville, MN: Liturgical Press, 2003). Copyright 2003 by Order of Saint Benedict. Published by Liturgical Press, Collegeville, Minnesota. Used with permission.

34. C. S. Lewis, *Narnia, Cambridge, and Joy: 1950–1963*, vol. 3 in *The Collected Letters of C. S. Lewis*, ed. Walter Hooper (San Francisco: HarperSanFrancisco, 2007). *Collected Letters*: copyright © C. S. Lewis Pte. Ltd. 2006. Extracts reprinted by permission.

35. "How to Be a Blessing Machine," *Bible in One Year*, https://www .bibleinoneyear.org/bioy/commentary/1021. Used with permission.

36. Saint Augustine, *Confessions*, trans. Henry Chadwick (Oxford: Oxford University Press, 2008).

37. Saint John of the Cross, *Dark Night of the Soul* (New York: Cosimo, 2007).

38. Raniero Cantalamessa, *Faith Which Overcomes the World* (Chicago: Alpha International, 2006). Copyright 2006 by Order of Saint Benedict. Published by Liturgical Press, Collegeville, Minnesota. Used with permission.

39. George Matheson, "O Love That Wilt Not Let Me Go," https://hymnary.org /text/o_love_that_wilt_not_let_me_go.

40. Corrie ten Boom, *Clippings from My Notebook* (Nashville: Thomas Nelson, 1982).

41. Raniero Cantalamessa, *Life in Christ: A Spiritual Commentary on the Letter to the Romans* (Collegeville, MN: Liturgical Press, 1990), 313. Copyright 1990 by Order of Saint Benedict. Published by Liturgical Press, Collegeville, Minnesota. Used with permission.

42. "Smith Wigglesworth Quotes," Goodreads, https://www.goodreads.com /quotes/621574-great-faith-is-the-product-of-great-fights-great-testimonies.

43. "Never Give in, Never, Never, Never, 1941," National Churchill Museum,

speech was given at Harrow School, 29 October 1941, https://www
.nationalchurchillmuseum.org/never-give-in-never-never-never.html.

44. "I'll Fight: One Hundred Years Since Booth's Final Address," *The Salvation Army: Doing the Most Good National Blog,* 2017, https://www.salvationarmy.org /nhqblog/news/2012-05-09-ill-fight-100-years-since-booths-final-address.

45. Art Buckwalter, *Interviews and Interrogations: Butterworth's Library of Investigation* (Boston: Butterworth–Heinemann, 1983).

46. Francis Collins, *The Language of God: A Scientist Presents Evidence for Belief* (New York: Simon & Schuster, 2006), 67.

47. "Abraham Lincoln Quotes," Goodreads, https://www.goodreads.com /quotes/3113771-better-to-remain-silent-and-be-thought-a-fool-than.

48. Rick Warren, *The Purpose-Driven Life: What on Earth Am I Here For?* (Grand Rapids: Zondervan, 2002).

49. "PR and the Christian Faith," Common Ground, http://www.seekcg.com /?page_id=26.

50. Shane Claiborne, *Irresistible Revolutions: Living as an Ordinary Radical* (Grand Rapids: Zondervan, 2016).

51. C. S. Lewis, *The Four Loves* (New York: HarperCollins, 2017). *Four Loves*: copyright © C. S. Lewis Pte. Ltd. 1960. Extracts reprinted by permission.

52. Jago Wynne, *Working Without Wilting* (London: InterVarsity Press, 2009).

53. Exact origins of this version of the quote are unknown, but John Wesley is believed to have said words to this effect in his 1799 sermons.

54. "Rick Warren: Hardest Criticism to Swallow Is Claim That All Megachurches Are the Same," *Christianity Today,* https://christiantoday .com.au/news/rick-warren-criticism-hardest-to-swallow-is-claim-that-all -megachurches-are-the-same.html.

55. George Angus Fulton Knight, *The Psalms,* vol. 1 (Philadelphia: Westminster Press, 1982), 117–118.

56. "Letter to the Bishops of the Catholic Church on the Collaboration of Men and Women in the Church and in the World," http://www.vatican.va /roman_curia/congregations/cfaith/documents/rc_con_cfaith_doc _20040731_collaboration_en.html.

57. Blaise Pascal, Pensees VII (1670), 425.

58. "Supreme Commander of the Allied Forces—Dwight D. Eisenhower," *Business & Leadership,* August 15, 2018, https://www.businessandleadership.com /leadership/item/dwight-d-eisenhower-allied-forces-supreme-commander/.

59. James Charlton, *The Military Quotation Book* (New York: Thomas Dunne Books, an imprint of St. Martin's Press, 2002), 83.

60. Linda Bloom and Charlie Bloom, "The Price of Success," *Psychology Today*, April 24, 2012.

61. *Guardian*, https://www.theguardian.com/lifeandstyle/2008/may/18/madonna.

62. Nicky Gumbel, *The Bible in One Year*, "1 February: Day 32" © Alpha International , 2018.

63. Will Carr, "The Last Temptation of Christ," *The International Anthony Burgess Foundation*, 25 April 2014, https://www.anthonyburgess.org /blog-posts/the-last-temptation-of-christ/.

64. "Bible in One Year 2017: Day 38," Bible.com, https://www.bible.com /en-GB/reading-plans/3420-bible-in-one-year-2017/day/38.

65. John Foxe, *The Acts and Monuments of the Church Containing the History and Sufferings of the Martyrs* (London: Scott, Webster and Geary, 1838).

66. Simone Weil, *Gravity and Grace*, trans. Emma Crawford and Mario von der Ruhr (London: Routledge, 2004).

67. Victor Hugo, *The Letters of Victor Hugo from Exile, and After the Fall of the Empire* (Honolulu: University Press of the Pacific, 2002).

68. John Bunyan, *The Works of That Eminent Servant of Christ, Mr. John Bunyan: Minister of the Gospel, and Formerly Pastor of a Congregation* (New York: Palala Press, 2015), 693.

69. Andrew Walker, *Different Gospels: Christian Orthodoxy and Modern Theologies* (London: SPCK, 1993).

70. Letter from Isaac Newton to Robert Hooke, 5 February 1676, as transcribed in Jean-Pierre Maury, *Newton: Understanding the Cosmos*, New Horizons (London: Thames and Hudson, 1992).

71. William R. Moody, *Record of Christian Work*, Vol. 32 No. 8 (East Northfield, MA: W.R. Moody, 1913), 513.

72. Charles Spurgeon, *Spurgeon's Sermons*, vol. 12 (1866), https://www.ccel.org /ccel/spurgeon/sermons12.html.

73. Joyce Meyer, "Wisdom Is Calling Out to You," Joyce Meyer Ministries, December 22, 2017, https://www.joycemeyer.org/dailydevo/2017/12/1222 -wisdom-is-calling-out-to-you. Used by permission.

74. Joyce Meyer, *New Day, New You: 366 Devotions for Enjoying Everyday Life* (New York: Hachette, 2007). Used by permission of Joyce Meyer, https:// www.joycemeyer.org/.

75. John Charles Ryle, *Practical Religion* (n.p.: Wisdom Books, 2018).

76. Christopher Jamison, *Finding Happiness: Monastic Steps for a Fulfilling Life* (Collegeville, MN: Liturgical Press, 2008). Copyright 2008 by Order of Saint Benedict. Published by Liturgical Press, Collegeville, Minnesota. Used with permission.

77. Aleksandr Solzhenitsyn, *The Gulag Archipelago, 1918–1956: Volume 1* (New York: Harper Perennial Modern Classics, 2007).

78. C. S. Lewis, "Hamlet: The Prince or the Poem" in *Selected Literary Essays*, ed. Walter Hooper (New York: Cambridge University Press, 2013). *Selected Essays*: copyright © C. S. Lewis Pte. Ltd. 1969. Extracts reprinted by permission.

79. Saint Augustine, *Confessions* 3.11.19.

80. *The Writings of Mother Teresa of Calcutta,* © by the Mother Teresa Center, exclusive licensee throughout the world of the Missionaries of Charity for the works of Mother Teresa. Used with permission.

81. John Stott, *Reading Romans with John Stott* (Downers Grove, IL: IVP Connect, 2016).

82. Lewis, *Mere Christianity*.

83. Corrie ten Boom, *The Hiding Place* (Ulrichsville, OH: Barbour, 1981), 235.

84. Charles Stobo Reid, Craig Morris Reid, © Warner/Chappell Music, Inc.

85. Russell H. Conwell, "The History of Fifty-Seven Cents," December 1, 1912, https://library.temple.edu/collections/scrc/hattie.

86. *Bartlett's Familiar Quotations* (Boston: Little, Brown, 2012).

87. "Saint Augustine (354–430)," *Lapham's Quarterly*, https://www.laphamsquarterly.org/contributors/augustine.

88. C. S. Lewis, *The C. S. Lewis Bible* (HarperCollins, 2012).

89. *The Writings of Mother Teresa of Calcutta,* © by the Mother Teresa Center, exclusive licensee throughout the world of the Missionaries of Charity for the works of Mother Teresa. Used with permission.

90. John Stott, *Issues Facing Christians Today*, 4th ed. (Grand Rapids: Zondervan, 2011).

91. Norimitsu Onishi, "Sinatra Song Often Strikes Deadly Chord," *New York Times*, February 6, 2010, https://www.nytimes.com/2010/02/07/world/asia/07karaoke.html.

92. Dennis Nafte, "Colonel Sanders Failed 1009 Times Before Succeeding," *Medium*, September 10, 2017, https://medium.com/@dennisnafte/colonel-sanders-failed-1009-times-before-succeeding-ac5492a5c191.

93. Benjamin Lang, "Christmas Day Training, Daley Thompson and the Path

to Glory," *Sports Gazette*, December 4, 2018, https://sportsgazette.co.uk /christmas-day-training-daley-thompson-and-the-path-to-glory/.

94. Oliver James, *Affluenza: How to Be Successful and Stay Sane* (New York: Vermilion, Random House, 2007), 52.

95. James, *Affluenza*, 52.

96. United States Army Recruiting Command, *Recruiter Journal* 49 (November 1996): 6.

97. Nelson Mandela, *Long Walk to Freedom: The Autobiography of Nelson Mandela* (New York: Little, Brown, 2008).

98. Andrew A. Bonar, *The Biography of Robert Murray M'Cheyne* (Hamburg, Germany: Tredition, 2012).

99. Henry F. Lyte, "Abide with Me," https://hymnary.org/text/abide_with_me _fast_falls_the_eventide, 1847.

100. Jonathan Bryan, *Eye Can Write: A Memoir of a Child's Silent Soul Emerging* (London: Lagom, 2018).

101. Eugene Exman, "God's Own Man," *United Nations World Magazine* 6, no. 1 (1952).

102. John Stott, *The Cross of Christ* (Downers Grove, IL: InterVarsity Press, 2006).

103. Meyer, *Everyday Life Bible*. Used by permission.

104. Quoted in David M Brown, *Transformational Preaching: Theory and Practice* (College Station, TX: Virtualbookworm Publishing, 2003), 558.

105. "How to Avoid Backsliding," Bible in One Year, https://www.bibleinoneyear .org/bioy/commentary/3056.

106. Philip Henry Stanhope, *Notes of Conversations with the Duke of Wellington* (London: 1886).

107. Lewis, *Mere Christianity*.

108. Pete Greig, *The Vision and the Vow* (Eastbourne, UK: Kingsway, 2005).

109. Edward Henry Bickersteth, "Peace, Perfect Peace, in This Dark World of Sin?" https://hymnary.org/hymn/AM2013/764.

110. Quoted in Nicky Gumbel, *30 Days: A Practical Introduction to Reading the Bible* (London: Alpha International, 1999).

111. Lewis, *Mere Christianity*.

112. Bear Grylls, *A Survival Guide for Life: How to Achieve Your Goals, Thrive in Adversity, and Grow in Character* (New York: Bantam Press, Corgi Books, 2013), 136.

113. Saint Augustine, *Prayers of St. Augustine of Hippo*, ed. Barry Ulanov (n.p. Seabury Press, 1983).

114. Francis Bacon, *Complete Essays* (Mineola, NY: Dover Publications, 2008).

115. Daniel M. Gurtner, "The Veil of the Temple in History and Legend," *JETS* 49, no. 1 (2006).

116. *The Writings of Mother Teresa of Calcutta*, © by the Mother Teresa Center, exclusive licensee throughout the world of the Missionaries of Charity for the works of Mother Teresa. Used with permission.

117. Francesco Moraglia, "St. Lawrence: Proto-Deacon of the Roman Church," Catholic Culture, https://www.catholicculture.org/culture/library/view .cfm?recnum=6098.

118. Lewis, *Mere Christianity*.

119. Lewis, *Narnia, Cambridge, and Joy*.

120. Mick Woodhead, "Foundations Daily," *STC Sheffield*, 27 February 2018, https://stthomascrookes.org/talks/27-february-2018/.

121. "The Breathless Wonder of Forgiveness," Bible in One Year, https://www .bibleinoneyear.org/bioy/commentary/816.

122. C. S. Lewis, *Surprised by Joy: The Shape of My Early Life* (New York: HarperCollins, 2017). *Surprised by Joy*: copyright © C. S. Lewis Pte. Ltd. 1955. Extracts reprinted by permission.

123. "Charles Finney: Father of American Revivalism," *Christianity Today*, https://www.christianitytoday.com/history/people /evangelistsandapologists/charles-finney.html.

124. Saint Catherine of Siena, Letter 368 to Stefano Maconi, in *The Letters of Catherine of Siena*, vol. 4, *Letters 231–373*, trans. Suzanne Noffke (Tempe, AZ: Arizona Center for Medieval and Renaissance Studies, 2008).

125. Sheppard, *Jesus Journey*.

126. Aleksandr Solzhenitsyn, "Godlessness: The First Step to the Gulag," Templeton Prize Lecture, May 10, 1983.

127. Basil Miller, George Muller: *The Man of Faith* (Minneapolis, MN: Bethany House, 1941), 49.

128. Gustave Flaubert, *Letters to Madame Louise Colet* (France, 14 June 1853).

129. Roméo Dallaire, *Shake Hands with the Devil: The Failure of Humanity in Rwanda* (Toronto: Vintage Canada, 2004), xviii.

130. Lord Byron, *Manfred*, 1.1.

131. Winston Churchill, "Plugstreet," *Pall Mall Magazine*, 1924.

132. "Feel God's Love," Bible in One Year, http://www.bibleinoneyear.org/bioy /commentary/1316.

133. Cantalamessa, *Life in Christ*.

ABOUT THE AUTHOR

BEAR GRYLLS has become known worldwide as one of the most recognized faces of survival and outdoor adventure.

Trained from a young age in martial arts, Grylls went on to spend three years as a soldier in the British Special Forces, as part of 21 SAS Regiment. It was here that he perfected many of the survival skills that his fans all over the world enjoy, as he pits himself against the worst of Mother Nature.

Despite a free-fall parachuting accident in Africa, where he broke his back in three places and endured many months in and out of military rehabilitation, Grylls recovered and later became one of the youngest climbers ever to reach the summit of Mount Everest.

He then went on to star in seven seasons of the Discovery Channel's Emmy Award–nominated *Man vs. Wild* TV series, which became one of the most-watched shows on the planet, reaching an estimated 1.2 billion viewers.

Since then he has hosted more extreme adventure TV shows across more global networks than anyone else in the world, including five seasons of the global hit TV show *Running Wild with Bear Grylls*.

Running Wild has featured Bear taking some of the world's best-known stars on incredible adventures. These include President Obama, Julia Roberts, Roger Federer, Will Ferrell, Zac Efron, Channing Tatum, and Kate Winslet, to name but a few.

His autobiography, *Mud, Sweat, and Tears*, spent 15 weeks at number one in the *Sunday Times* bestseller list and he has written over 90 books, selling in excess of 15 million copies worldwide.

He is an honorary colonel to the Royal Marines Commandos, the youngest ever UK Chief Scout, and the first ever Chief Ambassador to the World Scout Organization, representing a global family of some sixty million Scouts.

He is married to Shara, and together they have three young boys who also love adventure. They live on a houseboat on the Thames in London and a private island off the Welsh coast.

Bear's life motto is simple: courage and kindness . . . and never give up!